THE JAMES TAPES
BOOK ONE

JOEL OSLER BRENDE

COVER ART BY PATRICIA CHONG

To James, patient extraordinaire

CONTENTS

FORWARD

Can one actually identify and piece together an understanding of another's world of thoughts and feelings (emotional pain)? What is unique about the snippets from the ninety videotaped James tapes is the manner in which Dr. Brende helped to pioneer efforts to treat dissociative symptoms. He forged a pathway for James' physical and mental care. The James tapes reflect an earlier history of psychological care for dissociative identity disorder, when there was a lack of procedural treatment for dissociations. Dr. Brende uncovered, through medical, environmental, and family interactions, the client's secrets, repressed memories, painful physiological emotions, trauma, and loosely organized and displayed thought patterns. His therapy reflected a non-threatening, warm, responsive, and understanding tone of a one-to-one trusting therapeutic relationship. He used his medical and psychiatric training to connect his understanding of the client's background and experiences.

He and James encountered resistance while uncovering and understanding the client's pain through the use of psychoanalysis (techniques) and specific techniques garnered from Gestalt (empty chair), object relations (good/bad person fragmentation), psychodrama (protagonist), Adlerian (early childhood memories), art therapy (drawings), hypnosis (repressed memories), dream interpretations, traumatology (safety), and mind-body (brain) research existing at the time. During the period of the James tapes, recorded and published outcome clinical trials for effectiveness or efficacious treatment did not exist.

Dissociative states are observed during the session, and interpretations appear to be based on bodily reactions and the client's accompanying thoughts and expressed, or lack of, feelings. As these interactions take place during the sessions, Dr. Brende shares with the reader his clinical knowledge, experience, and after-session research to better understand the client for each of the dissociative states. He questions if these states interact and if they affect other states. The client had a history of epilepsy (seizures). There is known medical related symptoms for arm and leg automatisms that are observed several times throughout the therapy. As the automatism (changing a ring on one hand to the other hand) takes place, do they accompany each dissociative identity or are they only for James? Does the client's appearance at the initiation of each session reflect different dissociative states choices in dress (clothing) and style of hair (bun, ponytail, goatee, mustache, wig)? When body automatisms appear for the therapist, do different clinical probes stimulate leg over leg, muscular crossing of arms and/or arms raised above the head, smoking, matched with client comments regarding different sense modalities, especially color and smell. Pre 1900 history for cognitive assessment included differentiation in smell, hearing, light, touch, and color.

In reading the snippets one has to wonder what is the final outcome.

Gary L Arthur, Ed.D., LPC, NCC

Professor Emeritus of Professional Counseling at Georgia State University ~ Georgia Counselor Educator of the year in 2007 ~ Author of the widely used study course: *Study Guides for State Licensure Exam Preparation*

Introduction

It has been fifty-eight years since I graduated from medical school at the University of Minnesota, forty-eight years since I completed my training in psychiatry at the Menninger School of Psychiatry in Topeka, Kansas, fifteen years since I retired as a tenured Professor of Psychiatry and Department Chairman at Mercer University School of Medicine in Macon, Georgia, and two years since I retired as a part-time hospital psychiatrist in west-central Missouri. But most importantly, for the purposes of this book, it's been over forty-five years since I first met James, a patient I will never forget.

Can you believe an individual can have more than one personality in the same body? Or that his memory can be so fragmented he loses days, weeks, months, and even years from his awareness? Or that one of his personalities would be a little boy, another gay, another female, another unable to feel pain, another suicidal, another homicidal, and another psychic?

His given name is James, and he lived in a small trailer house close to his parent's country home, about an hour from the outpatient clinic at the veterans' hospital where I was a staff psychiatrist. He had been coming to this clinic every month to receive medication, most recently prescribed by the doctor who discharged him from the hospital four years before I met him. He was different from the other patients because he spoke intelligently and didn't appear remote, semi-rigid, or depressed, which was typical of many World War II veterans with chronic mental illnesses. He had been in the Air Force for ten years but was discharged in 1969 because of an intractable seizure disorder. Since then he had been treated for several different psychiatric diagnoses including anxiety disorder, depression, and somatization disorder.

I first met the patient in the winter of 1975 when I treated him for anxiety and depression with appropriate medications. During his follow-up visit I found him to be suffering from abdominal pain and nausea, so I referred him for a medical evaluation. The hospital specialist who examined the patient had him hospitalized. He returned to see me two weeks later, and to my surprise, he couldn't remember being in the hospital. I was curious as to why he had no recollection of this time, and also intrigued by the personality change I observed. For those reasons I asked if he would agree to meet with me for a psychotherapy session. He agreed to the session and signed a consent form for videotaping. We had no idea this would be the first of therapy sessions that would continue until August 1983.

It became clear to me during the first two therapy sessions that there was more than one alternate personality, whose names would not be evident until later:

JAMES: his given name, but not a predominant personality.

JAY: the predominant personality who generally acted and spoke quite normally.

JIM: the young boy named by his father.

JIMMY: the young boy named by his mother.

SHEA: a homosexual personality, present for a short time, and who would reappear later as a female.

JACK: the father, who would become apparent at a later time.

ROBERT RANDOM: a very transient and insignificant personality.

LATOT: the personality with a mystical origin who would eventually become the predominant personality.

CHAPTER 1

The First Session

March 24, 1975

James arrives at our first scheduled session in the recording studio wearing a white long-sleeved dress shirt, a light-blue sweater vest, and gray trousers. He is sporting a well-fitted dark wig with moderate length hair and sideburns. I introduce him to Tawn, a fourth year medical student from Creighton University who has spent the last two months in training with me, and is very interested in observing this session. I explain to James that the purpose for our meeting is to understand why he has no memory of recently being a hospital patient, and only remembers meeting with me in the psychiatric outpatient clinic.

"Do you remember my asking you about coming into the hospital?" I ask.

"You might have said that but I don't plan on coming into this hospital. You've asked me a million and one times to come into this hospital but I've always told you I won't come," he embellishes, not wanting to believe I had asked him on only one occasion.

"But you did come in this hospital a month ago and you were here for a week."

He denies it vehemently. "I wasn't here at all. That's what I

5

mean. You're trying to confuse me and I'm just not going to get confused."

Tawn asks him another question about his memory. "Do you remember coming to the last medication clinic you had with Dr. Brende?"

"I'm kind of foggy there," he replies casually as he brushes off the question with a hand gesture. "I only saw you about two seconds and then I got my prescription and got sent home."

It's clear to both Tawn and me that he has no memory for the duration of his week-long hospitalization for a medical problem, and possibly longer. For that reason I ask him if he is willing to be hypnotized in order to uncover what he's forgotten.

He shakes his head. "I can hypnotize myself. The old party tricks, you know," he laughs, and continues. "I made it seem like my arm was going to fall off. Parlor tricks like that."

"Were you any good at it?" I ask.

He shrugs his shoulders in an attitude of pseudo-modesty.

After explaining how I plan to use hypnosis he half-heartedly agrees. I ask him to close his eyes, extend both hands, and imagine that his right hand is wearing a heavy glove. At that suggestion his right hand spontaneously drops. I instruct him to use finger signals to answer my questions, but he suddenly breaks the trance induction, raises his head and looks at me, saying, "I don't like this game. I want to be somewhere else right now."

When I ask him to use his imagination to visualize a lovely scene his demeanor changes, and he tells me with an angry voice that he didn't like the doctor who treated him in the hospital. Then

6

he changes again and denies having any memory of being in the hospital. At this point he ignores me and begins to clean his fingernails. Suddenly his demeanor switches into a smiling, carefree individual who tells me he is enjoying life. As I press him for more details, his behavior changes suddenly and he drops his head, looks down at his hands, and begins folding and unfolding his jacket. This goes on for a few minutes until he switches topics and begins talking about a completely different subject, unrelated to my previous questions.

After a few minutes of animated verbiage he suddenly becomes silent. I ask what he's thinking and feeling, but he frowns and says he never feels good. When I ask for more information his appearance changes and he says, "I always feel good. Have you ever seen me when I didn't feel good? I think you're trying to pull something on me."

I point out that he had just said two opposite things but he only laughs. Then he pulls out a cigarette from his pocket and lights up, which is allowable in hospitals at this time. He lapses into small talk, accompanied by histrionic gestures using both arms.

Tawn asks him if he enjoys being in the spotlight.

"I always enjoy the spotlight. That's one place I am, no matter what it is. I can do anything there is in this world as long as there is a spotlight on me." He grins broadly, expresses disdain for morality, and brags that he doesn't like to follow the rules. "I can do anything I want to do, even go into a hypnotic trance if I want to or if I don't want to," he says.

"Why wouldn't you want to?"

"Probably because I wouldn't be in the spotlight, I don't know. Do you want to hypnotize me?"

"Yes, but only if you would feel comfortable."

"If you want to hypnotize me, then hypnotize me. You might be shocked. I might tell you to go to hell. Listen, I know all about hypnosis and I know you can do almost anything there is under hypnosis."

After bragging some more about his moral principles and desire to always tell the truth, he removes the cigarette from his mouth, puts it out in the ashtray on a nearby table, and continues to pontificate about the importance of being truthful.

I return to the subject of hypnosis and explain its purpose. "Hypnosis uncovers the other part of you that's under the surface."

"I've been told that. But uh…" He shrugs his shoulders and lifts his left hand as if to gesture "so what."

"Do you want to find out what the other part of you is like? Or do you want us to find out?" I ask.

He pauses for several seconds, then grins. "If I had another person, I don't think I'd like him."

"You don't know. He may be just as enjoyable as the other person. But, he'd probably be different."

"Well he probably would be different. There's only one me. There couldn't be more than one. There just couldn't," he insists.

"I know there's only one you but there may be different parts to you," I explain.

He looks at me incredulously and then turns his mouth down.

"I don't think I would like him. I just know I wouldn't. People have told me I'm selfish and arrogant. So what if I am?" He shrugs his shoulders, juts out his chin, and continues. "That's one thing that I'm the very best at. I'm arrogant and I know it. See, I am the very best. I'm conceited. I know that."

To challenge his grandiosity I point out that I have seen another side to him—sad, timid, and scared.

"I know I wouldn't like that part," he grins, and then expresses his disdain for anyone who shows weakness.

"What do you say that we agree that we should uncover the other side of you that you're scared of," I say.

"What other side? You mean that skinny little mousey little ass-hole? I mean person?" he scoffs.

It's been startling to see in just his first session James' inability to sustain a cohesive strain of consciousness. It's as if two parts of his mind are disconnected, and each part functions independently. This happens because of a psychological defense mechanism called dissociation, which splits James' mind and body into two. Dissociation can be a symptom of post-traumatic syndromes, as well as fugue states, and personality fragmentation. Although I have never seen a person with multiple personalities, I wonder if James could be that person. Fortunately I believe he will be a good subject for hypnosis based on the fact that individuals who dissociate have also been found to enter trance states more easily. If so, using hypnosis may help us determine the proper diagnosis.[1]

Before finishing today, James agrees to meet again tomorrow

for psychotherapy and hypnosis. I remind him today's session has been videotaped and I will gladly let him see the recording tomorrow.

I trust my ability as a trained medical hypnotist. I had received that training several years before I began my residency in psychiatry while I was a physician practicing medicine in northern Minnesota. As a primary care provider I used hypnosis for medical purposes—controlling pain, inducing general anesthesia, treating psychosomatic illnesses, and curtailing bad habits. It wasn't until I was asked to use hypnosis to treat a patient who suffered from chronic and persistent diarrhea that I learned there was a connection between her physical symptoms and her unresolved emotional problems. While in a trance state, she suddenly regressed to age five and remembered being sexually abused. That experience prompted my decision to seek specialty training in psychiatry at the Menninger Foundation in Topeka, Kansas. Among the many things I learned when I entered the Menninger training program in 1969 was that psychodynamic psychiatry could be traced back to Sigmund Freud and his use of hypnosis.

Freud became interested in this therapeutic technique in 1887, and received training from Bernheim and Charcot in France. His enthusiasm for hypnosis led him to translate Bernheim's textbook of 19th century hypnotherapy into German, entitled: *On Suggestion and its Therapeutic Application.* Although he initially found hypnosis useful for patients with hysteria, he later became frustrated by its transient effectiveness and shifted his attention to a lengthier process, which he called psychoanalysis.

I will not become aware that hypnosis has been used to diagnosis and treat patients with alternate personalities until I meet Dr. Ralph Allison in 1976, one of the pioneers in the recognition and treatment of multiple personality disorder, later referred to as dissociative identity disorder.[2] In fact, Dr. Allison described the hypnotically induced phenomenon as opening Pandora's box of emerging multiplicity.[3]

I will also learn that a number of other therapists will also successfully apply hypnotic techniques in cases of multiple personality disorder. Furthermore, when therapists have used hypnosis during the course of therapy, they have sometimes stumbled upon previously unrecognized dual or multiple personalities.[4]

In spite of hypnosis being recognized as an effective tool for the treatment of selected psychiatric patients, it has also had a controversial history. The presence of stage hypnotists, exaggerated depictions of the power of posthypnotic suggestions, and unethical uses of the technique have contributed to a disparaging of its medical value. Even respected professionals can be at risk to misuse hypnosis. Some mental health professionals will be accused of inserting false ideas about alleged personal traumas into their patients' subconscious thought processes while in a trance state. Some of these patients will file suit and win malpractice actions against the accused therapists. This will lead to the formation of an organization called the False Memory Syndrome Foundation in 1992. As a result several specialized treatment programs for patients with multiple personalities will close down, and a number of professionals will stop using hypnosis to uncover traumatic memories. The furor will eventually subside and the ethical use of hypnosis will be accepted once again as a powerful and useful therapeutic tool.[5]

My decision to use hypnosis with James was not only consistent with the experience of hypnotherapists like Ralph Allison, but also based on my own successful use of hypnosis with other patients. I trace my first use of the technique back to 1966, after receiving advanced training in medical hypnosis. The first application was with obstetric patients, initially with a woman I treated for the first time when she went into labor at full term. Hypnosis reduced the severity of her pain, with the help of a tape recorder. After a prolonged twenty-four hour time period she gave birth via caesarean section. I continued to use it for all my obstetric patients, including a woman who had five miscarriages before I saw her, but finally delivered a live baby. I also used hypnosis for pain control, bad habits, and assisting patients prior to surgery and during recovery. I maintained my skills through joining the American Society of Clinical Hypnosis, and securing certification with the American Board of Medical Hypnosis.

CHAPTER 2

Hypnosis uncovers three hidden personalities.

March 25, 1975

The medical student Tawn and I meet James in the studio on the following day. He is wearing the same wig and dressed neatly in the same gray slacks. He is wearing a blue short-sleeved shirt, and the same light blue sweater vest as he wore yesterday. He signs in with the name Jay. I ask him if he is willing to proceed with my plan to use hypnosis during this interview, and he asks if I am going to give him Sodium Pentothal. I assure him that I will not use Pentothal, and I will sit at a distance so that there will always be a space left between us. I also assure him that he will not lose control and is free to stop at any time. After I give him instructions about sitting squarely on the chair, he laughingly asks if I want him to take off his shoes and glasses. I tell him that won't be necessary.

I use a progressive relaxation technique and begin by instructing him to close his eyes, relax, and answer my questions using finger signals. He resists closing his eyes at first, and says he can't relax if he has to give up answering my questions verbally, because talking enables him to feel in control.

"What are you feeling?" I ask.

"I'm scared," he replies.

There is a long pause. After thirty seconds I hear a different and more subdued voice. "I'm not scared," he mumbles.

I ask him once again to use finger signals to respond to my questions, and instruct him to raise his index finger on his right hand to answer yes, to raise his index finger on the left to answer no, and to lift his right thumb if he doesn't know the answer. He starts to relax but then becomes tense.

"A part of you may not have any fear but there seems to be another part of you that feels afraid," I explain. Thinking that he may have a better sense of control if I focus only on one side of his body, I suggest that he relax his right side and allow the left side to remain tense. I give deepening suggestions and ask him to visualize a yardstick with the number thirty-six representing the deepest level of relaxation. He seems able to relax the right side of his body to the deepest level without any distress. When I ask if he would like to experience being in control of his left side he responds yes, so I suggest that he allow his left side to go as deeply relaxed as his right side. He stiffens up and cannot do this, indicating that each side of James' body is responding differently.

I wonder if the problem is caused by a lateralization process in the brain, which refers to the way some neural functions tend to be more dominant in one hemisphere than the other. In normal people the left hemisphere is linked to speech, cognitive organization, and right-handedness, while the right hemisphere is more frequently linked to emotional expression and left-handedness. Since James cannot relax the left side of his body, a lateralization process indicates that the right cerebral hemisphere that controls the left side of his body is malfunctioning.[6] Before finishing up I give him a posthypnotic suggestion that he will be

14

able to talk about anything important to him after returning to normal consciousness.

When he resumes normal consciousness he says he felt like he was asleep but had dreams he didn't like. "They're bawl-baby dreams. I'm scared of my own damn shadow. I'm just a fraidy-cat, that's all."

"What are you afraid of?" I ask.

"It's dumb, stupid. I'm afraid of everything. Afraid of myself I think."

Then I observe a sudden change in his demeanor and tone of voice. He takes a cigarette out of his pocket, gestures dramatically with his right hand, and tells me in a detached voice that he had a dream about a bawl-baby. When I ask this cigarette smoking individual, the same person I met yesterday, to describe the bawl-baby, he tells me he's upset that hypnosis allowed the bawl-baby to be released. "I don't like this crybaby and you told me there wouldn't be anyone in here. I don't like him."

I change the subject and return to the primary goal— continuing his psychotherapy and the goals we'd agreed on. He does not remember what we decided so I remind him. "We agreed that the goal in therapy is to help you find out about the other side of you, the fearful side. Today it appears that we can help you gain some control over that part of you."

"I'm always in control," he insists.

"You are sometimes. But I think you're not in control as much as you think you are. In order to accomplish this goal we'll have to have some regular meetings for at least three months, once or twice a week."

I ask him to make a commitment, and after struggling with his ambivalence, he finally agrees to return in a week. Before we close this session I ask if he is taking his prescribed medication. He tells me he's not taking the medication, so I ask him to resume taking it and to let me know if he has any disagreeable side effects. Finally, I ask him to write down any thoughts, concerns, or questions that may come to his mind, and to feel free to call me if necessary before our next meeting.

It had been a fascinating session. I believe that I observed three different personalities, including the frightened bawl-baby and the grandiose personality who says he is always in control. Another fascinating circumstance was the "lateralization" that took place, since he was unable to relax the left side of his body during the hypnotic trance induction.

There is very little published literature about multiple personalities that I can find to read, so I will have to depend on my therapeutic skills and intuitive instincts. I can't help but think that treating a patient with multiple personalities might be like putting together a jigsaw puzzle. First I must lay out the pieces—the personalities—see what they look like, establish a therapeutic relationship with each of them, and slowly fit them together. This will require time. I will eventually learn that the expected duration of time for successful psychotherapy for an individual with multiple personalities is a minimum of one year, with the likelihood it will take much longer. No doubt I am a very long way away from the presumed end point—a completed puzzle.

CHAPTER 3

The revelation of hidden aggressors:
Who's intoxicated? Who's in control?

March 27, 1975

I'm surprised to receive a telephone call from James' sister-in-law two days after the hypnosis session. "James has not been able to control himself the last two days. Something has gone wrong, he can't seem to remember what's happening and he can't maintain a normal conversation, particularly with me. He doesn't seem to be himself. And his behavior keeps changing all the time. Do you think he needs to be in the hospital?"

I ask her to bring him in to see me. When he arrives to the waiting room I notice that he is wearing dark glasses and his speech is slurred. I escort him down the hall to the studio and ask him to sit down and sign in. He complies and signs the name Jay.

"Have you taken too much medication?" I ask, wondering if he's under the influence of a drug or intoxicated from alcohol.

"I don't remember," he slurs incoherently.

"What seems to be the trouble?" I ask.

"Crybaby's coming out."

"What do you mean?"

"He's off some place."

"Where?"

"Lurking in the shadows. I'm worried he's going to kill me.

The other one eggs him on," he says.

I ask him to tell me more about the crybaby and how that is related to a possible medication overdose.

"Crybaby took 'em," he says.

"When did that happen?" I ask.

"He gave them to me about thirty minutes ago."

"Do you remember taking them?"

"I don't remember taking them but I saw the empty bottles. I got too much to live for. But someone keeps egging the crybaby on. Don't ever trust a crybaby cuz he'll sneak up on you," he warns.

Suddenly his facial expression changes and he casually reaches into his pocket to pull out a pack of cigarettes. "You don't mind if I smoke do you?" he smirks, clearly oblivious to this dramatic change in his behavior.

"Can you tell me what you remember about our last meeting?" I ask.

He vaguely recalls meeting with me three days ago. Then his eyes scour the studio in which he's sitting, which contains a table next to his chair and a window with a camera behind it. "This room seems familiar," he says. "Will you be my doctor when I'm in the hospital?" he asks, indicating that he knew his sister-in-law wanted him to be hospitalized.

"No. You'll be a patient in Building Four, and I'll work closely with your doctor there about your treatment."

He changes subjects and says, "You didn't hypnotize me the other day. You just talked and I just raised my fingers. I wanted to

18

talk but you told me not to talk. I remember the crybaby started to come out and I didn't let him come out. I told him to stay in until I wanted him to, but now he comes out even when I'm not summoning him."

"Why do you call him a crybaby? And why do you think he wants to kill you?" I ask.

"He bawls all the time and threatens me and this other guy eggs him on," he repeats.

"Can you tell me about him?" I ask.

"He has an Air Force uniform on. And he's as tall as I am," he replies.

"Can you tell me more about this individual?"

"Oh, he's pleasant on the outside but a mean son-of-a-bitch on the inside, pardon my language."

I frown with uncertainty about whom I'm talking with.

"I think his name is Sergeant James C. Kohlman," he states.

"And what's your name?" I ask.

"My name is Jay."

"What's your last name?"

"I don't have a last name. Don't you think Jay's enough?"

"It's all right with me," I reply.

"But I put Shea on all of my art work," he emphasizes, making sure I know Jay is not the same as Shea, which I assume is the pen name he uses for his art work. It will soon be clear that Jay and Shea are two different personalities.

"How come you're wearing dark glasses? Or do you always wear dark glasses?" I ask, recalling that I'd never seen him wear

19

these before.

"They're trying to kill me and I'm going incognito so they won't find me."

I hear him talk about several personalities, but remain confused as to which one might be a potential murderer. "Do you want to kill James?" I ask.

"No, I don't want to kill James. He's the only level headed one in the whole bunch."

He has revealed a number of personalities, but I'm not able to absorb this astounding information until later when I review the videotaped session.

"Can you tell me about James?" I ask.

Jay replies in a slurred voice. "Yes, he flares up once in awhile, but he flares up and then he soon forgets it."

"I would like to talk to James," I insist. After a long pause Jay's grin is replaced by an alert man with clear and succinct speech, not the slurs of an intoxicated individual.

"Are you James C. Kohlman, the Air Force sergeant?" I ask.

"Yes sir," he says with military precision.

"How do you feel now?"

"Marvelous. I feel a little tired, but you always feel a little tired, but that's no sign you're not making progress," he replies enthusiastically.

"How come you're tired?" I ask.

Then James begins to describe his mundane military life. "When you work in personnel flying clothes you have all the Air Force officers coming there and you have to make sure every detail is right. It's a little tiring."

"Where?"

"Where? Through the gates. You go through the gates and straight down to a great big hangar but you have a little room in the hangar." James precisely describes his military experience, although he continues to wear Jay's dark glasses.

"Why are you wearing those dark glasses, James? I've never seen you wear dark glasses before?" I ask.

"I don't wear dark glasses," he insists.

"Why do you have them on then?"

"Do I have them on?"

"Yes."

He scowls. "That's strictly your imagination." He takes the dark glasses off and places them on the table next to his chair.

"Yeah, you look like yourself a little bit, although you look awfully tired. Have you been having trouble sleeping?"

"Once in awhile I have trouble sleeping. But Jay kept coming into my room all the time saying 'go to sleep,' and when I went to sleep and dozed off, then Jim came in there," he replies.

"Tell you what, I've met Jay and he's kind of a nice guy. I'd like to meet Jim, Ok?"

"No, I don't like Jim," he replies and puts his dark glasses back on.

"I know, but I want to meet him anyway, I might like him."

"No, cuz he'll kill me."

"Not when I'm around he won't," I assure him.

James doesn't believe my assurance he will be safe, and

continues to resist my request to talk to Jim, so I decide to address him as if he were Jim, but he doesn't respond. I continue. "How are you? Is that your name, Jim? Now I want to talk to you for five minutes." He lowers his head but doesn't respond. "Are you frightened?" I pause. Still no response. "You don't have to be frightened." I pause again. "What are you frightened of?" I ask.

Suddenly he slides his legs together and pulls away from me. "Men in the dark," he mutters softly.

I'm fascinated by this change in his voice and body posture, and wonder if this person is Jim.

"You're frightened of men in the dark? Of what men?"

"Drunken men."

"Why would you be frightened of drunken men?"

"Cuz they do horrible things."

"Like what?" I ask. This information will have more specific meaning at a much later time, although now I am uncertain of its significance.

Suddenly his appearance changes once again and I find myself talking to the person I'd interviewed at the first—a man with slurred speech, talking as if he had never been absent from the interview. I believe I'm talking with the person who calls himself Jay. Our session is approaching fifty minutes, and I ask him how he feels about coming into the hospital. He tells me he doesn't like being in the hospital, and complains that he'll be given a bunch of drugs he doesn't like. I assure him that he will not be drugged by the doctor in the hospital, and then I ask him to tell me about the pills he took before he came today.

"I don't know if you took all the pills in your bottle or not, but I need to know if you did. Which one of you knows whether you took all of the pills? James, Jay, Shea, or Jim?" I ask.

"Jim did it," he replies.

"What did Jim do? Did he take 'em all?"

"Yes, he took them all. He doesn't like me."

"What time did he take them?"

"Ten o'clock or after."

I assure him that he's going to survive but also make it clear that I don't want him to overdose or do anything self-destructive. I also ask if he will be James, Jim, Shea, or Jay, or shift from one to the next when he's in the hospital. That question prompts James to emerge once again, speaking without any evidence of intoxication.

"Are you going to be James in the hospital?"

"That's my name. I feel marvelous right now, I'm a little tired, but that's no sense that I can't keep going for eighteen hours."

I'm amazed to see the difference between James, who is alert and speaks without evidence of medication overdose, and Jay or Shea, who came into the session with slurred speech. I am also surprised to see an identity switch between James, the primary personality, and Jay, Shea, and Jim, which was never reported when he was hospitalized several years ago. And now I hear Jay say to me that James is harmless unless he conspires with the crybaby.

After our meeting he is escorted to the psychiatric ward, where I will make contact with his hospital doctor to clarify that I learned the patient took the pills at approximately ten o'clock this morning. It's now about two p.m., and I'm unsure if this was a suicide gesture by overdose, but I doubt that, considering the fact that Jay told me Jim had given him the pills.

Although the need for hospital treatment is clear to me, I learn later that when James arrived on the ward he looked so normal that his doctor and nursing staff considered him to be one of their healthiest patients, and believed he didn't need to stay in the hospital in spite of the fact I said he had several personalities. In fact, the nursing staff accused James of trying to con me because they didn't believe he had more than one personality, or that one could be completely sober while another, in the same body, is intoxicated by a medication overdose.[7]

I will later learn that it is not easy to make a diagnosis of multiple personality disorder. Psychiatrist F.W. Putnam, a highly regarded specialist in this field, studied 100 cases of multiple personality disorder, and found an average of 6.8 years between the first contact with a mental health professional and the time a proper diagnosis is obtained.[8] Only a small fraction of therapists make an accurate diagnosis even when their own patients report symptoms of dissociation and fragmentation. About 40 percent of cases are discovered to have multiplicity during the course of treatment, but more than half will not be properly diagnosed until ten years of verbal therapy have elapsed. Fortunately, 15 percent of them reveal the presence of dissociated personalities during the first diagnostic assessment or early in therapy.

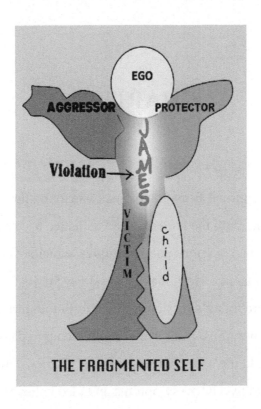

THE FRAGMENTED SELF

I have made a diagram labeled the fragmented self. The violation arrow points to James, although Jim will be seen as the trauma victim in later therapy sessions. James is the original personality who was discharged from the Air Force after ten years in military service. The "arms" signify two personalities—Shea, an aggressor, and Jay, whose primary purpose is to protect James from experiencing painful emotions. They both share ego functions (intact intellectual capabilities) and demonstrated evidence of intoxication when hospitalized at this time. The child personality is Jimmy, described as a crybaby who is afraid of the dark. He will be identified later as mother's child, and Jim as father's child.

CHAPTER 4
My name is Shea.

April 9-10, 1975

I have returned from a two-week vacation, during which time Tawn met with the patient. I had a chance to review the videotape of their sessions and am impressed with Tawn's professional manner. He'll make a good psychiatrist. He and I got together before today's session, and I briefly told him about my wonderful Colorado ski trip. He brought me up to date on what I missed and told me about his sessions with James. Tawn said he was fascinated by James' symptoms and also believes, as do I, that the patient demonstrates evidence of multiple personalities.

Today I'm struck by the patient's conspicuous physical appearance and behavior—a wig, histrionic gestures, and emotional flamboyance.[9] He announces himself with the name Shea, and says he doesn't have a clear memory of the time of our last meeting but thinks it was about seven months ago. "I don't particularly care for time 'cause time can take care of itself. I don't pay any attention to it. It doesn't matter. Time just doesn't bother me,"[10] he says casually.

When I ask if he can remember what's happened to him in the past, he pooh-poohs my question and tells me he doesn't worry about time or anything else. Furthermore, he has only a vague memory of the last time he was in the hospital, and can't remember

any specifics of recently spending a week in the hospital for medical purposes. We will learn later that he had been hospitalized for a considerable time on a psychiatric ward in this hospital four years ago, but only recalls fragments of that experience. After spending several minutes talking about insignificant trivia, I refocus our conversation on helping him remember his sister-in-law's concerns.

"She said I'd sleep nine or ten hours and that they'd be talking to me and all of a sudden they'd look over and I'd be 10,000 miles away from here and I didn't even know what she was talking about. See it's a bunch of malarkey as far as I'm concerned. Cuz I'm not that way. I felt a little woozy once in a while when I got up. But I think you changed my medication."

He tells me he's staying at the home of his older brother Clarence and sister-in-law Betty, who live about 50 miles away.

"How long are you going to stay there?" I ask.

"I'd really like to stay until I'm damn good and ready to go home but I don't know."

I ask him if he could stay closer to the hospital but he does not want to move to Topeka. He would rather stay with Clarence and Betty and I support his decision.

Suddenly I see his facial expression become a blank and I ask, "What just went through your mind?"

"Right now? To smoke a cigarette, I guess."

"You had a blank look on your face for a minute."

"Now you talk like my sister-in-law."

"Does she say that to you?"

"She told me I looked like that for hours," he answers, and goes on to explain it away as a bad acting job.

Toward the end of the session I ask him if he is willing to view previous videotaped therapy sessions in order that he can understand himself better. He agrees and I signal Dick, one of the technicians, to play a portion of the last session. As we prepare to look at the monitor Jay pulls out a cigarette and lights up. We see ourselves appear on the screen and he watches it carefully. After about ten minutes I request Dick to shut it down and ask Jay what he thinks.

"I don't like it," he says.

"What was it that disturbed you?" I ask.

"I look like some damn faggot up there, if you wanna know the truth about it."

I ask him to describe what he means by a faggot.

"The lowest class homosexual or queer you can get ahold of," he answers.

"And why did you think that you looked that way?"

"That's just the way I looked. Very low class."

"How would you like to look? If you could change your looks, what would you do?"

28

"That's a loaded question. I don't know. I always thought my looks were damn well pleasing."

"Your behavior? The way you talk? Or the look on your face?" I ask.

"That whole thing up there, the whole thing just looked ridiculous when I think about it. Really funny when I think about it."

"Well okay, that's better than being upset about it, I guess."

He continues to insist he wasn't upset but only amused. "I can't understand why you aren't laughing about the whole situation," he smirks.

The medical student and I remain quiet and listen as he also makes fun of my appearance on the videotape. "You looked as weird as me, and you're not Mike Douglas," he snickers. "The first time I saw myself, I didn't like what I saw. That was about a year ago, maybe two years ago. Well, actually I've been in movies, but I was always dancing or acting. I've never seen myself just in street clothes."

"You've never seen James Kohlman in real life?" I ask, wanting to clarify if Jay is aware of the presence of a different part of himself.

He pauses, reaches over to flick the ashes off his cigarette and his facial expression changes.

"Am I talking to Mr. Kohlman?" I ask.

"That's my father," he replies soberly.

"I can call you Jay, James, whatever you want," I say, and wait to hear if he's aware of his different names.

"My name is Shea. If you can't speak French, just Shea," he smirks.

"I can call you any name you prefer, and you should also give Betty permission to use whatever name you want."

He replies softly, "I like Betty. If she wants to call me 'shit ass' I don't give a damn," he sneers.

"Is it James she calls you?"

"Yes."

"Has she ever called you Jay?"

"Never," he snaps. He suddenly drops his arms behind his chair and looks down to his left. I see a vacant stare, indicating Shea has left the body. After a few moments I see his legs relax and his arms return to both sides of the chair and swing spontaneously from side to side. But he continues to stare vacantly into space.

"Can you tell me why you don't like being called by a different name than Shea?"

"Cuz I like Shea," he responds enthusiastically. But this animated appearance is short-lived as his body suddenly becomes rigid, his arms drop to the arms of his chair, his legs uncross, and his eyes lose focus and stare into space.

Then he begins to speak with a clipped voice. "I don't like Shea. My name is James C. Kohlman. I've been called many other things and I don't make a big deal of it." Then he stops talking, crosses his legs, lifts his arms, and takes a cigarette out of his shirt pocket. "You all don't mind if I smoke, do you?" he grins.

"Go ahead, it doesn't bother me," I say, uncertain if this is

Shea or a different personality. After hearing him complain about other people who smoke I ask this question, "What did your father call you when you were young?"

"Boy, I have to use my brain on that one. Dumb. Dumb. I don't know if he ever called me. Now that I think about it I don't think he ever called me."

"He never did give you a name?"

"Hell, when I was little there was too many other damn kids around, older and younger than me. There's fourteen kids in my family," he laughs. Then he flicks the ash off his cigarette. "At one time I was in the middle of the fourteen and then all of a sudden they all left and I was nowhere. You know that old joke about running away from home. Well I woke up one morning and my home had run away from me. When I woke up that morning they had moved out." He laughs. "No, it wasn't that bad. It took me three weeks to find out where they lived. Way out in western Kansas someplace." He laughs again.

After I express sympathy about his abandonment experience he nonchalantly calls it a good thing. "Everybody was gone and I had a room all to myself."

"You were abandoned," I assert, surprised by his lack of emotional response.

"Nobody was around so I packed up my clothes, went up and got me an apartment and that was it."

"Being abandoned…I can't think of anything worse than that," I emphasize more strongly.

I don't learn any accurate details from Jay or his family

about why he suddenly found himself alone in the house. Jay's description is like that of an emotionally detached observer who has blocked an unpleasant event out of his memory.

His other early life memories are vague. For example, he describes the duration of his childhood as first happy, then sad, and then ending abruptly, after which he transitioned into adulthood at a young age. I wonder what caused his childhood's abrupt ending. Was it a traumatic event that caused a dissociation and another personality to take over?

Our session ends on a positive note and we meet again the following day on Friday. When I ask if he would like to see the videotape of yesterday's session he agrees to watch it.

During the viewing of this tape, his facial expression takes on an annoyed and puzzled appearance. "That's not me. He's a sarcastic bastard."

When the viewing is over he expresses dislike for what he saw, but he's vague about remembering any content. Before ending the session I express concern when he complains about feeling over-controlled and over-protected by his brother and sister-in-law, and I encourage him to adjust to that environment and to be comfortable with who he is.

CHAPTER 5

James is going home.

April 14, 1975

This session includes James' brother Clarence and his wife Betty, who are prepared to take James home today, as he is being discharged from the hospital. Betty describes James as a normal, carefree young man who was been living in a small trailer less than one hundred yards from the family home. Clarence says his brother seemed to be very happy for a number of years after his discharge from the Air Force ten years ago, but then he began having mental problems that caused him to be hospitalized. When I ask about James' early life, Betty recalls a family tragedy when James was a young boy and his baby brother died of yellow jaundice. James had helped his mother care for the baby before he died. The death had a major impact on the family and it became emotionally fragmented. But James grew up, finished school, and joined the Air Force like his brother Clarence.

Clarence and Betty tell me James spends most of his time taking care of the garden during the day, but stays up watching TV in the main house all night. They've become concerned about his unpredictable behavior. Sometimes James is animated and seeks to be the center of attention. Other times he is childlike and withdraws like a whipped puppy. Betty says she notices moments when he waves his hand across his face, spaces out, and doesn't know where he is.

James sits quietly, listens to Betty's observations with a puzzled look on his face, and insists that she couldn't be right. But he acknowledges having memory problems and says he can't remember much of what happened to him during the past four years since he received electroconvulsive therapy (ECT) in the hospital.

When I ask James about his relationship to his parents, he refuses to talk about his mother and complains he never felt close to his father. Rather, he describes Clarence as his role model and family leader. When I ask what name his mother called him he's reluctant to answer, and becomes very anxious and withdraws from the discussion. But Betty remembers, "Mother always called him Jimmy."

"What are you thinking James? Would you like your mother to call you something else?" I ask.

His face becomes blank and his arms drop down. "My name is James. Of course they call me other things," he replies stoically.

"You can ask your mother to call you something else," I say.

"She has the right to. I don't have the right to ask my mother that. It says honor your mother and father," he replies somberly. Then he suddenly waves his arm in front of his face, looks at me as if he's unaware of what he just said, and speaks cheerily with a grin on his face. "I don't care what they call me as long as it isn't too late for supper."

Although James' behaviors are consistent with my belief that he suffers from a fragmented identity disorder, I don't mention that

34

to these two family members. I do ask if they are comfortable taking him home. James immediately turns to Betty after she nods yes and insists they shouldn't do anything special for him. Clarence agrees with his wife and makes it clear that they will treat him like a member of the family and be honest with him. "If we don't like something, we'll tell him."

Although I believe my patient's amnesia is caused by hidden and disruptive personalities, I can't yet make an official diagnosis. I am aware, however, that he's had several different diagnoses during his past hospitalizations. A previous hospital psychiatrist administered electroconvulsive therapy four years ago because he believed James had psychotic symptoms and depression.

Historically the numbers of reported patients with multiple personalities have been low. It was previously considered a rare phenomenon, with less than one hundred cases described before 1944. I have had no previous exposure to the disorder, and my interest in learning more about it is based on my personal involvement with James. My interest in multiple personality disorder has grown. So has the interest of many other professionals who, during the late 1970s and early 1980s, attended conferences and read articles about it. There will also be increasing interest within the general public stimulated by books and movies like *The Three Faces of Eve* and *Sybil*.

The established link to childhood sex abuse will prompt therapists to become more active in seeking out their patients' previously undetected memories of childhood sexual trauma. Many of these professionals who are qualified to use therapeutic hypnosis effectively will be able to make the diagnosis more easily. If they discover multiplicity, they should be able to treat their patients effectively. The prevalence of psychotherapy as the primary modality will enable these patients to be treated for extended periods of time without the restrictions from insurance companies that will take place in the 1990s. For all of these reasons the numbers of diagnosed cases of multiple personalities will grow immensely, and the incidence of this disorder will continue to rise sharply during the 1970s and 1980s. I will learn that the numbers of cases will reach 20,000 by the end of the century. Statisticians will estimate that 1.5 percent of the general population and 3 percent of those admitted to mental hospitals have the disorder.

The official diagnosis—multiple personality disorder—will be established in 1980, but its name will be changed to dissociative identity disorder in 1994. There will be an avalanche of case reports, books, articles, and conferences about it. An organization will be formed—The International Society for the Study of Multiple Personality and Dissociation (to be renamed later as the International Society for the Study of Dissociation)—and hold its first annual conference in 1984. Its official journal, *Dissociation*, will appear in 1988 and be replaced in 2000 by the *Journal of Trauma and Dissociation*.

In spite of the avalanche of discovered cases, a number of investigators will come to doubt the validity of the diagnosis of dissociative identity disorder. They will say that the multitude of cases reported in the 1970s and 1980s merely reflected a fad that will inevitably fade. They will claim that too many diagnosticians failed to recognize that the symptoms therapists thought were proof of dissociative identity disorder were really caused by other disorders.[11]

CHAPTER 6
I need to be independent.

April 21, 1975

The patient returns for a scheduled outpatient therapy session a week later. "I didn't want to come today. I was nervous about coming," he announces emphatically.

After he signs in with the name Jay, I ask how things were for him during the past week. He complains that he's not comfortable with Clarence and Betty being so over-protective, and would rather live alone in his small trailer where he recently laid down new carpet.

"Do you remember the meeting here last week?" I ask.

"My brother and sister-in-law were here, but I don't remember what we talked about," he replies.

"Do you want to remember?"

"Yes, unless it will upset me. I remember you cut my medication down to three pills and I feel better."[12]

He says he's willing to review the last session and I ask Dick to show it. While looking at the videotape Jay appears frozen in his chair by what he sees.

Upon hearing himself say "My name is James," and "people have the right to call me what they want to call me," he suddenly snorts, "He's a sarcastic bastard."

"Who is?" I ask.

"That's not me," he insists.

After watching for ten minutes he waves his hand in front of his face in disgust, pulls out a pack of cigarettes, and lights one.

"You said he's sarcastic and you didn't like him?"

"No."

I remind him that the goal of therapy is to improve his self-understanding and memory about things he's forgotten. Then I ask for his opinion after watching the tape.

"I looked stupid. I don't think this is my day."

After discussing this a little longer, Jay changes the subject and tells me he doesn't want to continue staying with his brother and sister-in-law, and ask them to drive fifty miles so that he can come to therapy sessions.

"You say you're not happy living there but I say you're not ready to be completely independent."

"I have independence. But that's not the point. It's their house. I don't belong there. Why should I butt in on my family?"

I clarify the reason they have asked him to live there is for support and honest communication with them.

"They think I'm crazy!" he exclaims.

"You're not crazy. Don't talk about it as if you were."

He doesn't answer.

I assure him Clarence and Betty want to make sure he is safe. Yet he can still assert himself and request more freedom while he's living there.

"That will be hard to do," he says and shakes his head.

I'm not surprised to hear Jay express his concern about being called crazy, a term frequently used to label a person who has said or done disturbing things. Furthermore, it doesn't surprise me since his sister-in-law had previously called me about his unusual behaviors and lapses of consciousness.

.

CHAPTER 7

I can't feel pain.

April 28, 1975

Our next therapy session is two weeks later. The patient arrives wearing the same wig and appearing quite effeminate, which is consistent with Shea's presentation. He eagerly tells me a number of interesting things about himself, the most unusual being that he lost the capacity to feel physical pain seven years ago. I will later learn that he suffered a major trauma at that time. When I ask for more details, he tells me he can't feel pain if he sticks his finger with a needle or if he has a cigarette burn.[13]

Shea is not interested in telling me if James also lost the ability to feel pain. He also winces every time that name is mentioned, but he's willing to talk about his memories of the lifestyle he and James lived in Tampa, Florida. He describes himself as a very active young man during the time he was stationed at McDill Air Force Base. He participated in a number of enjoyable activities during his free time, including becoming a Boy Scout leader. For the first time I hear him talk about enjoying his gay life style. "I used to go into this gay bar with my 'girlfriend' Poopsy. She comes in with a long black dress and dances on the counter. The vice squad comes in and jumps on this (cross-dresser) 'guy.' It took three men to take him down. The judge had him for impersonating a woman but dismissed him because he had a male organ."

After listening to this story that doesn't completely hold true, I ask if he had any relationships with the opposite sex, and he tells me about a girl he wanted to marry. He called her a Catholic virgin because they had no sexual relationship. He recalls that they discussed marriage plans even after she left Florida and returned to her home in St. Paul, Minnesota. They made wedding plans by mail and he flew there several times, but her mother intervened. He repeatedly tried to call her but she would not talk to him any further. He doesn't remember grieving the loss of that relationship and soon found another girlfriend. But that relationship quickly broke up and he stopped trying to get serious with girls. After that time they became objects and he always maintained emotional distance.

I ask if he ever felt sad about losing the girl from St. Paul, but my question triggers him to dissociate and I see a personality

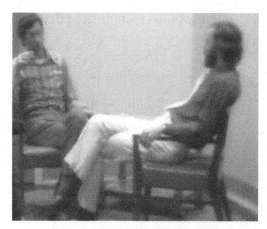

switch. He swings his left leg over his right, which I will later learn is significant, as it is associated with the dominance of one personality over another.

His failure to talk about feelings of loss makes me believe he needed to detach himself from the emotional pain of losing a meaningful love relationship.

42

As this session comes to a close, we review our therapeutic contract, which includes helping him recover lost memories, understand why his mind becomes confused, become comfortable with people, and discover why he had taken an overdose of medication.

CHAPTER 8
Memories and Memory Lapses

May 5-12, 1975

We meet one week later and Jay signs in. He describes his week as strange because he didn't feel all together and couldn't remember much. Rather than remain in Clarence and Betty's home, he stayed in a hotel in Topeka. But he's only able to recall checking in, talking to the maid, getting a Pepsi, and going to a restaurant. The rest of the week was a blank.

He tells me he tried to kill himself several years ago but doesn't feel that way now. He recalls being hospitalized, treated with Thorazine and Dilantin,[14] told his problem was cured, and sent home. He wonders why he is now having more memory lapses.

I remind him that one of our goals is to help him remember the things he has forgotten. I ask him what he remembers about his childhood and he doesn't remember feeling close to anyone in his family except his sister, who was two years older and with whom he spent a lot of time playing. He says he confided in her rather than his mother. He remembers his first job when he made twenty-five cents a week picking up mail for a neighbor lady when he was nine years old. He said he began to dance when he was seven years old and went to dancing classes with a married woman when he was older. He recalls little else except for the experience of being abandoned by his family at some point during childhood. He says he does not remember how he felt at that time even though he must have felt considerable grief. This subject will come up again during the course of his treatment, and illustrate the nature of his psychological defenses against experiencing painful abandonment feelings.

He talks about other past memories, including being a professional dancer in Tampa and using dancing techniques as a way of keeping in shape. When I ask about relationships to the opposite sex he tells me again about his one serious relationship with a girl who rejected him after they had planned to get married. He also tells me about Judy, a sexual partner during his twenties who he did not want to marry, and his first sexual experience when he was in seventh or eighth grade. I ask if his sexual relationships with women had been satisfying but he doesn't respond and appears anxious. After a minute I ask if he ever had sex with men and see a puzzled look on his face. After a long pause he says, "I guess I've had. But it was just a test. I wish I'd never done it."

"Why?"

"I had no need to do it. It wasn't good or bad. It proved something, that I'm not a homosexual. You can have men friends and love them and it has nothing to do with sex."

When I ask what his age was at that time he becomes anxious, waves his hand toward his head, and suddenly switches to a more flippant and carefree demeanor, denying that he feels upset.

Monday, May 12 is Tawn's last session. He meets alone with the patient, who signs in as Jay and provides additional history

45

about past medical problems, which include Bright's disease and scarlet fever when he was young. Six days ago he had stomach cramps, nausea, and was unable to eat anything, and last year he had episodes of chest pain and shortness of breath, which sound like panic attacks.

When Tawn asks what he remembers about this past week he says Betty heard him speak in a different sounding voice and he feels upset that he can't remember Tuesday and Wednesday afternoon. He recalls getting shock treatments in this hospital several years ago, and being held in the recovery room for two and a half days. That's why he dislikes coming here again. When Tawn asks Jay how he feels about Tawn's departure, he says he prefers being a "smart alec" so he can avoid expressing honest feelings.

Tawn says he plans to go to Hawaii, which triggers Jay's unpleasant memory about being abandoned by a previous therapist. When Tawn asks Jay if thinks he has made any improvement during the past two months, Jay says he's not as frightened of Dr. Brende. At the close of the session Tawn says goodbye and Jay responds appropriately.

CHAPTER 9
Motor Automatisms

May 19, 1975

I meet with Jay alone for the first time since Tawn finished his rotation. He appears extremely well dressed, wearing a long-sleeve silk shirt, gray vest and matching gray trousers. He's also sporting a full but well-trimmed beard and a wig. I arrive a little late and apologize for not being on time after missing the last two weeks. He says he thinks he's too much of a burden and expects me to discontinue our therapy sessions. "I'll never impose myself on anyone and I never will," he states clearly and firmly.

"I know you won't. You've said before that you don't like to be a burden on anybody. I don't consider you a burden at all."

"I don't think you do. It's just that you have other things to do."

His voice is low pitched and well controlled as he sits calmly in the chair. Then suddenly I see his eyes close, his right hand elevate and wave momentarily, then lower again. Then both hands spontaneously lift and come together over his head.

He soon regains control, opens his eyes and begins to talk. "You're leaving me, so I must plan."

In spite of my reassurance I see his eyes close again, his right hand swing across his face, and his left leg swing over his right leg. Then I see his hips shift to the left side of the chair, his body turn toward his right, and his head swing back toward his left.

I am witnessing automatic movements of his musculature that almost resemble a slow seizure and which, as I learn later, are called motor automatisms.[15] These are observed not only in patients who have multiple personalities, but also in persons with major mental illnesses, partial complex seizures, and fugue states with loss of self-identity accompanied by unplanned travel or wandering.

Then his eyes open and he looks at me. I'm seeing a different person, perhaps Jay, who begins talking in a more rapid, higher pitched voice about a completely different subject— planting his garden. I listen as he jokes and talks about growing and picking the vegetables, a topic that's in complete contrast to the content of his speech a few minutes ago.

This is not the first time I've witnessed James' automatisms during a therapy session, but they're occurring more frequently. They appear to be related to personality switches and seem to be triggered by memories or experiences he can't cope with, such as loss or threatened loss. In order to understand this phenomenon better I read about automatisms. They are an automatic motor or muscle movement lasting for several seconds to several minutes or longer, during which time the sufferer is unaware of his actions. Other examples of automatic motor behavior include sleepwalking and complex partial seizures (later referred to as focal onset impaired awareness seizures) caused by uncontrolled electrical disturbances in the temporal lobe of the brain. Automatisms can also be associated with dissociative states, as first described by the French neurologist Pierre Janet, in patients suffering from hysteria and emotional trauma.[16]

I ask him if he feels sad about Tawn's departure but he brushes that off as insignificant. However, he tells me Tawn had ordered an electrocardiogram (EKG) for him during my absence.

"What happened?" I ask.

"I was resting in the afternoon. I woke up and I was pure white, gagging, vomiting, and had chest pains."

Fortunately his EKG was normal.

Before our session comes to a close I mention I'll be changing our appointment time, but emphasize that I will continue meeting with him and ask him to return in two weeks on June 2, the day after Memorial Day. As we close I ask him to let me know if anything of significance comes up between then and now. (The meeting scheduled for Monday June 2 is not recorded here.)

CHAPTER 10

Discharged after a brief hospitalization for a
medication overdose he can't remember.

June 16, 1975

When I return from my time off I'm surprised to hear that James is back in the hospital. I learn that he was brought to the hospital emergency room a week ago because of a medication overdose which was, fortunately, not fatal. I see him enter the studio wearing slippers and a hospital gown, accompanied by a nursing assistant from Building Four. They had traversed a long hall connecting his ward with the video-recording studio in Building Two where our therapy sessions have been held for the past three months. He is sporting a full beard and his hair is in a ponytail. After signing in using the name Jay, he says other patients tell him he's acting crazy, talking nonsensically, and walking around angry. "I'm afraid I might do something and not know what I'm doing," he says.

When I ask why he took too much medication he can't remember doing it and denies being suicidal. I wonder if the medication overdose was an alternate personality's call for help.

His memory is unclear but he is able to recall a few things. "I don't remember Sunday. I remember being on a bus and laughing. It was crowded and I had to stand up. But I don't remember coming to Topeka. I think I came Sunday. I'm not for sure. I think

I came to the Jayhawk Hotel."

"You were at the Jayhawk Hotel Sunday and Monday night?"

"I don't know. I kind of visualize being there but someone told me that."

"Considering the fact that you can't really remember it, you do remarkably well because you didn't seem to have any trouble there (at the Jayhawk)."

"That's what I mean. I didn't have any trouble. If I'm doing this to run away from something, I wish that I could quit it. I don't know what I'm doing." He says he's afraid to be with his family because he might do something embarrassing, possibly explaining why he left Clarence and Betty's house and went to the Jayhawk Hotel.

I ask Jay if he recalls our last session when we talked about Jimmy (who may be an alternate personality) and my question triggers an automatism. The body sits straight up in his chair as his eyes close and his legs cross, uncross, and then land down on the floor. His arms raise and drop to the armrests. His breathing is irregular and his right hand suddenly elevates and swings across his face. His hand drops down and he opens his eyes. In spite of this lengthy motor automatism I don't see a personality switch. Jay regains control and complains about being continuously fatigued. He also says can't remember our last meeting so I clarify it was two weeks ago.

He remembers saying goodbye to the medical student but has no memory of taking an overdose, so he called his sister-in-law the

51

day after he came back into the hospital to ask what happened. "She said I was acting strange and was worried about me. I didn't know if I might do something weird so I decided to leave. And then yesterday this guy on the ward told me I sat in a chair without moving for a long time as if I was paralyzed. I don't always know what I'm doing. Maybe that's why I'm scared all the time."

"You said a few minutes ago that you were scared because you might do something," I clarify.

"I came into this hospital because I apparently tried to commit suicide. But I don't want to commit suicide. That's the last thing I want to do. I just don't know anything anymore. I know a lot but I can't put things together anymore."

He tells me he absolutely does not want to stay in the hospital so I ask him how he would feel if he were to go home today. He replies that it couldn't be any worse than being in the hospital where people stare at him all the time, or ring a bell and tell him it's time to do something. He tells me his brother and sister-in-law would not object if he came home to their place, but he doesn't want to burden them down with his problems.

Then after a pause, during which time there is a subtle change in his demeanor, I see him calmly reach into his pocket to get a pack of cigarettes. He puts one up to his lips as I've seen Shea do in the past. He inhales deeply and exhales a plume of smoke. Although his smoking is annoying I decide to let it go.

I ask if he can afford to travel by bus from his home fifty miles away. He tells me that would be problematic because his monthly income is $225 from social security and his retirement pension, but his expenses are eighty dollars a month for his trailer. It would cost him thirty-two dollars a month to take the bus weekly to Topeka and $150 a month if he stayed at the Jayhawk Hotel in Topeka.

He holds the cigarette in his right hand and gestures with his left hand while we continue to discuss whether or not he should return home. "I need to go home and take care of my garden. It's producing and why should I run off and leave a job half

finished? I don't think I should just drop it and let it go."

He smashes his cigarette in the ashtray as our session is about to end. Before we stop I question him again about his apparent suicide attempt but he emphatically denies wanting to kill himself. So I confront him with the possibility there is a part of him who is suicidal. "Maybe we ought to talk about the part of you that keeps coming to the surface that you don't like. Maybe the little boy from years ago. The part of you that feels sad. Jimmy, who you call the crybaby."

He suddenly squirms in his chair as his eyes close and head quivers.

"Did you hear what I just said?"

"What?" he frowns, clearly having blocked it out. I repeat myself but then witness an automatism. His left leg comes down to the floor followed by his right leg. His right hand begins to waver back and forth and reaches up to his forehead. Then both arms drop and swing from side to side behind the chair and drop down. Suddenly he waves his right arm across his face and reaches up to touch the top of his head. He sighs, shakes his head, and opens his eyes. The entire sequence of movements lasts twenty-seven seconds.

"Whew!" he announces as if he's completed a mile run.

"What happened?" I ask, not sure to whom I'm talking.

"I feel so tired. I guess I'm just not thinking straight. I apologize."

I can see that his state of mind is fragmented and I point out that there's a crybaby inside of his head that feels like crying, just like the time he was a little boy.

"I don't think I did (cry) when I was a little boy," he says.

"Wouldn't it be normal for Jimmy to cry?" I ask, believing that Jimmy is the crybaby lurking under the surface.

"Uh." He squirms, puts his right hand up to his head, uncrosses his legs and then re-crosses them. This automatism persists for a period of sixteen seconds.

"Would you repeat what I just said?" I ask.

"My name is not Jimmy," he exclaims. "You're doing the same thing to me that those people on the ward are doing to me. They're calling me names and getting me all upset. Then they're blaming me."

54

He stops talking but keeps his left leg tightly crossed over the right, as if a personality identified with the left leg is controlling the emergence of another personality identified with his right leg.

"You didn't answer my question," I repeat.

He briefly stares blankly, closes his eyes, sighs, moves his arms briefly, uncrosses his legs, puts his left leg back down on the floor, and swings his arm up across his face. "No. I couldn't repeat what you just said," he replies calmly.

"Ok, I'll say it again."

He smiles. "I think you're doing something to me and I don't like it. I'm getting tired." He moves each leg up and down slightly, then squirms and places his hand to his head.

"What would you not like me to say?" I ask.

He crosses his legs again and I can see that a different personality is present.

"Sorry. I wasn't paying attention," he says.

I suspect this personality is the one who calls himself Shea, the one who likes to smoke, although I'm not always certain about the difference between Shea and Jay. He begins to talk about a number of insignificant things and preens to the camera while asking if we are being televised. "The only thing I've got on my mind is to get out of the hospital. Are you going to call them up there and tell them I'm going to get out?" he pleads.

In spite of his recent hospitalization for a possible overdose, I'm aware that his hospital doctor would rather not keep him in the hospital because he's not demonstrated any evidence of suicidal behavior during the past week. Furthermore, many of the nursing staff believe he's conned me into thinking he has multiple personalities and they would prefer that he leave the hospital. It's important that I consider the following factors: Did he make a genuine suicide attempt or was it an indirect way for James or an alternate personality to call out for help? If so, which alternate personality was calling and why? Is he potentially suicidal now, and if not will he be safe if he returns home?

I believe one of James' alternate personalities felt abandoned after Tawn's departure and my absence. His sense of loss prompted one of the alternates to call out for help by taking excessive medications. Now that I have returned from vacation I feel comfortable that he's stable enough to leave the hospital, and he has loving family members who will make sure he returns to the hospital if necessary. I agree to call Jay's doctor and tell him I won't object if he wants to discharge our patient.

Before the session ends he tells me that he hopes to catch a late bus to his home. I ask him to reassure me that he will agree to accept help from his brother and sister-in-law, and ask him to promise he will take his medication.

"She will (make sure I take it) because she always asks me if I take my medicine."

"Are you telling a white lie? You told me you weren't taking it."

"I promise that I'll take it. I don't like it but it won't kill me I guess."

I ask him to return to see me next Thursday but to notify me if he has difficulties. I tentatively conclude that I will be providing outpatient treatment for James from now on.

CHAPTER 11

He acts too crazy at home.

June 19, 1975

Jay meets me in the studio three days later for our one o'clock appointment sporting a goatee and ponytail, and dressed neatly in gray slacks and a lime green T-shirt. After setting a suitcase on the floor by the studio door he sits down and tells me his brother and sister-in-law said he was acting too crazy to stay there and put him on the bus to Topeka early this morning. His hospital doctor and I were clearly wrong to have believed Jay was "together" enough to stay out of the hospital. When I ask him how he is doing he shakes his head and begins to have an automatism. The right hand swings across his face as he briefly appears to blank out but then quickly resumes control.

I ask him what he remembers about the last three days after being discharged from the hospital and he tells me, "Not much. I know I was in the hospital but I don't remember leaving Topeka. But I must have left 'cause I remember talking to my sister-in-law." He pauses a moment and apologizes for being unable to organize his thoughts. He goes on to tell me he knew he had worked in his garden but can't remember anything specific. Then he makes light of the seriousness of the subject by joking about the weeds in his garden.

"I guess Jimmy's left," I say.

"I don't know any Jimmy," he insists. "I just know there's something wrong, but I don't know what's wrong. Maybe I'm getting old."

"You don't know any Jimmy?"

"No, I don't know any Jimmy," he announces, triggering an automatism as he stares off to his right and his body becomes rigid.

"You're thinking?" I ask.

"Damn right I'm thinking!" he declares as his legs uncross and both feet plant themselves firmly on the floor, indicating a switch to a different personality who answers me with an emphatic voice I have not heard before. This individual has a different posture and leg position. I'm struck by the way his feet are planted firmly on the floor, which has significance. I wonder who this is. He is clearly not Jay and not Jimmy.

"What are you thinking?" I ask.

"Thinking that son-of-a-bitch ain't never coming back. That's what I think. Because I don't like that damn bawl-baby," he snarls. "He ain't never coming back!" He crosses his arms and remains sullen.

I make a comment about his anger but he denies being angry. Then I see his body stiffen, his eyes shifting downward, his head wavering, his feet shuffling slightly, and his body becoming rigid.

"What are you thinking?"

No answer.

"What are you feeling?"

To my surprise he answers me abruptly. "If I told you, what would you do anyway?"

I wait for his response.

"The same things you always do. Just pick my brain clean and then run off and leave me," he says.

"Run off and leave you? What do you mean?"

His eyes remain downcast and he avoids looking at me.

"Where am I going?" I ask.

"Hell, I don't know. You and Dr. Baird and everybody's leaving. So the hell with you."

"I am?" I ask, assuming the role of a previous counselor he seems to be talking to.

"Well, hell yes. You know he's leaving."

He crosses his legs—left over right—suggesting a personality associated with the right brain who desires dominance.

"When?"

"In about two or three weeks. The hell with him."

He uncrosses his legs, plants them on the floor, and folds his arms. When I try to be empathic he brushes me off as if I'm not there. "You can't be sad over spilt milk. I went along with you all. Where has it gotten me? The hell with you," he shouts. His head jerks as he continues to look down, avoiding my eyes, unaware of the reality of my presence in the room. "Been alone all my life. Nothing is wrong with that," he replies angrily as he remains oblivious to my attempt to be supportive.

I continue to express empathy. "I guess that would be normal to feel sad and feel like crying."

He ignores me. I see his head move back and forth and right arm swing across his face. His right leg swings down to hold down his left leg. This personality from the past, perhaps James, is angry with Dr. Baird for abandoning him, but now becomes confused as a switch takes place. I hear him breathe heavily and announce, "I've got to do something."

I ask this personality to explain.

"It's up to me to do it. No one's ever helped me. I'll do it myself," he replies.

I decide to test his reality at this point and ask him to tell me what year it is.

"I don't know," he says and sits quietly for a moment. Then he repeats, "I don't know."

"What's the month?"

"April, I guess. I don't really care."

"April? What year?"

"What difference does it make? This year," he complains.

"What year is this year?"

"I don't know."

"Where are we?"

"Oh we're going to play silly games. We're in your goddam office. Here in Topeka, Kansas. Today is Wednesday, 1969 or 1970. I don't really know and I don't give a damn. Is that all of your little games? Your twenty-one questions?" he asks sullenly, believing I am a former counselor or therapist.

"I guess being left is not very pleasant and I can understand why you would be mad."

"You're such a sweet person. You understand," he smirks. "Is that the reason you've put me through all this damn torture?"

"What have I done?" I ask.

"What have you done? I never told a soul until I told you. Now that I told you every goddam thing you ever wanted to know, you're going to pack up your old kit bag, and take off. No more. No more!" he exclaims loudly, venting his anger.

Suddenly, he crosses his legs, swings his arm across his face and a different personality returns to the body. When I ask what's happening he says he doesn't know. I'm uncertain who this is, but most likely it is Shea since he pulls out a cigarette. He glances at me with a puzzled look on his face, which is very different from the angry personality who had not looked directly at me.

He begins to tell me his concerns about the staff. "They say I act stupid. I can't quite remember. They said I did some bad things. I hurt someone but that's not true. I don't do anything bad. I don't

62

even have a bad thought in my mind."

As I hear him describe his idealized self-perception, I assure him that having bad thoughts only makes him human. He laughs and after a moment expresses concerns about things he's been told he's done on the ward, of which he has no memory.

"What I think has happened is that you feel you've been hurt by (two people) who have abandoned you," I explain, referring to Dr. Baird and an associate from a previous hospitalization.

Jay speaks clearly and very rationally now as he tells me he's unable to remember any details about the therapist he refers to as Gale, and Dr. Baird whom he recalls vaguely. He looks perplexed. "I don't think you'd be lying to me Dr. Brende but this upsets me."

He shakes his head while casually holding a cigarette in his right hand. His left leg continues to hold down his right leg. Although I don't fully understand its significance at this time, I'll later understand why his crossed legs have special meaning.

"I keep trying to think there's something I don't know."

This is the first time that he expresses a vague awareness that he's missed important time periods related to significant events in his life. I point out that he had expressed a lot of anger and was probably afraid of being left by his doctor but he flatly denies this. Then I see an automatism as his head begins to move, his arms swing, and his legs uncross.

"What's happening?" I ask the personality who has returned again for the third time.

This personality continues to believe I'm Dr. Baird and angrily talks about leaving the hospital today. "I'm thinking about getting out. That's exactly what I'll do," he exclaims as he folds his hands. "See. I'm very calm and collected. I can sit right here." He continues to sit upright in the chair, legs uncrossed, insisting he is not upset.

When I ask why he wants to leave the hospital he tells me that there is no reason for him to stay since he's convinced I'll be leaving him. His body starts to quiver and his arms swing. He is on the verge of losing control when I ask, "Are you feeling sad?"

That question provokes an immediate response as he suddenly jumps out of his chair and walks off to his right, catching me off guard. "You're not going to make me cry again. You'll never make me cry again. No one ever makes me cry," he exclaims loudly.

When I interpret his anger as a way of covering over sad feelings he vehemently disagrees, returns to his chair, sits down, and announces loudly, "I'm not sad! Not sad at all. Nobody else has to feel sad and nobody has to feel a damn thing because I'll never feel sad again." Then he waves his right arm across his face and dissociates to a different personality who, I believe, is Jay.

"I just feel tired. I don't know why Dr. Brende. This is what I'm talking about. I just feel tired." He describes how confused he felt about coming to see me today, although he had a sense he needed to go somewhere but didn't know where. After a brief silence I watch him uncross his legs and observe a change in his facial expression.

"What's happening?" I ask.

He doesn't respond.

"Are you thinking?" I ask, which triggers another dissociation. With his eyes focused straight ahead in a downward direction, he begins to relive a past experience with a person he calls David.

"David who?" I ask, attempting to clarify his reality.

He laughs. "Come on David. I'll just convince them."

"How are you going to do that?"

"I'll just be so beautiful in the group. I'll miss you. We'll see each other David," he replies in a dramatically different way compared to a few minutes ago when he expressed his anger about being abandoned by Dr. Baird and Gale.

"Where?" I ask, taking David's role.

"Around somewhere. It'll have to depend on you David. After all, I'm going to get out and if you get out I'll just come and see you. I've got a car." He smiles and nods his head.

"Maybe there will be other people who will miss you," I suggest.

"Nobody else will miss me," he says, indicating that David had been a special friend who had been a patient in the hospital with him four years ago.

"Won't Dr. Baird miss you? He must like you."

"I suppose he might like me."

"Like a son?"

"Oh, no. Not like a son."

"How?"

"I guess, as a crazy person, I don't know?" he grins devilishly.

"What's wrong with thinking of yourself like a son? One of his normal sons?" I ask, continuing to pursue the father-son theme, which may help me understand the nature of his relationship to his own father.

He begins to quiver and his head shakes. I ask him where he is but he doesn't respond. Then for a period of several seconds I observe a motor automatism as the body convulses slowly, arms move slightly and then swing.

"I…have to go…away," he stutters as his arm swings up to his face.

I observe a switch to a new personality who opens his eyes but seems confused and unable to tell me what had just happened. I suggest that he should relax and let his mind rest, but he tells me he can't do that because he has to use his brain all the time. He places his right hand on his head as if he were checking to feel if it was still there. Then he brings it down. He pulls out a cigarette, crosses his legs and sits quietly for a time.

"What's happening?" I ask.

"I've got to stay here but I can't stay here. I can't get help anymore here. I've got to go."

Although this response is similar to what I observed a few minutes earlier, I am not certain if I am talking to James, Jay, or Shea, so I ask him to tell me who he is. Rather than answer my question he talks to me again as if I'm Dr. Baird, and insists that I discharge him from the hospital since he believes he's been here for a year without getting any help. Then he stops talking. After a moment he sighs and his right hand swings across his face. A different personality suddenly returns again. I ask if he knows what we were talking about. But as before, he tells me he doesn't know.

Before the session ends, we discuss how he came back into the hospital after being discharged only three days ago. "Did I run away?" he asks, seemingly unaware of his own behavior, but then answers his own question by saying, "I did run away Dr. Brende."

When I tell him that we had just met for an hour he laughs and says, "It only seems like fifteen minutes." I tell him his mind is not clear enough at this time to go home and he needs to stay in the hospital. He quickly expresses resistance to that plan, although he'd brought his suitcase in case I wanted him to stay.

He seems relieved to hear me say we will meet in one week for our next session while he's in the hospital. He willingly leaves the studio with a psychiatric aide from Building Four who arrived at the studio after the secretary called his ward.

CHAPTER 12

I feel insane.

June 23, 1975

It is now a week later and the patient comes to this session dressed neatly in newly purchased dress clothes and wearing a beard with his hair swept back into a bun. He sits down, signs the permission form and crosses his legs with the right leg holding the left leg down and the right foot wrapped around the left lower leg. Although he signed in as Jay I suspect I'm meeting Shea based on his appearance and the way he crosses his legs. After reviewing this videotaped session at a later date I see that it is indeed Shea.

"I just don't know what to do, Dr. Brende. I'm sorry to be upset but it's beginning to weigh on my mind a little bit." Then he talks about his desire to withdraw from people who tell him he's acting strangely and ask why he is smoking two packs of cigarettes a day.

"How do you feel today?" I ask.

"Is this the calm before the storm? Or maybe I'm in the storm?" he asks.

"Yeah, you're in the storm," I reply, and reassure him it is important for him to be in the hospital and get help.

He continues to berate himself, talking about how ashamed he feels that he had acted terribly toward a nurse's aide on the ward. I encourage him to apologize and people will forgive him.

68

However his receptivity to that idea is tentative at best.

"I have a funny feeling all the time," he says.

"Can you describe it?"

"I'm just lost. I feel like I have done this before and that I know exactly what is going to happen. But I have never done this before!" he exclaims. "I feel insane right now as if I were an absolutely raving idiot."

"Do you have momentary feelings of being insane?"

"Just like right now."

"You're describing it very sanely," I say, and ask for examples.

He describes a disturbance in his perceptions when he smokes a cigarette. He describes the experience of lighting up the cigarette as different from smoking it. He lacks the capacity to experience what he is aware of, suggesting that his observations and experience of self are separated from each other.

After listening to him describe his difficulties, I suggest that he limit his crazy behaviors to the times he meets with me in therapy and maintain control of himself when he's on the ward.

"I think I am in control of myself. Now you upset me the other day when you said I was here for an hour yet it didn't feel that way."

"Tell you what. Why don't you accept the fact that you are in the middle of a storm where you are reliving memories of painful previous experiences."

Suddenly, his mouth quivers, his arms become tense, his appearance changes and I hear a different person speak apologetically with military precision. "I won't give you any trouble sir. No sir. I'm not going to give anyone any trouble."

In order to test his capacity to determine reality I ask how long we've been talking together. He says about ten minutes today and we have had meetings like this for about two or three months. Then I ask him if he can tell me what month this is and he replies that it is the first of the year.

"What year?"

"Oh, 1971, I guess." He puts his hand up to his head and turns away. I see him dissociate to a different personality who has a sneer on his face. "It doesn't make a damn bit of difference what year it is," he snarls, and then asks if I want to continue asking dumb questions. Then he turns his head the other way and slaps his hand against the arm of the chair.

It is clear he's unaware of the current sense of time, which also happened during our previous sessions. I later learn that a person's perception of the passage of time takes place in the basal ganglia within the parietal lobe on the right side of the brain, suggesting that the personality encountering Dr. Baird and Mr. Gale is linked to that part of the brain.

"Well, I've asked you some questions and now I want to offer you equal opportunity," I say.

"I'm not stupid!" he snarls loudly as he thrusts both arms downward, demonstrating how he devalued everything I had just said. "You may think I'm stupid, but I'm not," he adds.

"Well, I don't think you're stupid."

"You're so kind," he grins sarcastically as he waves his right

70

arm across his left shoulder, signaling the emergence of a different personality. I believe I'm now talking with Jay, who is clearly aware of the current time and place because he looks at me and sheepishly says, "I hope we're friends enough so that I don't have to apologize to you. It is because I have so many things on my mind I just forget my manners."

I have seen frequent personality shifts during this session, indicating the presence of personalities struggling for control. From a therapeutic point of view I know it's important for me to gradually gain more control over this dysfunctional patient and his personality shifts.

The session has come to an end. After I tell him our next appointment will be in one week he becomes very anxious and expresses a sense of desperation. "I just don't have it all together. I want to throw up my hands. This is just some foolish game that people are playing and I don't want to play it."

Since I know very little about the phenomenon of personality fragmentation and multiple personalities at this time, I look for articles about the subject. Unfortunately there is almost nothing for me to read in 1975 or 1976. But I can proceed optimistically as James' therapist because I've received training in psychodynamics and psychotherapy. I understand the importance of establishing a therapeutic relationship, maintaining boundaries and linking present difficulties with past conflicts. I will later learn that treatment recommendations for patients with personality fragmentation associated with a history of trauma begin with establishing safety, stabilizing and reducing destructive symptoms, educating patients about their diagnosis and symptoms, explaining the process of treatment, managing emotions, building stress tolerance, enhancing life functioning and improving relational capacities. After this initial stabilizing phase of treatment, guidelines become more focused on remembering and resolving past traumatic experiences.[17]

At this time I find it very helpful to draw on my experience of having been a patient in a therapy group in 1970, as well as individual psychodynamic psychotherapy two years later. The training requirements for doctors becoming psychiatrists in the early 1970s did not require obtaining personal psychotherapy. However a number of the trainees in the Menninger School of Psychiatry, including myself, chose to receive psychotherapy or a personal analysis. Psychotherapy sessions typically occurred two or three days a week for fifty minutes, and often continued for up to three years.

Psychoanalysis sessions were patterned after Sigmund Freud's own description of the technique he invented in 1896. The analyst sat just behind and out of sight of the analysand, who lay on a couch and freely expressed his or her thoughts. The analyst listened for forgotten childhood experiences, fantasies, and dreams that might reveal the presence of unconscious conflicts causing the analysand or patient's symptoms and character problems. His techniques would include a heavy emphasis on the interpretation of the transference (analysand's feelings projected unto the analyst) and countertransference (the analyst's feelings for the analysand). He would also be on the lookout for the patient's psychological

72

defenses erected to protect against revealing guilty secrets, unacceptable thoughts, and painful memories. The entire process was meant to improve insight, self-awareness, interpersonal relationships, and ability to achieve personal goals.

My personal experience of being a recipient of psychodynamic psychotherapy was very beneficial and educational. I particularly found it personally meaningful to understand the role of transference, an important tool I will use in my therapy with James. Transference refers to the significant positive and negative elements in the patient-therapist relationship that are linked to important persons in the patient's past. According to a former colleague from the Menninger Hospital and School of Psychiatry who will go on to become an esteemed psychoanalyst and author, Dr. Glen Gabbard, "A transference interpretation is a very important intervention in psychotherapy."[18] He maintains that it's important to understand that the patient's world of childhood relationships can be repeated in the here-and-now interaction with the therapist, and transferred into that relationship without the patient being aware of it. In such cases the therapist can interpret the transference situation in order to make something conscious that has been unconscious. My experience as a therapy patient, along with my professional training, has been foundational for my therapeutic work with James.

CHAPTER 13
Eight Automatisms

June 26, 1975

The patient enters the studio dressed casually. His hair is in a long ponytail and he is wearing a trimmed beard. After sitting down and signing the permission slip with the name Jay, he tells me for the first time he suspects he has memory problems. He describes hearing the recreational therapist tell him about the time they did some work together in the swimming pool several years back, but he doesn't remember it. I continue this theme and ask if he has any bad memories from the past. Jay says no and that is consistent with what I've learned about him—a person who blocks out painful or negative memories.

When I ask how things are going for him on the ward, he says everyone tells him he looks depressed but he denies that. "I say 'just calm down' and I try to think of something else." When I ask how he's sleeping, he says he goes to bed at one o'clock in the morning and gets up about six a.m. without feeling he'd ever been asleep. He pauses and puts his hand to his forehead, looking perplexed.

"What are you thinking?" I ask.

I witness an automatism as his body begins to stiffen and his right hand waves across his face to his left forehead. After this lapse in consciousness he answers the question. "I feel like I can figure out what's going on. But up on the ward when I used to work on a puzzle, I could put twenty pieces together in no time at all, but yet now I can be sitting there and two hours has passed and I sit there and think. But two hours of thinking? That's ridiculous."

"Two hours sitting there and not moving any of the pieces?" I ask.

"Yeah, that's ridiculous." He places his hand to his head with a puzzled expression on his face.

"What do you think about?"

He continues to ramble and says he thinks about things he's not thought about before. Suddenly he stops talking and begins a second automatism. He appears perplexed, and gazes off into the distance. His facial appearance hardens and his head drops.

"What are you thinking?" I ask, aware that a different personality has emerged.

"Not a dang thing," he retorts with annoyance. After a moment he continues to describe the things he's forgotten. He then shifts the topic to lost relationships, and I ask him if he can remember all the different times he's been abandoned.

He puts his hand up to his face and continues to look away from me. "Oh lots of times. What difference does it make?"

Then I witness a third automatism as he begins to convulse slowly with eyes closed. His arms swing back and forth behind his back, his head rolls slightly upward, and he opens his eyes, but they remain glazed over. Then his head rolls downward again. He sighs and folds his arms in a gesture of defiance.

"Oh, nothing," he says flippantly.

"What do you mean nothing?" I ask.

"Nothing!" He blurts more loudly. He stops talking, looks down at his left arm and begins to automatically pick away at it. After a minute or two he continues talking. "It doesn't do any damn good. You work physically and mentally and what becomes of it? Nothing! It's a waste!"

"Why is it a waste?"

"It just is. You work, work, work, and make a lot of money, and what do you have to show for it? Absolutely nothing. You think and you say something. And it's absolutely wrong. Or it's full of shit or something." He slaps his hands down on the arms of the chair, turns his head to his left and looks away with a disparaging look on his face. He continues to ramble on until he sneers, "I don't give a goddam anyway!"

After a moment he stops talking and I witness a fifth automatism as his legs and his arms begin to move back and forth. He closes his eyes, swings his right hand up across his face and around his neck and across to his left shoulder.

I then see a different personality, most likely Jay, emerge. "What?" he asks, completely unaware of what has just happened. He begins to talk with a singsong rhythm as if nothing had happened. "I just try to get along in the world and be nice and happy and everything will be all right. I don't get involved with anyone so that if they leave, I leave."

After hearing how he avoids relationships, I confront him with the fact that he must have become involved with people in the past.

"I don't have any past. That's gone. I only think about today," he insists while restlessly moving his arms and hands, folding his hands, and interlocking his fingers. "Today is today. And tomorrow, if it comes, will be tomorrow again. If it doesn't, I haven't missed it because I wasn't ever there."

I continue to listen without responding.

Then he extends his arms and hands in a gesture of carefree indifference. "I don't fret about anything," he laughs. "What's the sense in fretting?" Suddenly I witness a sixth automatism as his right hand moves automatically across his face and his eyes become vacant. The movements stop and Jay continues his carefree speech. "I like to be happy. If someone asks about the weather and asks if it's going to rain today, I always say, 'If it rains it rains. What are you going to do about it? That's Mother Nature and I don't care.'" He laughs again.

His carefree indifference is interrupted a few minutes later when I ask if he remembers telling me that two doctors had left him several years ago. This triggers a seventh automatism as his eyes close and his left leg, which had been very tightly crossed over his right leg, suddenly lifts and drops to the floor. His right hand swings across his face and over to his left shoulder. He blinks but I don't see a switch to an alternate personality. His left leg returns to where it had been, crossed tightly over his right leg.

"I've only known three doctors," he says.

"Who are they?"

He tells me about two surgeons and an anesthesiologist he knew while he was in the Air Force, but also insists he doesn't trust doctors.

My announcement that our time is coming to a close triggers an eighth automatism. His eyes close, his body becomes rigid, he straightens up in the chair, his right hand swings across his face and he grabs his left shoulder. Then he regains awareness.

"What just happened?" I ask.

At first he looks at his right arm across his chest and makes up a story to explain why his hand was there. When I repeat the question he answers by saying, "I don't know."

"You were feeling some anxiety?" I ask.

"I'm feeling it right now."

This is the first time he appears to have gained any self-awareness. Then he begins to talk about knowing people who went berserk, which seems to be a metaphor about himself. I mention that he is now in a safe environment where he can safely lose control of his emotions and behaviors, but he insists that he never loses self-control.

After telling me how much he misses his garden, I suggest that he call his sister-in-law and ask about it but he declines. When I announce that it's time for this session to end he minimizes the significance of our meetings, so I assure him these meetings are important and tell him we will meet next Monday and Thursday.

When I review the videotape of this session later I count eight different automatisms, several with personality switching. I also realize for the first time that the motor automatism characterized by the patient's left leg crossing over and holding down his right leg has special meaning. When Jay takes over the body he displaces James and interacts with me. His verbal skills are associated with left-brain functioning, something I would later learn in more detail when I study the phenomenon of "cerebral lateralization,"[19] whereby one side of the brain is neurologically connected to the opposite side of the body.

I've also been observing a change in the type of fragmentation present during our recent sessions. Compared with his first two sessions when I saw evidence of five different personalities—James, Jim, Jimmy, Jay, and Shea—triggered by the use of hypnotherapy, now, three months later, only two personalities, Jay and Shea, are fairly clear, although I am not always able to tell the difference. The other personalities are very unclear, with characteristics that seem more typical of differing ego states[20] than clearly differentiated personalities.

An ego state refers to a set of related behaviors, thoughts and feelings that comprise an individual's personality at a given time and for a specific purpose. When the purpose is to communicate or react to another person's behavior, this is called a transaction between ego states. The boundaries of ego states may vary from being flexible in normal persons to being pathologically porous or rigid in persons suffering from psychopathology. In extreme cases, a pathological child ego state associated with fear and shame caused by trauma becomes walled off from the rest of the personality, and lacking the flexibility of a normal boundary. These types of pathological child ego states may be a precursor to the formation of multiple personalities.

CHAPTER 14

Jay is surprised to see tears on his face.

June 30, 1975

The patient signs in as Jay today. He nonchalantly tells me he didn't eat or drink anything for the past three days. He also complains about the doctors and nurses on the ward and idealizes me as his only real doctor. I understand his feelings but I have received complaints from his hospital doctor that he has caused "splitting" on the ward. The term splitting[21] is used to describe the temperament on a hospital ward when a patient over-idealizes his therapist while devaluing the rest of the staff.

The fact that he is not eating or drinking is evidence of depression that I believe is related to his lost relationships. When I bring up this subject I see the beginning of an automatism. His eyes close, his arms lift up, his right arm swings into a strangle hold around his neck, and then it drops down. He opens his eyes, looks away from me and begins to talk. "So I'll do it myself. I'll do it. Quit pestering me about it. I'll do it!" he whines to someone from his past.

"You don't have to do it yourself," I reply.

"Well make up your damn mind. If I have to do it, I'll do it. If you don't want me to do it, I won't do it." He closes his eyes, moves his head, waves his arms up and then lowers them back down again. He swings his right arm across his neck to his left shoulder, then opens his eyes. I see tears and recognize that Jay was briefly replaced by an angry personality. He says he doesn't know what happened and insists he's not crying as he wipes his eyes.

I assure him that it's normal to cry but he brushes me off and tells me this is just a bunch of malarkey. He takes off his glasses, wipes the moisture away, and ignores my attempts to reassure him.

"That's okay. You can't be in control all the time."

"But I sure try, awful, awful hard," he insists as he views his hands and folds them, angelic like. "I keep things from getting the best of me," he adds as he continues to sit quietly with hands folded. "But I'm not perfect, I'm not God,"[22] he insists.

"No, you're not perfect," I agree.

"They told me (on the ward) I wanted to pick a fight. I may have a mean streak but I've got a yellow streak down my back that won't quit. My middle name is chicken." He laughs.

"You may have a mean streak but you don't sound very mean to me. I think that you feel mean when you're helpless and don't know what to do. Then you strike out," I say.

"I don't want to do anything. As long as no one bothers me then I'll not bother them. I can always get up and leave. Nothing bothers me except (the color) red and I'm making a big joke out of it," he sighs.

After several more automatisms he regains a sense of control and I ask how he feels compared to a half hour ago. He says he feels exhausted, refuses to compare himself to a half hour ago, but is concerned enough to request an escort to accompany him to his next session. "Just before I came down here I felt like I didn't need an escort but this thing keeps running through my mind that I do. I don't want to go out of here and lash out somewhere."

Before our session ends I remind him that important memories will come back to him when he is ready, and that he's in a trusting environment that will help him relax his defenses and remember things he's kept secret.

Childhood memories are potentially available to most people as far back as age three and a half years of life. That may not be true in individuals who suffered traumatic experiences, since those memories often remain repressed. When they seek help to recover from post-traumatic symptoms, their therapists will very likely help them retrieve their traumatic memories for review and assimilation so they can recover from their psychological distress.[23]

CHAPTER 15

Beginning awareness of two parts: one feels pain and one doesn't.

July 1-3, 1975

"I'm getting tired of counting to ten. I have to count every five minutes because of the patient (on the ward) who is drunk," Jay says shortly after sitting down. He tells me that a patient was recently admitted with alcohol on his breath, which was very frightening for him. In order to cope he tried to use a relaxation technique (counting from one through ten) that I had taught him.

When I ask him to make a list of the things that frighten him, he brushes me off by telling me he's only afraid of the dark. Then he insists on giving me a list of the reasons he should get out of the hospital. First of all, he doesn't like being the only patient who gets to have a therapist because that makes him feel guilty. Secondly he feels nervous about walking to Building Two. Third, he hates depending on other people. Fourth, he feels guilty about asking for an escort.

I tell him that he's not ready to leave the hospital and it's okay to depend on people. I also give him the unsettling news that I'll be gone for three weeks and a new medical student will meet with him during my absence.

Before the session ends we spend some time talking about a frightening nightmare last night that caused him to scream. We also talk about his anxiety after hearing someone call out the name

Jim to a new patient on the ward.

When we meet again two days later on Thursday, July 3, he is dressed neatly in a blue jump suit and white tennis shoes. When I introduce him to Jeff, the new medical student, he barely acknowledges the student's presence but becomes disturbed when I remind him that I'll be absent for three weeks. This news seems to trigger a subtle dissociation as he jokingly describes how he hates living on a ward where disturbed people drive him crazy. He takes a cigarette out of his pocket and I assume I'm talking with Shea. He lights up and tells me that the patients are dumbfounded when they see him crush a cigarette out on his hand without feeling any pain.

Then I see another subtle personality switch which I presume is Jay. He moves his hand to his face and begins to talk in a more subdued voice. "I'm even getting so I don't know what I'm doing," he says. Then he folds his arms, lifts his foot up, touches his little toe, and tells me he tries to help other patients. He mentions his concern for a patient named Kelly who is hungry all the time. "When I tell anyone else about him no one pays attention to me and that makes me angry."

"Do you think that he's not only hungry for food but for someone to care for him?" I ask.

"No, I don't think so."

"Don't you think that people aren't only hungry for physical but also for emotional nurturance? People aren't only physical beings but there's another aspect to them," I declare.

"Yes, Dr. Brende, I know there's that but I don't understand

84

emotions."

After we discuss the significance of emotions I tell Jay that I've observed two parts of his identity—one part feels emotions and the other does not.

"This is what I don't understand. You say there's two parts to me. Up on the ward they also say there's two parts to me. They told me that I crushed a cigarette out on my hand and I guess there's a little red mark there." He points to a spot on his left hand.

I find this information astonishing and explain the importance of being able to experience pain. "Feeling pain is a signal of a problem. It's also is a signal to ask for help. You can say, 'I'm having pain, help me.'"

Jay doesn't understand this concept and complains that he's tired of constantly struggling to lead a normal life.

"What would happen if you gave up struggling?" I ask.

"I did that one morning and I just sat down." He closes his eyes anxiously, rubs his forehead, and puts his left hand up to show me again the spot where he burned his hand. He says he would like to lie down and forget everything but he can't do that, particularly during the night when he gets scared.

"What are you scared of?" I ask.

"The other night it was scary because the nightlight was not on and there wasn't anyone (staff person) back there. I just can't turn to anyone any more."

"That's why we are meeting and that's why we have a nursing staff over there. You can turn to them and to me."

"You can't just turn to them over there," he disagrees.

"Why not?" I ask.

He can't give me a clear answer.

Before the session comes to a close I take time to prepare him for the fact that I'll be gone for three weeks and ask how he feels about having a new medical student during my absence. He closes his eyes and mumbles something, so I speak the words I believe he might use.

"I would imagine that you might say, 'It's awfully hard for me to trust anybody and it's taken a year to trust you Dr. Brende. How can you expect me to trust (another medical student)?'"

He smiles.

"What would you feel comfortable talking about with him?" I ask.

He puts his hand up to his forehead and tells me he'll think about it. After a brief silence I repeat my question again but he shakes his head and calls out to himself to relax. "Jay just behave yourself. Count to ten. Jay," he stammers. Then I see a motor automatism. His head snaps back, his face becomes rigid, his eyes glaze over, and his hands swing behind the chair.

"What is happening? What are you thinking?" I ask.

"I...I..." he stammers.

"What are you thinking? What's happening?" I repeat.

He continues to struggle as I repeat my questions. Suddenly his arms swing across his body and his face takes on a serious, almost intensely angry expression, indicating that a different personality has entered the body.

"I don't think!" he retorts.

"Who am I?" I ask, wanting to know if I'm talking to a specific personality who knows me.

"My God. Twenty-one questions every time I turn around. I really don't want to play that damn game. Oh yeah, I either answer you or else you'll throw me in the quiet room and give me another shot. I know all that crap. Okay I'll tell you."

"Okay," I reply.

I'm clearly speaking to a distinct personality stuck in a different time and reality, talking as if I'm Dr. Baird from four years ago. Not wanting to break his distorted reality, I assume the role of Dr. Baird and ask if I can help him. He tells me there is no way he can win against me, because I'm a large and forceful man. "They don't call you God on this ward for nothing. But we love ya anyway," James sneers while gazing into the distance. "I read what you wrote on that goddam card and I don't like it!" he exclaims.

"What was it?" I ask.

"I'm not a homosexual and I don't have homosexual tendencies. Because I try to get along with people, that's no sign I'm a goddam queer."

"Okay," I reply, assuming that Shea was present when Dr. Baird was his doctor.

"It's a goddam shame that other people will read that and I had to find it out somewhere else. If you're such a powerful person, why didn't you tell me yourself what you thought of me?" he grumbles.

Then he raises his hands up in despair, which triggers the beginning of a series of automatic movements of his hands and arms. His eyes close shut. He tries to speak. His head moves back and forth. Finally his right arm swings across his chest to his left shoulder.

His eyes open and he looks at me as if there is something wrong. I can see that Jay has returned. "I'd still like to go swimming. I'm so tired that I don't know what I'm doing," he says in a calm voice. Then he puts his hand to his head, sighs, and tells me he's trying to collect his thoughts. He briefly smiles self-consciously and finally frowns.

Our time is nearly over. But before we stop, he asks again if he can be discharged from the hospital. I have to tell him that I won't intervene with his hospital doctor's decision to keep him. Then his body begins another automatism until he finally regains self-control. Before leaving the studio he asks if our next meeting will be on Monday, but I remind him that I'll be on vacation and Jeff, the new medical student, will meet with him.

Fortunately I will have some time to visit with Jeff who, like his colleague Tawn, is also a knowledgeable and experienced medical student from Nebraska. I will arrange for him to see some video sessions before he meets with James while I'm on vacation.

I'll be away from work for three weeks because I'm taking my family to Colorado. Our eight-hour drive through the Flint Hills and across the open fields of western Kansas goes smoothly. Our first night in Denver is fulfilling after eating out at the Old Spaghetti Factory. It is also shocking. "Hey dad. Look!" my oldest son yells after we return to the motel. I'm startled to see a naked man streaking away from the front of our motel. The second night is marked by a drive into the Rockies and our arrival at a mountain cabin surrounded by a dozen peaks over 14,000 feet high with a lake close by where the kids can swim. I had arranged to rent this cabin from a colleague without knowing how picturesque it would be. The cabin has a front porch where hummingbirds flit back and forth. There is a kitchen and two bedrooms that sleep nine people, which is perfect since there are seven of us. Our three girls help their mother cook meals and all five kids swim in the nearby small lake. My youngest, a four-year-old boy, has a close call when he falls into water over his head, but fortunately I'm close enough to pull him out. We're nearby to Aspen and make a couple of side trips there. My oldest daughter says she has never seen so many hippies with long hair, beards, and mustaches—some playing guitars and singing. We have a wonderful time and leave the cabin after a week. The rest of our trip is mostly spent driving and making other stops. They include the Indian Cliff Dwellings at Mesa Verde; Santa Fe, New Mexico; and Deer Valley Ranch in southern Colorado. After arriving back home on July 27, I feel rested, and look forward to my session with James.

CHAPTER 16

James awakens from ECT—his first clearly defined presence.

July 24, 1975

Before meeting with the patient I review videotapes of the sessions that Jeff, the new medical student, had with the patient during my absence. In one of those tapes I could see Jeff effectively focus on James' feelings of loss. I saw several dissociative episodes with switches from Jay to James, angrily accusing Jay of controlling his existence. "God, he's going to come back and ruin everything. That snot- nosed queer. I'll get rid of him. I just have to make sure I stay here that's all. I won't think about him."

When Jay returned to the body he accused other patients of lying about him. "They said I was throwing chairs around in a rage. I never did that." Then Jay dissociated again after Jeff asked how he felt about my absence. When James emerged he relived a confrontation with Dr. Baird, whom he accused of lying. "You're using me like a guinea pig. I was suckered in by you people. You're not going to get anything out of me until it's time for me to do what I must do. You're all leaving anyway so what difference does it make. I'll take care of myself."

Today Jeff joins me during our session. We listen to Jay tell us the other patients have told him he's been going on violent rampages, tipping tables over, and swearing at people. But he is absolutely sure he didn't do any of those things. Jay also tells us that someone cut off his ponytail.

When I ask Jay if it's possible he did these things he waves his arm and dissociates to a different personality who appears to be James, whom I had just seen as I reviewed the tape of the last session. He avoids looking at us and begins a tirade. "I chased him off. I cut off his goddam hair and I'm going to get out of this hospital. That pipsqueak Jay won't be around now since he ran off and won't bother me. Next I'm going to cut his beard," he exclaims gleefully. Then he stares at the medical student and frowns. "Who the hell are you?"

James doesn't remember meeting with Jeff because it was the session when he relived an encounter with Dr. Baird. When I ask why he was so angry with Dr. Baird, James says Dr. Baird planned to give him ECT (electroconvulsive therapy) against his will. After this brief appearance, James dissociates to Jay, who suddenly looks around with a confused expression on his face and asks if he just had an epileptic seizure.

After completing this session I think about the relationship between James' disappearance from the body four years ago and receiving electroconvulsive therapy (ECT). This leads me to believe that ECT caused James' departure. How could that happen? ECT must have suppressed brain activity in the right cerebral hemisphere associated with James' identity. I review my own experience with ECT and remember my first exposure to it in 1965.

I was a short-term volunteer physician providing medical care to patients in a 300-bed mission hospital in New Guinea. A physician colleague at the hospital asked me to assist him while he gave ECT to a native who was openly psychotic. The physician put her in a straight jacket in a special procedure room, positioned electrodes on her head, and administered ECT while she lay on a mattress. She convulsed violently during the procedure and remained unconscious for a time until she woke up looking confused. The scene concerned me and I hoped to never be involved in a similar situation again.

My next unpleasant exposure occurred four years later when I was a psychiatric resident in training, and witnessed an attending psychiatrist administer ECT to a very depressed male patient while he lay on a mattress in a bare hospital room. The doctor placed electrodes on his scalp, injected him with succinylcholine to paralyze his muscles before giving the ECT, and then bagged oxygen into his lungs until the succinylcholine wore off. In spite of the crudeness of this procedure the patient benefitted from it.

I will have no subsequent exposures to ECT until thirty years later, when I observe a trained psychiatrist administer it to a depressed patient while an anesthesiologist provides a general anesthetic. After several more treatments this patient is no longer depressed. ECT will become a preferred treatment for a number of psychiatric disorders, particularly major depression, but also neuroleptic malignant syndrome, delirious mania, and catatonia.

I decide to look at the literature about ECT and its use in patients with multiple personality, and find an article at a later date

92

reporting the successful use of ECT on a patient with multiple personalities suffering from major depression. I will also discover an article reporting that ECT facilitated integration of alternate personalities after a two-year period of psychotherapy and medication. [24]

In spite of ECT's successes it must be noted that there have also been some side effects from its use that should not be overlooked, including some cases of permanent memory loss and adverse effects on the central nervous system.[25]

CHAPTER 17

He thought he killed me. He kept me locked up for many years.
But I'll get him!!

July 28, 1975

Jay sits down, signs in, and begins to complain about being a hospital patient. He also tells me he had a Sunday visit with his seventy-two-year old parents but doesn't remember much, and is surprised when told he'd been "belligerent to them."

Jay says he hates living on a ward filled with drunkards. He complains of being confused, doesn't know what's happening to his mind, and wonders if he should blot out all of his thoughts by going into a deep sleep. Then I see his facial expression become stoic, eyes glaze over, and one hand grabs the other hand. An automatism takes place and then an angry alternate personality emerges. James glares at me. "It doesn't prove a goddam thing you came back. They all run off sometime. That's no sign you won't run off again just because you came back," he exclaims.

James makes disparaging remarks about the alternate personality whose name he refuses to repeat. "That pipsqueak. I don't like to say his name. I'll get him! He kept me locked up for too many years!"

"You are very angry today," I say.

"Wouldn't you be? Goddam right I'm angry. He just wanted to get rid of me."

"How?"

"He thought he killed me. I played dead so he wouldn't think I'm around. He has a crooked mind. He made me relive some things I didn't want to relive."

"Killing is a pretty strong word."

"You bet it is. I was planning to kill that pipsqueak." He lets out a weird laugh.

"Have you felt this angry before?"

"Hell, yes! I won't tell you."

"How does he (the pipsqueak) feel?"

"He's an idiot. He's always happy."

"And you dislike him?"

"You bet. I cut off his ponytail, that's what. He's got me over a barrel. He's in this hospital."

"What would you like to do?"

"Just go, go, go, all the time, never settle down."

"What does that mean?"

"Never stay any place very long. Once I'm in power, I can go and he can't catch up with me."

When I ask if he can tell me who wants to control him, he begins to have an automatism, consisting of rapid respirations and head shaking back and forth. A voice yells "J…J…" Then James finally regains control and says. "See he just tried to get rid of me again."

Within a few minutes I witness another automatism triggered by my question, "Why does the other personality want to get rid of you?" This automatism, characterized by his arms waving back and forth and then wrapping themselves around his body, lasts for several seconds, as if it's an attempt to control his fragmentation. When the automatism ends I see that James is replaced by a personality, either Jay or Shea, who complains he doesn't feel well and doesn't understand what's happening. He looks at his hands and says, "I'm shaking. Maybe I have DTs?" He pauses and then asks, "Can I have a smoke, please?"

I deny his request for a cigarette and ask about his anger, but he denies feeling angry. I ask if he has a memory of being mistreated by his parents as a child but he denies that. "If my parents mistreated me, I'd remember. If I said anything bad to my mother, I'd remember. If I said anything bad to my father, he'd backhand me."

My therapeutic approach for patients receiving psychodynamic psychotherapy is to understand the relationship of their current behavior to past events. In James' case, my intent is to understand the origins of his anger, which has no meaning to Jay because his past experience is different from James'. I will continue to help each personality remember his past and ask what his relationship to his parents was like. Although I don't realize it now, I will also discover that each personality has a different memory about his parents.

After this session is over I review the tape and find it most interesting that Jay continues to deny that he locked James away. When I ask about ECT, he says he has no memory of receiving the "shock treatments" which suppressed James' existence four years ago when he received ECT. Dr. Baird apparently administered it to alleviate James' disruptive behaviors and mood swings and the treatment achieved that goal. Jay became the predominant personality and was soon discharged from the hospital.

When I see the movie *One Flew Over the Cuckoo's Nest*, based on the 1962 book of the same name, there are negative accounts of ECT. The author, Ken Kesey, once worked in a VA hospital and may have fallen back on his own personal experiences when he portrayed the book's version of a psychiatric institution. The patients were kept in line by a dictatorial "Big Nurse" who exercised almost absolute power over the patients' access to privileges, food, and basic necessities. If a patient acted out she punished him by withholding privileges or coercing the doctor into giving ECT. I will learn from psychiatrists, who will review the movie, that its traumatic portrayal of ECT would have a major impact on reducing its therapeutic use for many years.[26]

CHAPTER 18
Aggression, Self-mastery, and Tears

August 7, 1975

After Jay signs in today, he says he can't remember much of anything about the past few days and feels like he's coming out of a stupor. He can't understand why the patients are angry with him, but he's aware of considerable turmoil going on within and around him. He throws up his hands in despair. "I'd just like to forget," he says.

"Would you like to talk about what you'd like to forget?"

"But then you might spill the whole beans and my whole plan will go to pot."

"You were thinking of just running off?"

"No. I just want a discharge. They have to give it to me because I signed myself in."

"That's right. You're not here on a court order," I reply, and suggest I meet with him together with the hospital staff to discuss the matter. But he refuses because he's angry with the staff, who criticize him for always trying to help other patients rather than allowing the staff to help him.

"Does the staff want you to stop taking responsibility for others rather than yourself?" I ask, recalling that he assumed a parental role in the family by helping his mother and siblings.

"I've (taken responsibility) all my life, so I guess I always will," he claims.

I ask him again if he's willing to talk with the staff about this matter.

"No. You'll just spill the beans," he insists.

"If you say something to me and you're afraid I'll spill the beans, I can assure you I won't do that."

"I don't give a damn what you do," he replies angrily.

"You don't? We're trying to build up a working relationship so that you trust me. How are you going to trust me if I go spilling the beans, whatever that means."

As I reassure him about confidentiality, he withdraws, his eyes glaze over, and he begins to stare straight ahead into space. It appears to be James who, after I ask what he's thinking, remains silent, jerks his head slightly, and grasps his left wrist with his right hand.

I see his body remain rigid and his eyes stare straight ahead. Then I hear a voice declare forcefully, "If you all leave, then I'll leave. I'm just not going to let anyone go off and leave me. That's it. I'll not let you go off and leave me. If I'm not wanted, say so. To hell with it." I believe this is James emerging from abduction. He swings his arms back and forth and then behind his back until his wrists come to rest, crossed like a prisoner with his hands tied behind his back. He ignores me when I make an attempt at expressing empathy but then he complains angrily, "I was tricked into coming here in the first place!"

"You're not alone here," I reply.

"I'm never alone wherever I go because I have myself," he

99

exclaims. "I'm not afraid to tell you what I think about that mean-mouthed son-of-a-bitch who always thinks things through so goddamn clear and is so sweetish about every damn thing," he exclaims, then closes his mouth tightly.

"It's okay to be angry," I say, wondering whom he's talking about.

"I'm not angry."

"You are now."

"Why should you care? And here I needed help and you don't care. You're just going to push me off to the side, put a number on me and 20,000 years from now you'll push a button and maybe you'll say something to the poor slob."

"I can understand your feelings about being abandoned," I reply empathically.

He sits quietly for a moment, then his breathing becomes harsh and rapid, his head shakes back and forth, and he begins to talk to himself. "By God, James. You know where you are. It's starting all over. You know it is. Behave yourself James, get ahold of yourself. Just let it go. Go elsewhere."

"What's it like to feel alone?" I ask.

He remains silent and withdrawn while breathing rapidly and staring straight ahead with arms crossed behind his chair, ignoring me. Finally he speaks. "I know what I have to do and I'll do it," he insists firmly.

I echo his words: "You know what you have to do and you're doing it."

"That's right. I've even urinated for myself and I've picked up those goddamn son-of-a-bitchin words he (Jay) uses. And I tell you. I haven't done it for years. It felt good. It felt marvelous."

"To urinate?"

"I went in there and took a good healthy piss. That's what I did and it felt marvelous," he exclaims while looking away from me.

James is expressing delight about controlling his own bodily functions for the first time in four years. He is also telling me how much he enjoys defying Jay for keeping him a prisoner. "I'll do it myself from now on. If I have to kill the son of a bitch, I will. I'll do anything," he rants. He gazes into the distance as if remembering events from the past. He suddenly he yells out, "I'm right here. I'm right here…. Right now, I'm right here. Right here." He struggles to maintain his presence as his arms begin to swing wildly, until they finally return to their resting place on the arms of his chair. "I'm right here and he's not going to make me go away. He's not going to come. He's not going to because I'm going to stay right here, goddamn it. I know I'm right here."

"Yes you are," I state, clearly acknowledging his presence by reaching over to touch his shoulder. He jerks away and nearly jumps out of his chair as if bitten by an asp.

"I'm right here. I'm staying right here. I'm right here," he shouts.

"I touched you so that you would know that you're here," I explain.

"No one touches me! No one! I'm not allowing anyone!" he yells.

"All right. Don't allow anyone to touch you if you don't want them to."

His head begins to move from side to side and I can see the beginning of a struggle between James, now claiming the body, and Jay, who wants to replace him. His chest, shoulders, head, and neck begin to writhe slowly as his speech slows down and softens.

"I'm right here. I'm ..." he trails off.

"You're here. Who am I?" I ask.

His eyes begin to fill with tears. I hear inarticulate sounds, watch arms and hands convulse slowly as they hang from his shoulders and then beat back and forth against the chair. Then I see his arms begin to raise straight into the air and his head turn slightly toward his right. He cries out, "I want to stay here. I want to stay." He breaks into sobs as his hands move together and clasp the top of his head. Then his body bends forward until his head nearly reaches his lap. He continues to sob uncontrollably.

I tell him I understand his pain and reach over to touch his shoulder.

"Why do they do this to me every time? Why? Why can't I be free? Why don't they leave me?" he sobs, and then moans about demons controlling his body. I am convinced however that the demons he fears are really other personalities who want to control the body.

"You're not alone now. You're not alone, you're not alone," I say as I attempt to break through his cries. I keep my hand on his right shoulder as he continues with a mixture of sobs and occasional words reflecting his bewilderment about what's happening to him. After about a minute I witness an automatism as his head and body straighten and an alternate personality opens his eyes and looks around, clearly unaware of what had just happened.

"You're all right. Let me get you some tissue," I say, leaving my chair to find a box of tissue in another part of the studio.

He appears very perplexed.

I ask him if he feels better after allowing himself to cry and he looks at me in amazement. "What? I haven't been crying," he snickers while wiping the tears from his face.

"Join the human race," I say.

"I've always been in the human race. Something's funny here." He shakes his head, pulls a cigarette from his pocket, and lights up. "C'est la vie," [27] he grins and shrugs his shoulders.

"That's okay. It happened. You're you," I reply.

"I know I haven't got a cold," he says, trying to understand the moisture on his face.

"Those are real tears. Real genuine tears. I'm not kidding," I point out.

"I have no reason to cry. Nothing to cry about."

"It's a good feeling to be able to cry. A normal thing," I say.

"Yeah, people have said that they've cried and felt better. But I haven't cried since I was a little boy."

"That long ago?"

"Sometimes I've wanted to. But …" Jay shrugs his shoulders in bewilderment. "This reminds me. One of the patients up there said he saw me sitting in the corner bawling."

"I think it's commendable that you've allowed yourself to

103

cry. You trusted me enough to show that part of yourself to me."

He shrugs it off, says he doesn't understand what I mean, and momentarily puts his left hand up over his eyes. Then he picks up a pair of glasses that were on his lap and puts them on.

"They told me I did a bunch of other stuff. Oh well, I don't know what they said, I just feel exhausted."

Nearly every therapy session I spend with James and his alternate personalities will last fifty minutes, although each chapter in this book will comprise only a portion of an individual session. During training my supervisors established this as the accepted time frame. It followed the example of Sigmund Freud and psychoanalysts after him who believed that fifty minutes was the time necessary for "unconscious processes" to unfold. This gave rise to the phrase "the 50-minute hour," which became the norm for the majority of therapists until it eventually became modified, in most cases, for business reasons. I feel comfortable with this time frame, although there are occasions when I shorten the time to thirty minutes.

CHAPTER 19

Don't leave! I've got to have another chance.

August 25, 1975

Jay is dressed casually in a white T-shirt and blue and white striped pants. He's preoccupied about a recent meeting he had with his parents and some of the hospital staff. He says his father became extremely upset because he's convinced that Jay can't manage his money properly, and had allowed his nephew to misuse his funds. Jay, however, is unconcerned about his money and more concerned about the turmoil within his family that has interfered with his plans to go home.

"If he is stealing it, I would know it. But I don't think he is," Jay says, expressing sympathy for his nephew who was recently divorced and short of money. He also says he doesn't have a need to spend money for anything except to make payments on his trailer. What mainly upsets Jay is hearing his father call him incompetent and mentally retarded, and believing I knew about this but didn't tell him. I assure Jay I know nothing about it and hope he is able to control his own funds.

Fortunately Jay uses this incident to justify staying in the hospital. "Actually, I thought I would only be here about two or three weeks, but I can't go home now with my father like this."

"Do you remember the conversation we had last winter when I asked you to move to Topeka?"

"Yes but I can't do that. Do you know what I have caused for my father? And my family? I've caused him to accuse people in my family of things that aren't true."

I ask him if he wants to move away from his parent's home but he says his father would get a court order to prevent that. He goes on to tell me that he found himself very "shaky" the day his parents came but doesn't want to talk about it, and continues to bluster about his father having everyone, including the whole town of Strong City, population 485, in an uproar. "He's got the postmaster, the assistant postmaster, the banker and also the social security people, believe it or not." He tries to shrug it off by laughing but can't dispel his sense of helplessness about being caught in the middle of this turmoil. He says he tried to abate his father's tantrum by telling him to stop turning the VA disability checks over to his nephew, who has been making payments on James' trailer with the money.

Talking about these reality issues reveals a number of things. Jay is distressed about his father's anger and wishes he could prevent it. He's ashamed about causing his entire family and community to be upset. He is very concerned that his nephew might misuse his funds. Then Jay makes a surprising admission that he doesn't recall buying the trailer and doesn't care what happens to it or to his money.

"How come you don't know?" I ask.

He shrugs his shoulders and asks me a question. "How come I don't know what happened Friday at the meeting in the ward? They told me I was there and they voted me in as vice president of the ward."

Although his amnesia for these events is a serious matter, he laughs about it and makes a flamboyant gesture to describe his own lack of involvement with what has gone on. "I got a little teed off because I got voted in as vice president. I didn't have time to campaign or say I deny it. But they voted me in," he says comically. "And one of the nurses aides said I was there."

"You're a pretty important person but you just don't want to remember it," I say as we both laugh. In spite of our laughter, it's probable that Jay was replaced by Shea when the patients voted him to be vice president. As we discuss this, Jay tells me about his concern for his father.

"I care about him. He's my father."

"That's the first time I've heard you express that kind of concern about him."

"Well I don't want him to have a heart attack but I don't like what he's doing to the whole family, just over a dumb check. I'll tear it up or something if that will help. I've got to get him straightened out. I've got to get out of this hospital and go far, far away. I don't want him to be upset." He frowns and turns his head to the left.

"I'm glad you're concerned about him but why don't you like others to be concerned about you?" I ask.

"Why should they (be concerned about me)? In fact, I was going to ask you a direct question. Do you want to see me, or not?"

"Why do you ask?"

"Because the last couple of times, it was 'hi-goodbye.' And

107

the aides up there say that I shouldn't be seeing you in the first place because I have a doctor up there on the ward."

"You do have."

"Big deal."

"Can't you have two doctors?" I ask.

"Ok. But if you don't want to see me just say so and I'll make my plans and go on about my business." As he talks about possibly ending our therapy sessions his eyes suddenly close, his body becomes rigid, his mouth makes puckering and unpuckering movements, and his breathing becomes rapid. He suddenly raises his right hand to his face and back down. Then I notice a momentary change in his facial appearance before he regains control.

"Did you just have a memory? It looked to me like you were fighting off a painful memory," I observe.

"No, I was just fighting off sleep. The only painful memory is of my father. And I've got to make plans to curb all of this."

"You can't change your father. If he wants to get upset about this, you can't change that."

He continues to deny his problems and claims that staying in the hospital will only get him in deeper. But I share my observation that it would be important for him to remain in treatment in order to understand how the split in his personality affects his relationship to his father. "There's a part of you that is very afraid of and angry at your father, and another part of you that is concerned and wants to please him."

"No. Whenever my father is sick or isn't getting along I help

108

him the best I can. After that, what else can you do? He's on his own. But I don't want other people to be helping me or be concerned about me. I'll help myself!" he insists.

With a grim face he nods his head and informs me he is going to find a way to leave the hospital. Then his body becomes rigid again, his arms shake, and his eyes open briefly as he looks upward and to his left. A dissociation takes place and James begins to shout, "I'm going to stay right here! I'm going to stay right here in this hospital. He's not going to talk me or anyone else out of going, that's all there is to it!"

Then I see him take a deep breath.

"What are you remembering?"

He cries out his own name, "James! James!" After a brief pause he continues. "That son of a bitch might just give one person a chance and that's it. I've got. I've got to have…I've got to have another chance, that's all. I've got to have another chance." His eyes blink. Then he closes and reopens them. Finally they glaze over and stare into the distance.

I wonder if he is he having a seizure. If so, what kind would it be? It may be a petit mal or absence seizure. An absence seizure causes a person to lose consciousness for a few seconds, during which time he stares straight ahead blankly without responding to questions. An absence seizure can be diagnosed by finding abnormal brain waves on an electroencephalogram (EEG). If he is having a non-epileptic seizure (NES) or pseudo-seizure, there will be no abnormal EEG findings. An NES is also called a dissociative seizure, which can be caused by repressed traumatic experiences.

109

James' dissociative episodes might be considered dissociative seizures. Hypnotherapists frequently use hypnotic age regression, also referred to as regression and revivification, in such patients to help them recall and relive trauma experiences.[28]

"What are you remembering?" I ask, aware that James is experiencing a spontaneous age regression and revivification.

"I'm going to stay right here. I've got to have another chance," he says.

"What kind of a chance?"

He breathes heavily, his head quivers, and he struggles with his words. "I've got to have that chance," he sputters.

"What chance?" I ask again.

He continues to struggle silently as eyes close, head turns to the right, and body convulses slowly.

"What's happening, James?"

He continues to struggle but then suddenly yells out, "God damn it. I've got to have a chance. I've got to have…" He opens and then closes his eyes. His head moves to the right and back to the left as his breathing continues to be irregular. "God, they can't do that to me again."

"Do what? What are you afraid they're going to do, James?" I ask.

"They just can't. They can't kick me out when I really need them."

"Did your family kick you out?"

"They just can't do that now when I need them. I'm not going to let them talk me out of it, that's all there is to it." His eyes close and tears stream down his cheeks. He continues. "I'll get rid of him. I'm here now. I'm here. I'm here. And I'll fight. They're not," he sputters, and his head begins to convulse slightly back and forth. Then he moans, "I feel sick."

"Did your family kick you out?" I ask again, but rather than talk about his family he relives his past hospital experience with Dr. Baird.

"Baird can't do that to me. I have a chance now. Goddam it!" he exclaims as he begins to sob. His hands fly upward helplessly and his arms wrap around his neck as if attempting to choke off his emotional expression.

I see a dissociation to a different personality—Jay. After he collects himself he says he has a feeling he's not had before. "I've got that feeling Dr. Brende. I don't like it. I've never had it before."

"Do you know what the feeling is?"

He shakes his head. "I think I know the word. I'm just a little shook up. I just get tired. Shaky. Weak."

"You're letting yourself feel things that you haven't felt for a long time."

"I've never felt this before," he says.

"Part of it is sadness," I suggest.

"I don't think so."

"What do you think it is?"

"I'll take a wild guess. I had it first on Friday, then Saturday and Sunday. And I've never had this feeling before. It's strange. I really don't want to be alone, but..." He doesn't finish the sentence. Then he frowns, opens his eyes, and closes them quickly. I suggest there is a relationship between his feelings and my absence but he denies it. "I'm not afraid. No. Maybe I'm scairt."

Then I suggest he has a fear of the unknown. "You're afraid that something bad might happen."

"Afraid isn't the word. That's a word that means something might happen but you can do something to stop it. Scairt is a better word and I've never been that way," he insists. Then he asks if I'm afraid of him.

"No," I reply. "I'm not scared but I wonder if you're afraid I won't be able to manage you if you were to lose control."

He doesn't answer.

CHAPTER 20
The Host and the Inner Self Helper

August 28-31, 1975

As has been typical, Jay arrives and signs in. I have come to see Jay as the personality who is primarily in control. He has the capacity to think and speak clearly and is able to control all emotional discomfort. He is the personality who, as I will later learn from other therapists, is referred to as the host, or the inner self helper (ISH).[29]

I will learn that the ISH becomes a "protector" by taking over and replacing the victim personality to avoid experiencing or remembering painful, traumatic emotions. He is also frequently referred to as the host personality because he is predominant and tends to appear normal. He appears to be able to carry on an ordinary existence because of his ability to speak clearly and make rational decisions. Before learning about the characteristics of the ISH, I had already discovered that Jay served a protective purpose because he felt no emotional pain and had no memory of past traumatic events. I will learn that Jay first became a protector at the time of James' first trauma by taking over and saving him from experiencing painful emotions. Although it is not clear at this time, I will come to believe this happened at age seven.

Although Jay lacks awareness of alternate personalities he has begun to sense the hidden presence of someone he can't define.

And that makes him anxious. He blames his anxiety on having to listen to other patients complain about the doctor and staff members.

During the middle of this session I witness a dissociation and see Jay replaced by an alternate personality who seems to be a young and anxious boy. "I'm going to fight and I won't let anyone run me off," he exclaims.

I recall seeing a young boy named Jimmy during our third therapy session, so I ask if his name is Jimmy. That question triggers an automatism and the shedding of tears. Jay returns, in his protective capacity, and wipes away the tears with a large towel.

Before the session comes to an end I remind Jay again that he is not ready to leave the hospital and he does not object.

Three days later Jay arrives at the studio and signs in. He proudly announces he's been elected president of the ward but complains of fainting episodes, a loss of appetite, and inability to sleep. He also expresses alarm that I wasn't here yesterday for our scheduled appointment. I tell him my secretary called to reschedule our session for today because of a conflict. Obviously Jay didn't get the message because he walked all the way to the studio and then to my office only to discover I wasn't there. When I ask if he felt upset he doesn't answer. Then he appears to dissociate, although I'm unsure which personality is present.

"Are you Jimmy?" I ask.

He suddenly pulls his chair away from me.

"Are you Jimmy?" I ask again.

"I don't like that word," he replies stoically, indicating that Jay has returned to the body.

"I can see that there is a part of you who has missed me and tells me he is afraid to be alone, but there is another part of you who is afraid to show any feelings about it," I say.

"I know I put on a front and that makes me feel tired," he replies.

"What would happen if you didn't put up a front?"

"I'd walk off forever."

I clarify once again that there are two parts of him—one part who gets upset easily and another part who appears normal enough to be elected president of the ward.

The personality who is easily upset may be Jimmy, the boy Betty told me about during an earlier session who was his mother's favorite. I will see additional evidence of a boy personality several times during the course of therapy, but it will not always be clear to me if that boy is Jimmy, named by his mother, or Jim, named by his father. What is clear at this time, however, is that Jay cannot tolerate the mention of the name Jimmy. I'm puzzled by that fact.

Before the session comes to a close I ask if he can agree to a joint meeting that will include his hospital doctor. He does not object.

Dr. Yoon is one of the hospital doctors, primarily responsible for maintaining a therapeutic milieu and prescribing or changing patients' medications. He leads daily team meetings and discusses each patient's problem and treatment goals with the staff. The members of the staff include several registered nurses and aides who interact with patients supportively, provide a safe environment, and attend to patients' basic needs. I rely on Dr. Yoon to provide James with appropriate medications and maintain a therapeutic milieu where there are patient group meetings and assignments to special therapies in education and art. It is important that Dr. Yoon and I have a good working relationship, as it is important for James' recovery.

CHAPTER 21

James says angrily, "I don't want to go back there."

September 8, 1975

Jay arrives today accompanied by a psychiatric aide. He's casually dressed in a lime green T-shirt, blue and white striped pants and tennis shoes. He sits down, signs his name as Jay Kohlman and then tells me he is experiencing a new and unfamiliar emotion. "I'm scared to death. I've never felt that way before, but I am. I don't know why."

Then he complains about a problem with his family. "They think I'm incompetent and wanna take over my disability checks!" he exclaims. "I'd like to disown 'em."

"It sounds like you're pretty angry."

"I'm not angry. I'm just scared," he says, and goes on to say he started feeling this way three days before his parents came on Friday.

"I think I should get out…out…of the hospital," he stutters and then becomes silent. I see his body become rigid, his eyes glaze over, and his hands clench the arms of the chair, which appears to trigger a dissociation.

"Are you remembering something?" I ask.

A loud but different voice speaks out as he sits rigidly while staring straight ahead. "See, he's doing the same thing he's done before!"

"What?" I ask.

"I don't wanna go back there!" he insists.

"Where? You don't want to go back where?"

"I'm not going back in there. I'll…I'll fight and I won't go back in there!"

"What are you afraid of?" I ask.

"He's doing it and I'm not going to let him."

"Who's doing it?" I ask.

"J…J…Jay is going to put me way back there. I'm not going back there!" His body remains rigid as his eyes continue to stare straight ahead. "I'm not going back there and I'll kill the son-of-a-bitch if he makes me! He's not going to put me back there again! He's not going to!" he exclaims loudly.

"I won't let you kill him," I reply to the voice who may be James, the personality who first appeared on March 27, described himself as being in the Air Force on April 9, and appeared most recently on July 28 when he complained about the shock treatments that shut him away.

"I won't let him put me back there! I don't…I don't want…I don't want to be put back there," he demands.

When I ask if Jay put him there he begins to struggle with his words and then stops speaking. His arms suddenly fly up over his head, swing back and forth, and become wrapped around his neck to choke off his sobs. Silence takes over. After several seconds, his eyes pop open, and Jay emerges.

"Why are you so frightened?" I ask.

He tells me he doesn't know why he's scared but his body

118

language speaks volumes. I see his arms wrap tightly across his chest and his hands hold onto each shoulder as if he's trying to hold himself together.

"You said that you didn't want Jay to put you way back there. I wonder what that means?" I question.

His body relaxes slightly and appears to dissociate but he doesn't lower his arms. I hear a voice. "I'm Jay. I'd be going back where?" he answers, clearly unaware of the distressful words "I won't let him put me back there" spoken moments earlier.

"You just said you're Jay. Would you prefer to be called James?"

With the mention of James' name, he becomes anxious, catches his breath, and closes his eyes. "Jay! Jay! Jay!" he announces loudly three times in an attempt to maintain control.

"You don't want to be called James?" I ask.

"Please, I don't like that name!" he yells.

"Your name is Jay?"

"Yes, but I don't know right now who I am. I'm scared of who I am right now. I think I'm an idiot right now."

"We don't want you to leave the hospital!" I emphasize again.

After a brief silence he says, "I'm sorry. I'm tired. I'm cold. I'm frightened. I don't feel like I'm myself. I feel like I should be hit over the head and knocked out to make my body come back together. My body feels like it's splitting apart."

"You're holding yourself together right now I see," referring to his arms stretched across his chest and his hands holding down

119

both shoulders.

He quickly puts his arms down, lowers his head, and apologizes for being upset.

I assure him that even if he feels like he's going crazy he isn't. I urge him to acknowledge his need for help.

"I've never had a problem," he insists.

"You have a problem. You just said that you were feeling like you are going to fall apart. Why not share that?"

"Why share such a horrible thing like that with anyone? It's my problem and my responsibility." After a pause he says, "I wish I could feel pain. I just wish I could feel pain."

"You are feeling pain, but you won't let yourself feel (experience) it."

"I wish I knew what the matter was."

"I can tell you. If you let yourself feel pain it would just be too horrible a feeling. There was a time when you were a little boy you felt pain. Remember when your sister and brother and family talked about the time you were left behind all alone. You felt pain then."

"Not really. I used to joke about it. It didn't really hurt," Jay replies, indicating that the personality split in his mind had already taken place before his family's abandonment, which prevented him from being able to experience pain from that event.

"You know, Jimmy was left alone when he was a little boy," I say.

"Please, please. I can't cope with that name," Jay replies anxiously. "I want to get up and leave. I'm too upset. I've blocked

120

that name out."

"That's why you're so tired. It takes a lot of energy."

"The reason I'm here is they think I'm incompetent," he complains sadly and slowly shakes his head. He says he's unable to logically understand what is happening to him. Although he knows he has much in common with other hospital patients, he realizes his problem is very different from theirs. He begins to experience a motor automatism and suddenly I see a personality switch.

James emerges and stares past me as if I'm not in the room. "I've got...I've got...See what he's trying to do? He's trying to convince you. Like he...d...d...did," he sputters.

"What are you referring to?" I ask.

He continues to stare into the distance without speaking.

I reach over to touch him but he quickly backs away. Then he yells out dramatically. "I'm not going to have any more shock treatments. I'm not going to. And he's not going to drive me away." His head nods back and forth as he raises his arms and waves them above his head. A moment later they drop down and wrap themselves around his neck, which triggers a personality switch again.

"See Dr. Brende, I know I'm going crazy. Look at me. Look at me," Jay announces as he watches his arms slide downward across his chest.

"I know you're afraid of falling apart."

He remains silent.

"Do you see that you moved back six inches?"

He looks down and recognizes his chair has moved away from me.

"You backed away when I touched you. Why was that? Have you been hurt by someone in the past?" I ask.

"I don't know Dr. Brende. Who would have hurt me?" he replies in a low-pitched voice.

"You backed away from being helped. I have the feeling that you would like to cry out for help but you don't think anyone would hear."

"I've asked for help (on the ward) but they say, 'that's your problem, your responsibility,'" Jay replies.

"How about saying, 'I feel that you aren't helping me and I want more help?'"

Jay continues to deny that he needs help and insists that all he needs is the magical treatment of a needle. "Maybe I should just ask for a shot of Sodium Pentothal and I could go to sleep and maybe I would wake up as a normal person."

I ignore Jay's suggestion to put him to sleep and focus on the fact he wants to feel pain, which is in contrast to the time he says he stopped feeling pain in 1968, a time, as I will learn later, which was the date of a major traumatic event. "You've felt helpless and depressed. You say that you would like to feel pain. You've obviously been feeling it. When you are walking around holding yourself together, that's obviously feeling pain."

Then he makes a significant observation that there is a split within him. "I feel like a part of my body is going to leave me."

"Which part?"

"I don't know." He hesitates and adds, "The only thing I know is that my right arm sometimes feels like it's ten miles long and weighs 500 pounds or something."

I find it interesting to hear him describe his right side as distorted and not fitting in with the rest of his body, which is consistent with my observation that Jay's presence is linked to his right side and left hemisphere functions. This appears to be a breakthrough—he can finally acknowledge that something is wrong without joking about it. It's also notable to hear him say, "I'm afraid. But I don't know what I'm afraid of."

Before the session ends we discuss his fear of being made legally incompetent. When I ask if he can stand up to his family members he says, "No I don't wanna do that."

"What do you want?" I ask.

He shakes his head. "I don't want anything. I've had it all and I've given it all away."

"You're complaining about people taking and not giving to you."

"Why should people give to me? I don't want anything."

Indeed, he is not able to tell me what he needs or wants. However, I will continue to hear Jay express his fear—that James wants to kill him.

CHAPTER 22

Jay says he is no longer needed.

September 11-13, 1975

The patient hesitates signing in today because he's unsure about his name, but finally signs Jay Kohlman. He says he's losing his mind, feels overwhelmed by an abundance of memories, and is frequently upset by other patients on the ward.

After a few minutes he struggles to maintain himself but loses control, dissociates, begins to cry, and an alternate personality emerges. "Dr. Brende, I don't want to go. They're pushing me out. I don't know why they're doing this."

Within a brief time he dissociates again and, to my surprise, Jay returns to the body and appears to be shedding tears although he feels embarrassed about it. He says he remembers crying when he was young but can't remember details.

Although the patient has just shed tears they may be a spillover from the personality who fears being pushed out. I would not expect Jay, who has been emotionally detached, to shed genuine tears unless he is experiencing a loss.

Tears usually are a response to grief and emotional pain, but can sometimes be a sign of emotional relief and stimulate the production of endorphins, which have positive mood altering effects. [30]

Before our time runs out I ask if he'd like to view a tape of our last session but he declines. I also ask if he feels any better after talking about this emotional breakthrough, but he says he's afraid he'll feel worse when he leaves the studio.

"I almost passed out after our last session," he says.

We meet again two days later, and Jay immediately says he's been looking forward to seeing me today, something I'd never heard him say before. He tells me he's been fighting with James for his very survival but is afraid he's losing because he feels weaker. "James told me I shouldn't be here any longer."

When I offer to help him with this he replies, "I don't need help, but I think the child needs it. He's immature. He's a normal teenager who thinks he knows everything."

He tells me his existence suddenly began many years ago for the purpose of taking care of James. He always felt like an adult and never questioned why he had never felt like a child. "I never needed anyone to help me grow up," he states.

He had previously told me his family moved out and left him alone when he was a young preadolescent. Thus Jay's entry into James' life was to assume the role of caregiver. Although Jay's protective role can be viewed as a component of multiple personality disorder, his role in the family can also be understood as parentification. This is a phenomenon whereby a child is prematurely forced into the task of being the "parent" because the actual parent is inadequate or untrustworthy. According to Object Relations theorists, the child's sense of self, blocked from maturing in a normal way due to abandonment or traumatization, is replaced by a "false self." Because a parentified child tends to act like an adult he or she is perceived as having grown up rapidly in order to become a family caretaker.

Unfortunately, this parentified child's memory of early life will have many holes and contain few normal emotional responses to loss. Since Jay became parentified at the time he took over his protective role, James did not have the opportunity to experience loss in a normal way. Consequently he is prone, as I have already seen, to experiencing abandonment depression with real or threatened losses.[31]

I ask Jay if I can help him, but he resists my offer and tells me it's been his role from the day he was born to take care of James because he was always unhappy.

"I made a promise that I would never cry. There was more to it in a radical way. For me to protect him I had no feelings. I had to keep him from getting hurt. I took his pain and I took his emotions."

This is the first time Jay tells me his purpose from the very beginning of his existence was to protect James from all emotional and physical pain. That meant that Jay lacked the capacity to feel normal emotional and physical pain. James remained a lonely victim cut off from the other parts of his identity and from all early childhood memories. He was also cut off from the positive emotions associated with the relationship to his own mother.

Before the session ends, Jay tells me James believes he can get along without him. He says he isn't needed to take care of James any longer and wants me to take over. I tell Jay it's very

126

loving of him to entrust James' care to me at this time, and I will take on the parent role rather than Jay.

Jay tells me his purpose has been fulfilled and bids me farewell. "I don't think I'll see you again."

CHAPTER 23

I don't have a name.

September 15, 1975

The patient appears lost today. He tells me he can't sign the permission sheet because he doesn't have a name. When I ask him why, he has no clear answer other than to tell me he can't get his thoughts together. I'm aware that the last session was very significant because Jay told me his purpose had been fulfilled and that he didn't expect to see me any longer. So this is not Jay. I wonder who it is.

When I ask him again to sign his name he hesitates and says, "I'm supposed to do something but I don't know what to do."

"Just let your right hand write whatever comes out," I reply. He looks vacantly at the sign-in sheet and tells me again that he doesn't have a name.

"Is there a name you'd like to have?" I ask.

"I'm supposed to know something but I don't know anything except I know I'm supposed to be here."

"Where?" I ask.

"Here seeing you, Dr. Brende."

I continue to ask if he can remember his name but this line of questioning is a dead end. I ask him if he knows the name on his birth certificate but that only confuses him.

"Didn't your mother give you a name?" I ask.

"I'm thinking back but there's no back."

"You look puzzled."

"I was supposed to be there but now I'm here."

"Do you remember what happened last session?" I ask.

"I don't remember."

"You let yourself shed some tears," I remind him.

He appears upset by that information and begins to have an automatism, but after a brief period of time he regains control.

"What happened?" I ask.

"I was some place just a minute ago," he says, and bites his arm to see if he really exists.

"Is crying an emotion?" he asks.

"You said you wished you could feel things. You said you haven't felt pain and would like to."

"I'd like to know what kinds of feelings are associated with feeling lost?" he asks.

"That it would be feeling frightened or scared," I reply.

"I don't know what these feelings are," he says. Then he adds, "This would make a marvelous TV show. A little kid lost. No other characters. Just him and his thoughts."

I agree with his observations.

Before our relatively short session comes to a close he says, "I'm upset because I wanna go home but I'm not going to 'cause I don't know where it is."

James doesn't know where home is and doesn't know his name because his identity is in a state of flux. What does a name mean for a normal person? A name equates to having an existence.

It means being part of the history of a parent or parents, as well as family members with that same name. It is the guarantee of the existence a person puts down on paper to sign letters, pay bills, write checks, and sign contracts. Having a name provides the basic meaning to an individual's profile as he connects with other people. Fortunately Jay will return in the future, and James and each of his alternates will once again tell me their names.

CHAPTER 24

Jay feels fragmented but holds himself together.

September 18, 1975

When the patient arrives I'm not sure who to expect since during his last visit he didn't know his name. Furthermore, during my last contact with Jay he told me he had completed his purpose and would no longer see me. I notice today that he appears more adult-like with a mustache and goatee. He is also wearing glasses I've not seen before. He seems hesitant about signing in but finally signs the name Jay.

I notice a cyclic quality to his speech and behavior. Sometimes he smiles, sometimes he sneers, sometimes he closes his eyes indifferently, sometimes he frowns, and sometimes he twists his mouth from side to side. He picks on his fingernails and makes derogatory remarks about his hospital doctor's English because he was born in Korea. He tells me his doctor ordered a neurological test and wonders if I can tell him the results.

"I wasn't aware of this test."

"That's strange. I'm confused. Aren't you in charge?" he asks.

I assure him that each of us has different roles to play, but I'm in regular communication with his hospital doctor. I ask him to tell me about his relationship to the hospital staff.

"I don't particularly like the staff, because I don't trust them," he says.

"What are you afraid they might do?"

He finds it difficult to answer me and anxiously brushes some lint off his pants. Then he says to himself, "Jay calm down."

"Why do you have to ask Jay to calm down?" I ask.

"Because I'm upset…or anxious. I don't know. I've been having this funny feeling. I'm scairt. I'm not afraid but I'm scairt." His voice becomes softer and more serious as he talks about not knowing what he has to be scared of. Then he tells me he's afraid the staff might take advantage or even get rid of him.

"Does that remind you of anything in your past?" I ask.

His head remains downcast. I see it begin to quiver and his hands stiffen. "Jay, Jay, Jay!" he shrieks, calling his own name to maintain control.

When I repeat my request to remember the past he remains downcast, silent and rigid. But then his hands tightly grasp the arms on his chair and I hear a different voice begin to stutter. "He…he…he…"

I wonder which personality is struggling for control and encourage him to talk, but the words are caught in his throat, as his body remains frozen in the chair. Then I ask him to talk about his situation. "You seem to feel so scared that you're hanging on to your chair and you're tense all over. What's happening? Who's here? Who else is here?"

He doesn't reply. His head hangs down, his eyes remain closed, and his hands begin slow, restless movements. Rather than

132

switching to a different personality his body continues to respond with automatisms. Finally I break through by asking him to tell me who is in the room with him.

He does not look at me but speaks in a relatively controlled voice. "I'm not scared of any of you."

He seems to be reliving a past experience, so I ask again if he can tell me who is here. He turns his head slightly to the left and asks if I am one of the staff who treated him four years ago. He gives me a couple of names, and I ask him to go back in time to any other events that caused him to be even more scared.

His head begins to shake from side to side and he lifts his arms above his head. 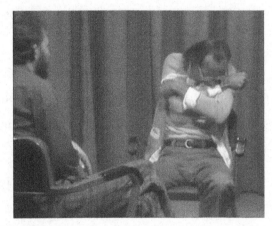 I ask him again to remember but his head shakes more vigorously and shifts rapidly from side to side. Then his arms drop down and he lifts his right arm over his head.

I assure him that he's all right but he doesn't seem to hear me. I see his head bend forward, teeth bite into his right wrist, left arm cross over his chest in a wrap-around motion, and right arm cross to cradle his body, which rocks slowly back and forth.

I ask him what he is feeling right now and that question

seems to jar him back
to reality. His head
suddenly lifts, his
arms come down, and
the person I met at the
beginning of the
session looks at me
with a confused
expression.

"What happened?" I ask.

"I was going to ask you," he says softly as he gazes off to his left.

"You were trying to remember something when you were young and very scared, and then you bit your wrist," I clarify.

He frowns, shakes his head, and begins to pick at his fingers.

"Are you curious to know?" I ask.

"Dr. Brende, nothing ever happened to me when I was young," he exclaims softly and continues to look down.

I repeat myself and tell him again that something serious must have happened, but he looks at me with a frown on his face, and sighs. Then I suggest his biting behavior could be a physiological memory of an earlier experience that he can't consciously recall. But he shakes his head slowly and continues to pick at his fingers.

Then he clasps his hands together while continuing to shake his head. "I'm sorry, I'm thinking about what you said," he says.

He looks at his wrist again, acknowledges he'd bitten it before, then describes a strange feeling like the time when he'd felt that he'd fallen apart—it was the feeling of not being here, although he knows he was. He has difficulty explaining what he's feeling but I believe he's becoming aware of the split between two identities.

"You mean you just felt that again a few minutes ago?" I ask.

"I just put myself together. That's another thing I notice," as he grabs himself again like a few minutes earlier. "I've crossed my arms...or I've hugged myself...Oh!" he says in exasperation. "See what I mean? They're just all messing me up."

"Yeah, this is a puzzle. Your need to hold yourself together. Are you saying that you weren't there for awhile? Is that what you're saying?" I ask, wondering if he had left his body.

"No. I'm always here. It seems as if I'm going all ways." He gestures in both directions with his arms and hands, indicating his sense of being fragmented. "I'm just feeling like I'm falling apart."

"Like you were scattered off or pulled apart in different directions?"

"In a sense yes, but all the parts were together as they were flying apart. Whew, that doesn't make sense." He places his right hand up to his forehead. "It's a feeling anyway. A feeling of falling apart."

"The kind of a feeling a little baby can have when he's less than a year old?" I ask.

He smiles at me while insisting he couldn't be an infant. "I wish I could remember. It would be marvelous to tell," he laughs.

"If you do remember, you'll probably forget about it, which is okay. Let me suggest that you don't work at it too hard and just let yourself remember when you're ready."

He laughs. "That's a marvelous idea. I never do work at anything and it always turns out right." He smiles at me and lifts his hands to his forehead while telling me he can't understand what's happening.

Before our session comes to a close I clarify our future meetings will be twice a week—Monday and Thursday.

This was an interesting session that I hope to understand in view of the previous session when Jay told me that his purpose—protecting James from the awareness of emotional and physical pain—had come to an end. Today it appears that Jay's protective purpose has not yet ended, although it seems to be breaking down. He described an unfamiliar feeling of being scared, perhaps due to a beginning awareness that there are events in his past he doesn't want to remember. Furthermore, it may not be possible for him to continue suppressing those memories. Rather than revealing the truth about what lies under the surface, Jay's body resisted in the form of automatisms that were triggered by abnormal electrical impulses emanating from the temporal lobe, most likely within the right brain. The only evidence that an alternate personality was fighting to emerge from his fragmented identity occurred when Jay returned to the body and discovered bite marks on his wrist. He tried to gain a sense of control by wrapping his arms around his body. When that didn't seem to help he said he must escape all of this by leaving the hospital.

136

CHAPTER 25
Frightening Dreams and Visions

September 22-25, 1975

In this session Jay describes a dream of a vicious animal with human characteristics who loses control of himself. When I ask him to give the animal a name Jay resists, although he now seems to think the animal is a person called James. But his anxiety has not lessened and he continues to think about running away, and tries to talk me into letting him leave the hospital. I refuse. Jay must face the stark reality that he is "trapped in the hospital," which prompts a dissociative episode. An alternate personality emerges whom I assume is James, although he is not angry like the dream indicates. I wonder if he is Jim or Jimmy, because he tells me how scared he is of being abandoned. When I ask him to identify who will abandon him, he stutters with difficulty, J -J -J - Jay and begins to sob.

We meet again three days later and he hesitatingly signs in as Jay Kohlman. Jay tells me he knows James wants to kill him but I explain very clearly that neither I, nor the hospital staff, will let that happen. I see that he's depressed and losing weight. Although he has no memory of being aggressive, he tells me other patients told him he had been particularly violent yesterday. "How can that be?" he asks. Jay is aware there is something wrong with him and reports that he had a vision of three violent dark figures. "I know there were three people there fighting, struggling, kicking. They were grown people. Dark figures. I don't know if they were men or women."

I ask him if I'm one of the three dark figures but that doesn't make sense to him.

I ask if there's anything from his past that might be related to this but he vehemently denies it. "I'm getting depressed, because you keep bugging me to remember," he protests. He asks me to tell him why he's having these experiences, and wants me to prevent him from hurting someone. I assure him that I won't let that happen. I also assure him that Dr. Yoon and the nurses on Ward 4-2-C will prevent him from hurting anyone. During this session I observe a seizure-like dissociative episode that concerns me, and I ask Jay to tell the doctor about it, but he says he doesn't trust Dr. Yoon. After our session is over I walk over to 4-2-C to talk with Dr. Yoon and the hospital staff about James' current symptoms, as well as his ill-advised desire to leave the hospital. They assure me James won't be allowed to hurt anyone or leave the hospital.

I research the literature about the dreams of individuals with multiple personalities and find articles that describe distinctive dreams.[32] I find reports from the 1800s that alternate personalities communicated with their hosts or protective personalities during dreams. Sometimes host personalities experienced recurrent nightmares during the night triggered by their alternates. In some cases host personalities went to sleep and other personalities woke up with nightmares. In some individuals with multiplicity, dreams

138

seemed to facilitate the integration of their personalities, as reported by Chris Sizemore, the woman who was the actual multiple personality patient depicted in the book *The Three Faces of Eve*. Ms. Sizemore eventually wrote a memoir to detail her life story.[33]

CHAPTER 26

Dr. Jekyll and Mr. Hyde and the Corpus Callostomy

September 29, 1975

During this session there is continuing evidence of the conflict between two alternate personalities, which Jay refers to as his own Dr. Jekyll and Mr. Hyde. I observe two brief dissociative episodes, the first occurring when a personality I believe to be James emerges to tell me he's only thirty years old.

I pursue more information about James' early life, and he tells me things I have not heard before about both his childhood and older years. He recalls suffering from scarlet fever at age eight, having thirteen brothers and sisters, helping his brother's wife deliver their son, and spending time in military service. I find it most interesting that he grew up as one of fourteen children. It would have taken extremely capable and well organized parents to raise children in such a very large family.

When he says his parents aren't concerned about him, I respond with my observation that I heard his mother say he was the most talented of all their children. But he dismisses her comment because he recalls that she described his older brother the same way. When I tell him his parents are worried that he's giving his money away and won't be able to support himself, he minimizes his parents' concerns, but becomes anxious and begins to lose control. It appears that a personality switch just took place. I hear

140

him mumble about James.

"What about James?" I ask.

He remains silent for a time. Then I see an automatism. His arms swing behind the chair for a short time until an alternate personality emerges and looks around with a fearful expression.

"You look frightened. Is your name James?" I ask.

"Yes," he mumbles.

"Relax and tell me about yourself. You have your hands behind your chair, like they're tied."

He turns his head to the side but seems unable to speak. When I ask what he remembers, he squints as if he's in pain. When I ask what is so painful he mumbles, "Nothing." He continues to look confused. Then I ask him to identity me. He looks up and states, "You're everybody."

I raise my eyebrows and wonder if he can describe his sense of reality if I ask pointed questions about his current circumstances. "Are you in the army now?"

"No, I'm not in the army," he replies.

Then I ask him why his hands appear to be tied behind his back "Are you a prisoner? You seem to be helpless."

He closes his eyes, shakes his head slightly, and cries out, "Jay!"

I see a brief dissociation without an automatism and Jay suddenly emerges, replacing the personality I believe was thirty-year-old James.

"See what happened?" he complains.

"Would you like to review the videotape to see what

happened?"

"I don't know," he says with hesitation.

"You're afraid of something? Are you upset about James?" I ask.

He struggles to answer and stutters his own name, "Jay, Jay," as a way of maintaining his presence in the body. Then I see him lose control and another personality appears who looks around and then at me. "I'm upset," he exclaims.

"What upsets you?" I ask, uncertain which personality I'm talking to.

He does not explain why the name Jay upsets him but he's willing to tell me more about James' memories of being in military service.

"I was in South America, Puerto Rico. I was six years in service (Air Force) before they kicked me out because I had epileptic seizures."

"That's interesting," I say.

"I was going to go to Japan. Greenland was hell on earth. I was in South America, Puerto Rico and Cuba. The only time I've ever used the word love was about the Air Force. I loved the Air Force. Now I'm bored."

According to James' medical record, he received a medical discharge from the Air Force for intractable grand mal seizures. I am aware that he has been receiving an anti-seizure medication, Dilantin, for many years, but that medication could not control intractable seizures. So what is controlling this more serious seizure disorder? I would later learn about the surgical procedure,

142

corpus callostomy, which consists of severing the corpus callosum that connects the left and right cerebral hemispheres, and effectively prohibits intractable seizures.

This procedure was made famous by Drs. Michael Gazzaniga and Roger Sperry, who won a Nobel Prize in 1981. Their research revealed that when individuals with severed corpus callosi lost the connection between right and left hemispheres, each of them functioned as two different brains. They studied the unique qualities of these two and found that the left hemisphere specializes in speech and language computation, while the right specializes in visual-spatial processing, facial recognition, and the primary emotion of fear.

After learning that a corpus callostomy "splits" the two halves of the brain, I came to believe James had experienced a spontaneous physiological blockade within his corpus collusum when he was severely traumatized. In other words, it's entirely possible that James' intractable seizures were prevented because the trauma "split" his brain into two separate parts: James linked with the right part of the brain and Jay with the left part.

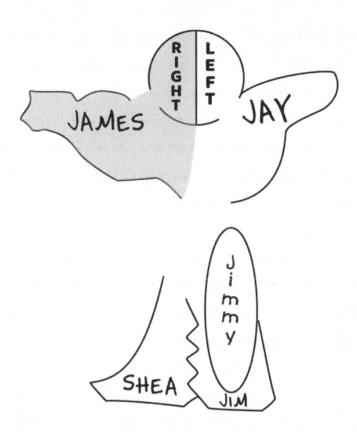

The diagram shows how James' identity and mental functioning is closely linked to the right cerebral hemisphere while Jay's mental functioning is linked to the left hemisphere. The presence of the two child personalities, Jim and Jimmy, stay somewhat hidden due the absence of intellectual functioning. Shea's presence as a distinct personality is unclear. He will later reveal himself as gay but the extent of his sexual aggressiveness will not be revealed until a later time.

CHAPTER 27

They tell me I've been violent. I don't know what I'm doing.

October 2, 1975.

When Jay signs in I notice that his goatee is neatly trimmed and he's smartly dressed—tan turtleneck, light blue and white V-necked sweater, light blue slacks, and tennis shoes. Shortly after signing in he says that after he attended a patient meeting he could only remember a few things. He also remembers that there was blood on his arm. "I saw blood on my arm and I thought that I had bit myself or that one of the other patients had hit me on the mouth with his fist. I went back to the meeting but I was foggy about what was going on and the next thing I know is that the patient who hit me on the mouth was fighting with this other patient. One of them had an ashtray and the other one jumped up."

He talks softly for a time until the speed and volume of his voice picks up. "The only thing that really sticks in my mind is that I had on this torn shirt."

Although unsure about what had happened, he became upset when the staff told him he was one of the patients fighting. "They said I didn't hurt the other patient but I had him on the floor. I can't believe it."

I ask if he bit himself or was bitten by a patient but he can't remember.

"Mr. Young explained what had happened. They said that

145

when they took the other patients out of the room and tried to talk to me I wasn't really there. I kept hollering. 'No one touches me! No one touches me! No one touches me!' I just went in there and the last thing I know is I was reading the blackboard. That's the last thing I remember."

I observe his deflated body language and see he's depressed. Then he tells me about the cuffs. "They told me they'll have to put me in cuffs so that I don't harm anyone, or I'll have to go to a different locked unit."

He sits with his head down, ashamed that he has no control over his rage, but I am encouraged that he's beginning to have awareness of the presence of an aggressive alternate personality within his body.

"Who do you think it is that does all of this? You can't remember what you do. The last time we met you were talking about another part of you. You didn't want to use a name."

"Of course I don't like that name."

"Are you talking about the name James?"

Saying the name James triggers an automatism as his eyes close tightly, body tenses up, muscles begin to writhe, hands clench and unclench, and speech comes in short spurts. "No… uh…uh."

I ask what's happening but he doesn't respond. His breathing becomes irregular and his arms start to jerk behind his chair as if tied there. Eyes peer down and away from me. Then a switch takes place and a different personality emerges.

"Is your name James?" I ask.

146

"Yes!" he declares, continuing to look down and away, avoiding my eyes.

"What are you thinking about?" I ask.

No answer.

"Who am I?"

No answer.

"Am I Dr. Brende?" I ask.

No answer. His head is moving in tight spasms up and down. Then he begins to talk. "Doctor! Doctor!" he cries out.

He responds very slowly while continuing to look toward the floor with glassy eyes. "Doctor Brende?" he repeats with a question in his voice.

"Yes, that's who I am," I say with assurance.

After I assure him that I'm here he looks at me and repeats my name. "Doctor Brende?"

"You looked at me. That's my name. Where are you?"

He looks up at the ceiling and after a moment he asks, "Doctor Brende?"

"Yes. What are you thinking?"

He doesn't answer so I continue to encourage him to speak.

Finally he breaks down in tears and his

head slumps forward. He sobs for a few seconds and stutters, "Go...Go...Go...Go away...."

I see a sudden personality change, his eyes open, and Jay appears in the body. He gazes at me with a puzzled look on his face. "I can't go through this anymore," he moans.

He sits quietly for a moment, with his chin resting on clasped hands. At first he complains about the difficulty he feels trying to maintain control. Then he describes something  new I haven't heard him complain about before. "I keep seeing things. But they're backwards. And they're not."

"What do you see?" I ask.

"Things that are supposed to be on the right are on the left. They don't last long. Not long enough for me to see. They keep coming and going. I'm losing my mind," he says. I have postulated that Jay's identity is linked to the left side of his brain and the right side of his body. Thus, as Jay's presence is increasingly being invaded by James, Jay feels the loss of his sense of permanence. This may explain why things that were on his right side now seem to be on his left.

He says he's afraid of walking down hallways because he gets confused about the directions. "When I think I'm walking down this way, I should have been walking this other way," he says, holding up his left hand and pointing over his right shoulder.

148

"And I'm not crying. I know that there are tears coming out but there is a lot of dust in the air and the tears are washing it out. I'm just upset. I don't know what way to go. I can't go right, I can't go left. I can't go forward. I can't go up. I can't go backward. I can't go down," he cries as he places his hands over his eyes.

I suggest he tell his hospital doctor what he's experiencing, but he says he doesn't know how to do that. So I provide a sample of the words he might use. "You could say, 'Dr. Y. I feel like I'm going crazy. I can't sleep. I'm upset. I'm scared. I need more help.'"

"I'm beginning to feel just like those other people that were transferred over to that lock-up ward. The basket cases up there," he says, referring to a ward in the hospital that houses the more severely disturbed and potentially violent patients.

Before the session ends I empathize with his distress and confusion about not knowing what to do and remind him to share his feelings with the hospital staff. But he resists my recommendation and says, "They're too busy to listen to me. And I'm not that important."

My closing words are, "You're important. I want you to ask for more time with the staff."

Jay's description of the issues he faces on the ward concern me. I will call his doctor on 4-2-C because it's important to coordinate our treatment goals. But I also want Jay to speak up and make his requests known to his doctor and staff. I'm mindful that he will benefit from his interactions with other patients, as well his involvement in ward activities, and participation in group therapies.

149

CHAPTER 28
Who shaved off my beard?

October 6, 1975

In this session, Jay tells me that he had a memory gap for the preceding weekend and doesn't know how his beard got shaved off, but is beginning to think another personality may have done it. He also is aware that he loses time and has large memory gaps. "I don't remember anything about Friday, Saturday, or Sunday." He says he gets upset about trivial events and sees things backwards like the windows and TV. And he is most disturbed about the bite marks on his arm. In spite of this he insists he's never consciously been aware that someone else takes control of his mind or body. Yet he has a premonition that a real person is going to take over and "eliminate" him.

I ask how he can explain these things. "Were you somebody else?"

"I hope not. I say I forget. But I don't know about it in the first place."

"What ever happened didn't register in your brain. Did you put it (your brain) to sleep?"

"I guess so."

"However, the part of you that was not sleeping shaved off your beard. How do you explain that?"

"I just shaved it off. Probably shaved it Sunday,

automatically, like brushing my teeth." He tells me he has never missed a day of shaving since he was in the Air Force. Then he changes subjects and talks about his premonition that someone will die within the next twenty-eight days.

"Who will die?"

"A male."

"Are you predicting an event that will happen to you?"

"I have the feeling of death and (the number) twenty-eight hours or days or years."

"You once said that if a crybaby named Jimmy once got loose he might kill you. What did that mean?" I ask.

He suddenly becomes anxious when he hears the name Jimmy and exclaims to himself, "Jay! Jay!"

"You said, 'Jay.' Did you feel out of control?"

"It makes me come back (into my body) to say 'Jay.' I'm telling myself to listen," he explains.

"It would be important to figure out why you were leaving and had to say Jay to come back."

He doesn't answer.

I continue. "You left for three days during the weekend and now you came back."

"I didn't leave," he corrects me.

"Jay is sitting here. I'm talking to him," I affirm. "If it wasn't Jay on the ward Friday, Saturday, or Sunday, might it have been someone else?" I ask.

He shrugs.

"You were there but your mind wasn't there. Maybe that

happened for three days. People saw you there. Maybe you were a different personality then. Somebody who isn't Jay?" I wonder if Shea might have been the personality people saw.

He looks at me, puzzled.

"When I would say a different name, you lost contact with yourself," I say, referring to the times I spoke the name James or Jim or Jimmy.

"Maybe that explains a lot. I remember things but they're often backwards. The windows and TV set are on the other side," he says, referring to his distorted perceptions once again. "Why would I get so upset about going down to work in the ceramics or go down to do exercises?" he asks, changing the subject. "I find myself having to run out. I have bite marks on my arms," he continues.

"If what we're saying is true and you change into a different person, that part of you bites your arm," I explain.

"God forbid."

"Why do you say that? Are you afraid?"

"Yeah. Then I have no control over myself. My only protection is to be here in the hospital."

"You need other people to keep you in control when necessary. To help and not hurt," I say reassuringly.

"I have never heard of someone controlling them for their benefit," he insists.

"Haven't you been in a controlled environment before?"

"I've had obligations going to school. I went to dancing and theatrical school, things which held me in control. But no one

152

person has ever let me be in their control," he insists.

I listen.

"Time has (control). That's why it doesn't mean anything to me." He pauses, then continues. "I've been feeling down for two weeks because I keep thinking about everything."

"Thinking and figuring it out is your way of keeping yourself in control. Thinking and figuring out so that nothing happens again."[34]

Then I express my concern regarding his premonition he's going to die.

"I've had this feeling for the past week," he says.

"Last weekend one of your personalities took over," I say.

He nods yes.

"You hate the part of you that loses control and takes over for three days, and you don't know what happened. I suggest you be less tough on yourself. Don't hate yourself."

"I don't hate myself," he replies.

"No, but you hate James," I clarify.

He reacts with a frown and headshake. "Jay. Jay doesn't hate anyone," he says to himself in order to maintain control.

"Let's open the door so that Jay may be able to accept James," I say.

He pauses, looks around, and says, "A whole bunch of things went through my mind."

"Tell me next time," I reply as I look at the clock on the wall and see we are out of time.

"I don't have much time, but that's funny because time

doesn't mean anything to me," he replies.

"How much time do you have?"

"Time is something a million miles off and something that's right here," he replies. "I picture everything. I dream in Technicolor."

CHAPTER 29

Jay acknowledges for the first time that James exists.

October 9, 1975

Today he comes to the session laughing and wearing a bright blue sweater. He signs his name as Jay Kohlman. I ask him how he is doing and then remind him that as we discussed in the previous session, we will not meet next Monday.

He ignores my message and tells me he can't explain why strange things are happening and wonders if I'm right. "I remember what you said about another personality. If that's true I don't have to worry about haircuts or shaving because that part does it," he smirks.

After this acknowledgement, he tells me he can't understand why staff and patients accuse him of picking fights and cursing all the time, because he would never do those things. Furthermore, he asks me if I can tell him why he has teeth marks on his right arm.

I speculate that the teeth marks on his right arm are actually James attacking Jay, and ask him what he's going to do about it. Jay replies that he's going to think it away or hypnotize himself. Then he changes topics and complains that his father cashed his social security check, but he doesn't want to think about that because he's more worried about something else, although he can't pinpoint what it is.

I give him credit for recognizing he has a problem serious

enough to warrant staying in the hospital, but he doesn't agree and returns to the subject of his government check.

"Why don't you give the money to them as a gift?" I ask.

"They don't need it. Not my mother or father. I'll either manage it or give it to someone," he says angrily. Then his anger shifts direction and he accuses me of not helping him, and his brother and sister-in-law for turning against him.

I point out the enormity of his anger today and ask if he is afraid of losing control. He answers by crying out, "Jay, Jay," and struggles to keep from dissociating.

I confront him with the bite marks on his arm and point out that this seems to be evidence of the presence of another personality. He reluctantly agrees, but asks why he was so angry that he would bite himself.

Our session comes to an end and I remind him again that I'll miss our next session. As Jay leaves the studio I hear him complain to his escort, "Dr. Brende is always leaving."

Jay has told me today that he found teeth marks on his arm. I am quite sure it's because James bit him. Why? Perhaps it is James' attempt to prove to Jay that he exists. Or it may be James committing an aggressive act against Jay. As I review the literature about multiple personalities, I find one alternate sometimes inflicts pain on another alternate for aggressive or revengeful reasons. However, I also find that self-harm or self-injurious behavior is not limited to patients with multiple personality disorders. In fact, this behavior is found in individuals with a variety of psychic disturbances. More recently, it's been

156

found in persons diagnosed with borderline personality disorder. These individuals may bang their heads against walls, but more often cut or burn their arms, wrists, legs, or abdomen at stressful times. Although the risk of suicide is higher in such patients, their acts of self-harm are generally not attempts to kill themselves. More often they have been victims of childhood trauma. Their brains produce chemicals such as endogenous opioids to block the experience of physical and emotional pain in order to enhance their capacity for survival. Having become conditioned to feel numb during times of stress or perceived danger, they will also feel numb if they have painful traumatic memories. Thus they inflict pain on themselves to break through intolerable feelings of numbness and prove they are still alive. [35]

CHAPTER 30

Jay has a dream of four personalities.

October 20, 1975

Jay comes to today's session clean-shaven and dressed in old pants and tennis shoes. While he talked about his beginning awareness of an alternate personality during the previous session, Jay immediately picks up the same theme but now wonders if there is more than one other person doing destructive things. He says he woke up Thursday morning to find his pants had been cut up while he was asleep.

"I'm going nuts. I found my pants all cut up. And I'm sleeping too much."

"Something's happening when you're asleep that's tiring you out?" I ask.

"I dreamt about four cute puppies. Two black, one white, and one black and white with a black cap on his head and a spot of black on his right shoulder. I looked at the black and white one the most. I dreamt in color and there was green grass."

"Would you give them human characteristics? How would you describe the black ones?"

"Proud and defiant."

"The white one?"

"They wagged their tails, nice and lovable."

"The white and black one?"

"There were no definite markings."

I will think about this later and speculate that the dream portrays four alternate personalities who are not yet mature. I surmise the puppy with a black cap on his head and spot of black on his right shoulder symbolizes an immature James. The black spot on his head is symbolic of his more mature mental capacities and the black spot on his right shoulder represents emotions. I theorize that the two black puppies represent the defiant qualities of James and Shea.

After a brief pause he changes the subject. "I want to take a pass (leave the hospital)."

I insist that he remain in the hospital and return to a more important subject. "Last time we had a serious conversation about another personality," I say earnestly.

He makes an attempt to brush this statement off but then tells me what concerns him most. "He comes out at night."

"Do you know who it is?"

"I don't want to know him."

"Give him a name," I request.

"I don't cuss," he replies.

I repeat my request.

Then he says, "I'd cuss him. The other one is an ass...I'd call him under my breath."

"Describe his age."

"Nothing comes to my head."

"I'd like to get to know him better. He may be an interesting guy," I say.

"You'd be sorry from what I've learned." He squints at me and then changes the subject to the color of my shirt. "You look unnatural. I don't like red. It's an unnatural color. That (color) makes me sick to my stomach. I used to think red was beautiful. I used to be carefree then."

Rather than discuss his distaste of the color red I continue to pursue the previous topic. "Give me a name," I request again.

He's not able to provide a name so I ask for his age. He responds by saying, "He's learning things and crawling and is close to walking."

"That's six to nine months," I say.

"I mean adolescent learning, learning to ride a bike, getting girls," he corrects himself. He adds, "He had a red car and traded it in." His sense of excitement about the adolescent's red car quickly vanishes. "I can't stand red."

"What is your association to red?" I ask.

"Throwing up in the bathroom," he replies. "I don't want to remember all those things back there. It took me a long time to do it but I put it out of my mind."

"You're paying the price because now there's another personality. Can we get to know the other personality?"

He continues to insist he has tried to put it out of his mind.

"If that would have worked, you wouldn't be in the hospital," I assert.

"Wouldn't it be nice to let him come out in this session?" I ask before this meeting comes to a close.

"No!" he retorts. "I don't trust him."

160

It has become apparent that Jay's capacity to maintain denial and protect James from pain by not remembering his past had come at a significant price—a split personality. But as he's losing his capacity to maintain the split he feels like he's going crazy.

CHAPTER 31
You gotta blow his head off. That's the only way you can help.

October 23-30, 1975

During this meeting three days later, Jay tells me he has not slept for four nights. He also says he had a seizure. We have a brief session, during which I hear a continuing theme about the escalating conflict between Jay and James, which stirs up so much apprehension that Jay says he's afraid to go to bed. James appears briefly during this session and tells me he hates the SOB (Jay) because he's planning to leave the hospital. "If he leaves then I'm lost."

During our next meeting a week later Jay signs in. I am very interested in understanding why Jay is frightened and whom he's afraid of. When he tells me there's a boy that bothers him I ask if

he's referring to either Jimmy or Jim. Jay shakes his head, scowls, and tells me that he doesn't want to hear those names. I reply that there must be a reason and ask if he will agree to allow me to make contact with Jim.

"Okay if you have to," he replies sullenly.

I decide to use the empty chair technique. I place a chair in front of Jay and say, "Tell Jim not to bother you."

Jay obediently responds and talks to the empty chair. "Don't bother me."

Then I ask him to sit in the empty chair and take the role of Jim. "Let yourself be Jim. He's telling you to get away from him."

 Jay reluctantly sits in the empty chair but refuses to talk. An automatism begins to take place but he quickly pulls himself together. I ask if he remembers our last session and he replies, "No, I don't wanna remember that." When I ask if he recalls what happened the last time he was in the hospital four years ago he gets very anxious.

"Jay, calm down!" he cries to himself.

"You're all right," I assure him. "But there's an inner struggle between the parts of you."

"I kinda know what you're talking about. I found myself standing outside your door Tuesday."

I'm surprised to hear him say he came to my office the day after our last meeting even though I told him I would be away. "Why?" I ask.

"Maybe James wanted to meet," he replies, but then begins

163

to lose control. In an effort to keep himself together he exclaims, "Jay" and then frantically counts "One, two, three, four, five."

I ask him to sit in the other chair but he seems frozen and then begins an automatism. I watch him switch to an alternate personality who exclaims loudly, "I'm right here! Right now!"

"What's your name?" I ask.

He does not answer.

"You look tense, you look afraid."

"Dr. Bren...Bren...Brende..." he stutters then suddenly yells out, "James! James!"

"Are you James?" I ask.

"Right now, I am!"

"Are the others bothering you?" I ask.

He ignores me but after a moment he cries out, "Dr. Brende!" He looks confused but then asks me if I'm Gilbert.

"Does it seem like I could be Gilbert too?" I ask.

"Yes," he replies. When I ask him more about Gilbert he doesn't answer. After a brief pause he frantically speaks out, "He won't let me think."

"Who?"

"Jay."

I believe I am talking with James, who suddenly stands up, shoves the chair away, and begins to rant. "How can anyone like a sneaking SOB like him? I'm here right now. He's doing the same thing! He wants to leave! He took me on a long trip. He wouldn't let me know or let me see," he cries.

"When?"

"Yesterday. A hundred years ago. Last week. I don't know. He made me forget." He shakes his head slowly and then says, "I remember right now. I was in this hospital. Think, Jay," he says to himself.

"Are you Jay?"

"I'm not. Never!" he yells.

"Do you think? Or is it only Jay who thinks?"

"Yes. I think. I'm not going to let him hide me away," he insists.

"How can I help?" I ask.

"I want you to help me. But Jay won't listen. You gotta blow his head off! That's the only way you can help." He pauses, then adds, "I've got to stay here. I can't go."

It's clear that James and Jay have a serious conflict, and James feels torn apart. When I ask the two of them to come to an agreement this triggers a dissociation, and within moments Jay returns to the body. He seems confused.

I immediately tell Jay about my conversation with James, and ask Jay to be more accepting of James' presence, but he resists that idea. Instead he says, "I feel tired, like I've been in a deep sleep."

Before our session comes to a close Jay tells me this is the day before Halloween and last year at this time he saw death. I ask if he has a premonition of dying but he brushes me off. I remind him we will meet again on Thursday.

I used the empty chair technique today, a technique I learned during a psychodrama training program at the Moreno Institute in

1972. Psychodrama relies on dramatization and role-playing as a method of psychotherapy, and was first used by Gestalt therapists in the 1940s. It is a therapeutic exercise that places the person who the therapist is addressing in an empty chair. The therapist encourages dialogue between the empty chair and the person in therapy in order to engage the person's thoughts, emotions, and behaviors. I applied this technique to help clarify and promote communication between alternate personalities.[36]

CHAPTER 32

James struggles to exist. "I'm here. I'm here."

November 3, 1975

Jay comes to this session and tells me he is struggling with strange feelings that he can't understand. He is aware that there seems to be something going on within him but can't accept the possibility there might be an alternate personality. I ask Jay if he will allow me to talk with James and he closes his eyes. Within a short time James appears after a lengthy automatism. He immediately becomes agitated and stands up with his arms outstretched but remains silent.

I tell him my name and he repeats it loudly. "Dr. Brende. Dr. Brende." He struggles to maintain his grasp of the current reality and repeatedly says, "I'm here. I'm here." I reach out my hand so he can  grasp it, and after several attempts he touches it. He remains in this standing position for a period of time until I confront him with the fact that there is another part of him that also exists.

After a struggle, Jay returns to the body and stands there for a time, talking with me in a lower tone of voice. He remains confused and doesn't understand how he arrived in this standing position.

I confront him with the reality of what had actually happened, and he finally seems to accept the fact there is another personality who takes over his body and that personality had just

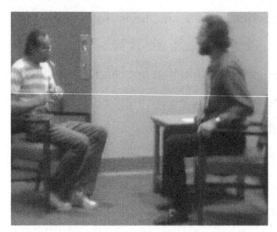 been standing there. With an embarrassed grin on his face Jay sits back in the chair and lights up a cigarette. After discussing the fact that he is not in control of

his behavior I emphasize that he needs to stay in the hospital.

When I review this session later I'm uncertain which personality had stood up. Was it James? Or was it Jim or Jimmy? Are these two sub-personalities, one of which reached out to touch my hand to assure himself and me that he existed? I've previously learned that Jim was the name used by his father and Jimmy was the name his mother called him. Does this mean that James, Jim, and Jimmy are part of a family system? I believe it does. This fact will become clearer when other family alternates emerge, one by one, in the future.

I will later review the literature and learn that family therapists who have experience with multiple personalities tend to find it easier to understand these patients than therapists without family therapy experience. Thankfully I was exposed to family systems and family therapy during my last year of psychiatric training, which was helpful indeed. It helped me understand how family relationships, both positive and negative, impact children's emotional and cognitive development. I learned how a family may become dysfunctional when an individual child is either scapegoated or over-idealized. I witnessed the family Oedipal triangle play out when an over-protective mother enhanced her mother-son attachment by repeatedly criticizing her husband's attempt to discipline him. When the son's acting out became more uncontrollable, his parent's marriage deteriorated. I had not yet obtained a consistent picture of James' relationship with his parents or his role in the family.

I am beginning to realize that I am part of James' family of alternate personalities, so to speak. For example, during this session I was much like a "mother" when I provided an empathic touch and verified the young James' right to exist when he reached out to touch me.

CHAPTER 33

James warns me that Jay wants to sneak out of the hospital.

November 6, 1975

When Jay comes to this session he finds it difficult to talk, but soon tells me he's preoccupied with changes taking place inside of him he's not felt before, including the fact that he lost his temper for the first time.

"Are you angry at me?" I ask.

"No," he replies, but after a moment he becomes anxious and blurts out his own name, which has become the most frequent way he tries to maintain control.

When I point out there are two parts of him, both struggling for control, he changes the subject. He tells me I'm wearing his favorite color blue, and looks away from me. But he soon loses control and begins to dissociate. James emerges, looks at me fearfully and exclaims, "He's been lying again. He's going to leave, Dr. Brende."

I ask James if he can remain in the body but he shakes his head sadly and says, "He won't let me. I'm trying to stay but he won't let me stay."

I ask him to recall what happened during the last session.

"Everything was backwards," he replies.

He continues to complain that Jay is going to send him back into the darkness. I want to talk directly to Jay for clarification but

I have not yet learned how to reliably control the personality switches, so I use the empty chair technique again and ask Jay to appear and sit in the specific chair I've set up for him. This maneuver does not work.

"He doesn't listen. He won't talk to you," James exclaims.

I call for Jay again and he finally opens his eyes and looks around. I ask him if he can let James stay in the body but he says he can't give me a truthful answer. Then he becomes anxious and wraps his arms around his head, seemingly torn apart by the presence of two personalities struggling for control. After a difficult dissociation he transitions back to James, who looks up and loudly declares my name several times as if to affirm that I am really present. James continues to express his conviction that Jay will leave the hospital. He tells me that he must come up with a solution. "I'm going to have to do something," he announces.

"Tell me," I insist.

"He's leaving, he's planning to leave."

"How?"

"He lies."

"What kind of lies?"

"He's already told them. He said that he is going to leave and move in with his nephew. And I won't have the strength (to exist) once he leaves here."

"We won't let him leave," I assure James. "He'll only be angry at me, not you."

I ask to talk to Jay once again but James resists and cries out, "God, help me."

"Relax James," I say.

James is not able to hold on. He puts his hands on his head and a dissociation takes place. Jay returns to the body.

"You can't leave the hospital," I assert.

"I know it."

"How'd you know?"

"I've been told. They (the staff) said, 'We'll lock the door so you won't sneak out.' But I'll ask to go downtown to see a doctor," he says, revealing his plan to manipulate the staff to let him out of the hospital.

"You'll feel better when you know you can't sneak out," I tell him, and add that it would be self-destructive if he did. I follow up with a call to his hospital doctor to alert him to Jay's plans.

Jay wants to leave the hospital but I can't agree. When a psychiatric patient escapes from the hospital against medical advice it is generally referred to as an elopement. I review articles about psychiatric elopements including reasons why patients elope. Since the majority are hospitalized voluntarily, it is easy for them to simply walk away from the hospital if they choose. One study found a 20-30 percent suicide rate in patients who eloped but hid their suicidal plans beforehand. Another in 1968 found an elopement rate of nearly 9 percent, usually occurring early in their hospitalizations, or when given more privileges. Almost half came back to the hospital within twelve hours, most often on their own or when retrieved by staff. One-third were returned by the police, and a small minority were brought back by relatives.

CHAPTER 34

You've allowed yourself to say you are afraid of him—who's him?

November 10, 1975

The session today is very interesting. First of all I notice that Jay's beard has been shaved off. Then I hear him complain about the red color of my shirt, which he says makes him nauseated. "Please Dr. Brende. I feel like I'm going to vomit."

The session then proceeds to reveal a number of significant events that took place during the past four days that Jay can't remember. Other patients told him he acted weird and the staff expressed concern that he fainted twice, left blood on his pillowcase and sheets, and became enraged toward his parents when they visited him.

I ask Jay to tell me about his anger but he denies having any feelings whatsoever. Yet I can see he's clearly depressed today. He believes he is at risk to hurt other people as well as himself. When Jay asks why he has bite marks on his arm, I point out that there's another part of him who is responsible. I mention the name James again and Jay begins to lose control, repeats his own name several times and counts, "One, two, three, four, five," as an attempt to regain control.

"What are you afraid of?" I ask.

"I thought I saw fear in your eyes. I didn't know what to do. I saw it in your eyes and I was afraid I could hurt you."

"No one will let you hurt anyone. I think it's important for you to find out why you're afraid."

"Ok, I want to find out. I don't know how but I want to know. How do I find out?"

"You took the first step. You said you want to find out why you are afraid."

"I am afraid," he insists. "Too many things are happening right now. I don't know what's happening to me on the ward. They are giving me the run around. They aren't giving me any assignments. See, I'm mad," he exclaims as his voice gets louder.

"It's healthy that you're expressing your feelings. You have allowed yourself to say you're afraid of James. So at least negotiate with him," I recommend.

"What?"

"Recognize him!" I insist.

"Who's him?" he says, maintaining his denial that James exists.

"The other part of you," I clarify.

"You've lost me. There are only two parts. Front and back. I don't know what you're talking about," he exclaims.

This denial surprises me because he'd previously told me he believed there was another personality. I try to convince him he has an alternate personality named James, but that only causes extreme anxiety. I encourage him to relax but he seems confused by my request, and I see the onset of a dissociation. Within seconds an alternate personality emerges with head hung low and arms swinging behind the chair.

I acknowledge that he is sitting in an awkward manner with his hands hanging behind his chair. He doesn't respond so I inquire about his thoughts. "What are you thinking?" I ask.

He struggles to recognize me. "You're not Gilbert? You're Brende?" he asks with broken speech. After looking around he anxiously tells me we're in a small room.

"When were you in a small room?" I ask.

"March…sixty-nine…sixty-nine…" he stutters while remembering the time he relived this experience (March 1969).

He still appears uncertain which reality he is in—the time he met with Gilbert, or the present where he is with me.

"No. No. No. I don't want him here!" he exclaims while struggling to escape from the memory of Gilbert in 1969. "That's what happened. He came and I went away," he adds sadly.

When I ask him to tell me what he's talking about he says that someone shut him out. "He blocked me. Shut me out. Closed the door."

"Who?" I ask.

I mention the name Jay, and the name triggers considerable anxiety. He calls out his own name, "James!"

"How do you like your name (James)?" I ask.

"I don't care. My mother gave it to me. I didn't have any say," he complains.

"What name would you pick?"

"Robert," he replies. I've not heard this name before but I will hear it again in the future.

James brings his arm up to his mouth and bites down. This

appears to be a signal for Jay to return. "I'm disgusted, I don't know what's going on and it's driving me up a wall," Jay complains.

I see tears in Jay's eyes, and I assure him there's nothing wrong with crying. But he insists that he's not crying. Rather he says he's confused and frustrated about things happening that he doesn't understand. I attempt to reassure him that he exists no matter what name he gives himself, but he continues to talk about his confusion and unhappiness about being a hospital patient. When I tell him I understand his feelings of helplessness and desire to run away, he tells me that I don't understand what he's feeling. There is clearly no closure to his sense of frustration and confusion as our session ends, and I ask him to share his feelings with the staff.

As therapy progresses I am beginning to see glimpses of the aggressive nature of the hidden personality who calls himself James. Jay appears to be afraid of this part of him. I am aware of the possibility that one alternate personality can attempt to hurt another, since it already happened on March 27, when one of the personalities gave Jay an overdose of medication. It will be important for me to monitor the possibility that this might happen again as therapy progresses. I later find articles reporting that aggressive behavior involving one personality hurting an alternate personality is not uncommon. There is very little literature about the subject available at the present time, but I will later read a review of 100 cases of multiple personality disorder wherein 70 percent had a violent alternate personality. I will find another author report that in 53 percent of cases one alternate personality attempted to kill another.[37]

I am not concerned for my own safety since James doesn't appear to be a threat to me, but time will tell. I will later hear about multiple personalities who were homicidal. Males have committed every reported case of murder by multiples. Generally speaking there has never been adequate evidence of multiplicity to convince juries of their innocence. I will read about the case of Mr. A, who was accused of murdering, decapitating, and dismembering his girlfriend. He had been in treatment for ten years for a diagnosis of multiple personality disorder, but the psychiatrist apparently had no direct interaction with the alternate personality by the name of Billy Ray, who Mr. A said was the murderer. During the trial his attorney presented testimony by a friend of Mr. A's who knew him as a nice guy, but sometimes violent. The defense also presented evidence of written conversations between the two personalities pertaining to Mr. A and his psychiatrist, whom Billy Ray despised and hoped to undermine in their therapeutic relationship.

Evidence presented about Mr. A's mental health at the trial was based on a complete psychiatric evaluation. He was given a diagnosis of major affective disorder, bipolar with multiple personality disorder, manifested by seven distinct personalities. One of the personalities, Billy Ray, is a vicious sociopath, and whose behavior is highly bizarre, dangerous, and violent.[38]

The jury found the accused not guilty by reason of insanity and he was incarcerated in a forensic hospital.

CHAPTER 35

I want to feel pain before the end comes.

November 13, 1975

Jay Kohlman signs in. He is preoccupied with two concerns. The first is his concern that he will blank out and another person will take over. His second concern is that he can't experience emotions or physical pain. He wants to be able to feel both.

"Tell me about your fear of blanking out?" I ask.

"I raised my voice and screamed and hollered. Then afterwards I blanked out. The whole afternoon was gone," he moans.

"What do you think happened when you blanked out?" I ask.

"The other guy shaved me. And he cut my hair off."

I suspect the other guy is James, who wants to take over the body. If that happens Jay will relinquish his role as a protective personality. Does he want to feel pain and emotions so he can become a whole person?

"I've been practicing crying for the last three weeks but I still don't have any feelings. I know there were tears but there was (no emotion)," he replies as he points to the right side of his body (the side of his body associated with Jay).

"Do you feel empathy for James?" I ask.

"Define empathy."

"It is being able to share the same feelings as the person you have empathy for."

"That's too much. No human being is physically able to feel that much. You would be overwhelmed," Jay insists.

When I ask him to give me an example he abruptly stands up and walks around the room. "Time is running out. There is not much left anymore. Time's running out and it's almost empty. My life will be over with. That sounds morbid. But there you have it. My life means nothing," he cries.

"What do you mean when you said if you were to experience all of James' feelings, it would almost kill you?"

"I've never had the feeling like what a woman has when giving birth to a child. My mind can't grasp it. I'm not supposed to," he says, describing a real birth rather than the psychological birth of an alternate personality. "I want to make a decision. I want to feel physical pain and remember these things. I want to have a feeling and feel the pain that goes with it. I want to feel good or bad."

"This will happen. But I don't want you to hurt yourself," I emphasize.

"I'm not stupid. I do things logically. I wouldn't do that."

Then Jay asks me what a headache feels like, and adds that he wants to have the experience of pain before the end comes. "I know there's going to be an end. I want these things before the end."

"Changes are scary," I say. "You and James are on the verge of accepting one another."

But he disagrees and says, "I'm not supposed to."

I believe James and Jay may be on the verge of fusing into one personality, but my experience is limited. I will later review the literature and find that a therapist should not plan to fuse fragmented personalities into a unified person too quickly, although it is an ultimate goal. When a fusion occurs too early in the course of therapy, or is attempted under extreme pressure, it always fails and results in the patient relapsing. According to psychiatrist Richard Kluft, who has conducted research on patients with multiple personalities, relapses occur when several things take place: a previous alternate returns, a new personality emerges, or there is a new traumatic event. The therapist may believe a fusion has taken place only to discover additional hidden personalities. Fusion, also referred to as integration, is most likely to be achieved when there have been at least three stable months of continuous personality existence, there is no evidence a new alternate personality will emerge, the patient feels a subjective sense of unity, the therapist cannot find additional personalities after re-exploration, and the patient does not believe there are any more alternate personalities.[39]

I will later review articles and find a blog on dissociative identity disorder where the author believes, based on her personal experience, that a few alternate personalities can work together in a cooperative relationship. "Becoming aware of my various personalities has often been painful and occasionally paralyzing. On the other hand, (having multiple personalities) has a positive side, one which I am having trouble letting go of. Without a doubt

180

I have accomplished a great deal because of—rather, in spite of—my ability to dissociate into various personalities. For example, I am fully capable of watching television, reading a book, and writing a lesson plan simultaneously."[40]

CHAPTER 36

He has a dream that he died.

November 17-20, 1975

Jay arrives clean-shaven, wearing a jump suit. He sits down and signs in. I can tell by his demeanor and that he is depressed. He says he feels the presence of violent emotions inside of him and he had a dream about his own death. "I'm afraid someone else is going to take over my body!" he exclaims.

"Are you afraid of losing yourself?" I ask.

"If that happens I could care less."

I'm not convinced that Jay's expectation of dying will take place, so I promote a plan for both personalities to exist. "We need to give both parts of you a chance to express themselves," I say.

He doesn't reply.

His dream worries me, so I express my concern and ask if he will let me hypnotize him. He agrees. I proceed by using a progressive relaxation technique to induce a trance. I instruct him to relax, close his eyes, and use fingers on both hands for each personality to signal answers to my questions. Because I had previously learned that Jay's presence is linked to the right side of his body, I expect him to answer from fingers on his right, while James' answers will come from his left fingers. I instruct Jay to raise an index finger on the right hand for yes and his thumb on the right hand for no, and ask him to tell me what he is thinking.

"I'm thinking about this dream," he replies verbally.

Then I ask, "Do you have any emotions?"

Jay raises his thumb on the right hand indicating a no response, which is consistent with being emotionally detached. He opens his eyes and says he thinks he's been tricked and feels like vomiting. Although it's disappointing that hypnosis didn't clarify more about the origin of his dream, I suspect that his resistance means he doesn't want to reveal any more.

As the session comes to a close I say, "Maybe there's more to this than we know. Maybe something (emotionally painful) happened in your past."

Reviewing the literature about the subject of emotionally painful trauma during childhood, I learn that trauma was considered a major cause of psychiatric disturbances more than a century ago. Psychiatrist Bessel van der Kolk, a brilliant researcher I would get to know personally, reviewed the history of trauma in psychiatry and reported that the first book about sexual assaults on children was written in 1857. During the rest of that century prominent neurologists and psychiatrists recognized that the psychiatric disorder of hysteria, with its exaggerated physical symptoms, selective amnesia, and emotional outbursts, was linked to a childhood history of trauma. The focus on trauma related disorders was diminished as Freud's theories gained popularity.

During the 1960s psychiatrists regained an interest in the subject as patients with dissociative disorders were discovered. As new findings are published I will read that patients with multiple personality disorder are severely traumatized in almost all cases.

Cornelia Wilbur, Sybil's therapist, will report on cases she treated who were all subjected to sexual abuse in early childhood. During the 1979 American Psychiatric Association annual meeting, she will quote psychiatrist Richard Kluft's description of the seriousness of this subject. "I see multiple personality as a syndrome which follows child abuse. Most multiples as children have been physically brutalized, psychologically assaulted, sexually violated, and emotionally overwhelmed." Kluft will also report on thirty-three cases in which the majority were subjected to trauma which included sexual abuse, physical abuse, psychological abuse, family violence, exposure to the deaths or dead bodies of others, and witnessing murder and violent death.

I will be fortunate to have a conversation with Dr. Wilbur at the same meeting, and I'll describe my videotaping project with James. She will provide a welcome response. "Don't let anyone keep you from continuing to record those therapy sessions, because no one else has ever done what you are doing."

As my therapy with James and his alternates progress, I will learn more about his traumatic experiences. At this time however, the patient who primarily comes to therapy is Jay. In our next session in three days, Jay says he can't tolerate James, and maintains his fear he'll die if James should appear.

"I can't talk to James or have anything to do with him," he announces.

"Why is that a problem for you?" I ask.

"Things didn't go well yesterday. Everything is mixed up. I had another dream that I died. But I'm not going to worry about

184

it."

"You said you were very confused yesterday. Can you say why?"

He can't explain why but says he had a convulsion and urinated in his bed.

"What do you think is going on inside your head?" I ask. When he tells me he's angry, I ask him about the little boy Jimmy, whom I remember was associated with feelings of anger.

The question upsets him and he calls out his own name, "Jay! Jay! Jay!"

"Upsetting feelings are better than no feelings at all," I say.

He asks what I mean by upsetting feelings, so I remind him he's been upset in the past about subjects such as love and sex.

"Sex is an animal instinct. I think all sex habits are strange," he replies, and goes on to say that sex is meaningless between a man and a woman. "I don't ever remember masturbating and sex doesn't enter my mind," he insists, but then becomes very anxious again and repeats calling to himself, "Jay! Jay! Jay!"

When I ask him what's entering his mind now, he tells me he's had disturbing conflicts with James for several weeks but doesn't like to talk about it. "I'm not supposed to have anything to do with James," Jay emphasizes. After a long pause he says, "The dream about dying keeps coming back. I see myself on a stretcher."

His dream is very concerning so I say, "I think you're afraid James will hurt you. Can we ask him? Will you sit in that chair and be James?"

"I'm not supposed to," he insists.

"Will you try to let James come?" I ask again.

"I can do this but I'm not supposed to think about the subject," he replies emphatically.

"I'll give you permission. Will you give me that authority?"

He refuses to allow me to use the empty chair technique again, and is also resistant to my suggestion that his fear of dying originated in his past. "Perhaps a parent or someone else in your family said 'I wish you were dead, or why don't you go away and never come back, or I never want to see you again.'"

"No that never happened," he insists.

Before this session ends he tells me that he feels guilty about arguing and fighting about everything, but I commend him for asserting himself as a way of keeping himself alive. Then I remind him that our regularly scheduled therapy session for Thursday can't take place because that's Thanksgiving Day.

Jay's dream of an impending death is troubling. Is it just a dream or is it a prophetic dream to be taken seriously? Does Jay have a good reason to fear his own death? Perhaps so; I will pass on my concerns to his hospital doctor. I will also explore other accounts about dreams of impending death, the most remarkable that of President Abraham Lincoln. Three days before his death the president told his wife and a group of friends about the dream:

> About ten days ago I retired very late. I could not have
> been long in bed when I fell into a slumber. I soon began to
> dream. There seemed to be a death-like stillness about me. I
> heard subdued sobs, as if a number of people were
> weeping. I left my bed and wandered downstairs. There the

silence was broken by the same pitiful sobbing, but the mourners were invisible. I went from room to room; no living person was in sight, but the same mournful sounds of distress met me as I passed along. Where were all the people who were grieving as if their hearts would break? I was puzzled and alarmed. Determined to find the cause of a state of things so mysterious and so shocking, I kept on until I arrived at the East Room. There I met with a sickening surprise. Before me was a catafalque, on which rested a corpse wrapped in funeral vestments. Around it were stationed soldiers who were acting as guards; and there was a throng of people, some gazing mournfully upon the corpse, whose face was covered. Others were weeping pitifully. "Who is dead in the White House?" I demanded of one of the soldiers. "The President," was his answer. "He was killed by an assassin." Then came a loud burst of grief from the crowd, which woke me from my dream. I slept no more that night; and although it was only a dream, I have been strangely annoyed by it ever since.

Two weeks later, on April 14, 1865, Lincoln was assassinated by John Wilkes Booth. As in his dream, his casket was put on view in the East Room of the White House.[41]

I will soon know that Jay's dream and his fear of dying is indeed based on a real event soon to take place.

CHAPTER 37

"I know I'm going to die."

November 24, 1975

Jay arrives at 9 o'clock this morning, which is not his usual time. I see that his hair is in a ponytail today. After signing in he takes out a comb and brushes it back, then he spends several minutes telling me his family is trying to deal with financial matters he doesn't understand. He says government checks are coming to the house and his father wants to assume control. He pulls out a cigarette and rationally tells me he plans to sign the checks over.

He says he has looked forward to coming over today because he is curious. People on the ward have been talking about the *Three Faces of Eve* and told him that he's got three personalities.

I point out that it must be scary for him.

He agrees. "I'm losing myself. I'm losing, losing, losing. People are taking my stuff. I have to guard everything from getting stolen."

When I ask if he thinks he has other personalities he becomes upset. He asks if I believe he has other personalities and I nod my head.

"Do you know them?" he asks.

"I do."

"What are they? Is it all this garbage they tell me? Biting and screaming?"

"I haven't seen those qualities but I've had a conversation with him."

He puts his hand to his forehead. "I'm losing myself," he moans.

"What if you lose your identity and become James?"

"I'll end up in a straight jacket!" he exclaims. He begins to count to ten to control losing himself. "From what I've heard I've been him for hours."

I ask if he would like to look at videotape and see for himself what this other personality looks like. He shakes his head, tells me that scares him and starts to count to ten again.

I assure him that he hasn't lost himself and that he is still here but he tenses up, lowers his head, breathes rapidly, waves his arms behind his chair.

I ask if he needs to keep his hands behind the chair and he answers loudly, "I know where my hands are!"

He remains very tense and I ask again if he can relax with his hands in front but he doesn't seem to grasp my request.

Finally he brings his hands forward and says, "I'm here. I'm not there. I don't want to be there."

"Where is there?" I ask.

"They all lied to me. They didn't want to talk to me anymore." He brings his hands to his head.

I lean forward and ask who lied to him.

"Old fatass Brende!" he exclaims. Then apparently realizing that I'm sitting in front of him he yells, "No! No! No!"

"No what?"

He brings his hands down and in a loud voice announces, "You're Brende. You're right here."

When I ask if he can talk about being lied to by people who didn't want to talk to him, he says that he wants to talk to me.

"I'm glad you want to talk. That's the reason I'm here." Then I ask if something had happened to him when he was young which involved being left by his family.

The question stirs up anxiety and he puts his hands up to his head.

"Why are you holding on to your head?" I ask.

"I'm trying to figure it out."

The look on his face reveals that he must be suffering, and I point out that I can see the pain in his face.

"There's no pain when they give you electro shock treatments," he says.

"What are you feeling?"

"I hurt all over!" he exclaims. Then I see his hands rubbing his head.

"Dr. Brende I've got to talk to you. Because I'm here now."

"I know you want to be able to stay here."

"I'm gonna stay. I'm gonna stay. I'm right here!" he exclaims repeatedly.

"Yes you're going to stay. And your name is James."

"Yes my name is James. Why not call me that name."

He now has his hands behind his back, as if they are tied there. "You're not gonna hurt me and then vanish. I'm not going to let anybody vanish anymore. I just wanna be here right now!" he exclaims. "I can't go back to the ward."

"Why not?"

"They sneak up on you. They take advantage of you. They lie to you." He says there's no one he can trust including the doctors.

"I'm a doctor and you can learn to trust me."

"Yeah. Can you take away my pain?"

"Where is your pain?"

"Everywhere. My back. My legs. My head. I ache all over."
He also says he's sick of his emotions but it feels good to cry. "I

sorry I'm crying but it
feels good. But it's not
good. They made me
cry and I cried and
cried and cried."

He expresses his
fear of being
abandoned and bends
over. I can see the
tenseness in his arms.

I reach over, touch his shoulder and assure him he'll now be
able to relax.

He pulls away from me.

"Does touching scare you?" I ask.

"It makes me sick!"

I ask him to explain but he doesn't know why he can't stand
to be touched. Now he's fearful he offended me, and asks me to
stay because he's afraid he'll lose himself if I leave.

"I'm here right now. I'm here. I wanna open my eyes and see
but I'm afraid. I'm so used to the dark. I saw light once but it was
too bright." He keeps his hands on his head. "I'm right here. I'm
right here."

I can see the anguish in his face as he tells me he is afraid to open his eyes.

"There must be some fear in what you might see," I say.

He puts his hand to his mouth as if he is going to vomit. Then his body bends backward as I ask him to relax. But his head remains bent backward almost as if some force pulled it back.

Then I see a switch. His expression becomes softer. Jay opens his eyes. "I don't like this anymore."

"What don't you like?"

"I don't feel so good."

"What do you think just happened?"

"I don't know for sure. I have an idea. I'm losing."

"What are you feeling?"

"That I should go away someplace by myself and get some strength."

I explain that it is important for him to understand that the other part of him is also him. "What you think you're losing you're not really losing, But I know this is painful," I explain. "But it's important that you learn about it. If you don't accept the other part of you, that will force him underground. That's why I want you to look at a videotape."

Although he's curious to see the videotape he's also afraid of what he'll see.

"I should just accept the fact that no matter what happens it will happen."

"What are you afraid will happen?"

"I don't have much time. I'm going to die. I don't know how. But I'm going to die."

CHAPTER 38

The day he died.

The day after Thanksgiving –
Friday, November 28, 1975

I should have been more prepared given the signals that had
been emerging for several weeks. Jay had been telling me about
his fear of an impending death and today his fear is almost
realized. I'm not scheduled to meet him for therapy in the studio
today because of the vacation holiday. Thankfully I did not take a
long weekend, because Jay arrives at my office door at eleven
o'clock in the morning unaccompanied. I invite him to come in,
and within a few minutes of sitting down in a chair in my office he
collapses to the floor. I summon Betty, the outpatient nurse, to
bring a stethoscope. She responds quickly and is alarmed to see the
patient on the floor. I apply the stethoscope to his chest and listen
for a heart beat. She checks his radial pulse, but neither of us finds
evidence of a heartbeat. I'm very apprehensive. Then, after nearly
a minute he suddenly sits up, looks around, and says, "I had to kill
him. I had no choice."

"Kill who?" I ask.

"Jay. That's who."

I'm confused. Who is sitting on my office floor? "Tell me
your name," I say.

"James C. Kohlman," he replies in a matter-of-fact voice.

I'm dumbfounded. "When were you born?" I ask.

"July 23, 1936."

"Do you know Jay?" I ask to clarify he is not the same person who came into my office ten minutes earlier.

"Not anymore. I killed him. Call in your cops if you have to! I had to kill him. It was in self-defense!" he exclaims.

"I will listen to you without your having to kill Jay," I reply.

But he doesn't listen. Rather he scowls, looks away from me, and begins to speak as if talking to someone else in the room. "I'm here. Go away. I just want to be here!" he announces to no one in particular. He closes his eyes briefly before opening them again. He looks around in an attempt to orient himself and then looks at me. "I know you!" he exclaims. He looks at me more intently and proclaims, "I don't like your red sweater." Then his voice softens. "I don't feel so good. I didn't think it would be so hard. It's been a long ways for me to get right here and it's going to be a long struggle to stay here and to put things back from swirling around!" he exclaims.

"Can you be more specific?" I ask.

"I just remember sobbing. They cut me down until I was nothing. Then they left me." I wonder if he is recounting an abandonment experience from the past, something he's talked about during previous therapy sessions. I see his eyelids begin to flutter as he begins to fade. "We need to get him back to Building Four," I call out to Betty, and summon the hospital aide who is seated nearby. We quickly get James on his feet and escort him down the hall through this building, then through a long covered walkway to Building Four. Upon our arrival we take the elevator to Ward 4-2-C on the second floor.

James can barely stand up so I immediately ask for help to lift him onto a hospital crash cart for transporting bedridden patients. I take his vital signs, finding a very low blood pressure and thready pulse. "We've gotta get him to Intensive Care," I announce and quickly push the crash cart, with the help of two staff persons, to the elevator. We ride down to the first floor where we find the walkway and propel it with a running gait to an elevator in Building One. When we reach the ICU on the second floor James is now unconsciousness, but personnel had been called to expect us. They quickly proceed with life-saving procedures—intubation, breathing machine, and intravenous fluids. He's going to live, but it had been a close call.

When the toxicology report comes back the next day it confirms the presence of high blood levels of his prescribed medications. It's clear that James had been saving up pills and hiding them in his room in order to give them to Jay, without realizing both he and Jay would die.

The medications James had been stockpiling were Dilantin (phenytoin), an anticonvulsant, and Librium (chlordiazepoxide), a benzodiazepine. Librium is a widely prescribed tranquilizer but there will be other more popular benzodiazepines in the future for the treatment of anxiety disorders—Xanax (alprazolam), Ativan (lorazepam), and Klonopin (clonazepam). They will be potentially addictive, particularly Xanax, and also potentially lethal, particularly when taken with other drugs, including Dilantin.

CHAPTER 39
The Fearful Experience of Being Alive

December 1, 1975

I meet with James five days after he's transferred from the ICU back to 4-2-C. I see him dressed in hospital attire as he's wheeled into the studio by Dr. Yoon, his hospital doctor. James struggles to sign his name, James C. Kohlman, and then holds his hand over his eyes. Although I tell James he's free to drop his hand down, he complains the light hurts his eyes, which I assume is related to the fact that he's been shut up in the dark for the past four years. He also complains that he's confined and isn't free to do whatever he wants after escaping from Jay's control.

"You can trust the people around you," I say.

"No you can't. No you can't." He pauses and then asks, "What year is this?"

"It's 1975," I reply.

"It seems like 1970 or 1971." He goes on to say he believes he was in the hospital at that time.

I point out that he is a patient on 4-2-C now. "It's important for you to trust the staff. They care."

"Is that where Richard is?" James asks.

"Yes," Dr. Yoon replies.

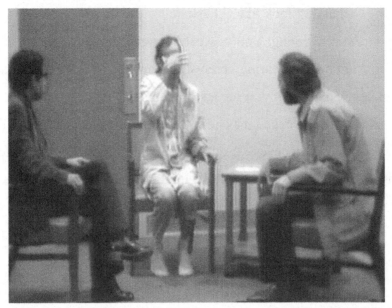

James appears confused when he hears the doctor's voice so I clarify. "Dr. Yoon is your doctor on 4-2-C."

"I don't know him."

"He's sitting right next to you,"

James turns his head toward Dr. Yoon and squints while keeping his right hand over his eyes.

"It's important that you learn to trust Dr. Yoon," I say.

James reacts angrily, "I see what you're doing. I see what you're doing."

I assure James I won't leave and turn him over to a new doctor, but he has painful memories. "I cried and I cried and I cried and the next thing I knew they all ran off and then I was just gone."

I remind James I'm here to stay but he tells me he only had brief glimpses of me during the past month or so. One time he says I appeared to be ringed in gold and another time I looked like I was white-hot. And today it hurts his eyes to look at me.

"What do I look like?" I ask.

"You're young. You're wearing green."

I am in fact wearing green slacks and a tan jacket. "Take a look at me and see if you see anything else," I say.

He lifts his head up as he strains to look at me, but keeps his right hand over his eyes. "You just look like spring." He chuckles and then complains again that the light hurts his eyes.

"I guess you're happy to see me today," I say.

"Yes. 'Cause I'm alive. I'm free. But they don't want me to be that way."

"Who's they?" I ask.

"All they want to do is shoot me full of dope and burn my brain out again," he replies, referring to the staff on 4-2-C.

"Nobody is going to shoot you full of dope," I clarify.

"Yes they have!" he asserts loudly, and then pulls up his left sleeve, looks down, lowers his right hand and points to where the IV was inserted in his left forearm.

"That's what kept you alive. You were in intensive care Friday. That's where you got that IV. You gave Jay all those pills you know. It had a bad effect on you."

He continues to look at his arm.

"You almost died!" I repeat clearly.

"Me? I didn't take any pills," he answers loudly.

"You thought you gave those pills to Jay. But you and Jay are the same person. You're the same man," I insist, although he doesn't understand me.

"Jay? Jay's not a man!" he exclaims.

"What do you think happened then? Why do you think you went to intensive care?"

"I was never there," he insists.

"Sure you were. And I was there with you. We put all those tubes in you—down your throat to help you breathe. You remember that?"

"No!" he exclaims repeatedly.

"Well, you came close to dying. We saved you and we're very happy we saved you. We didn't want you to die."

"I'm happy to be alive," he replies in a softer voice. He looks at Dr. Yoon and asks, "Why did they lock me up there?"

"We never locked you up. We were just watching you so we could help you," Dr. Yoon replies.

James sits quietly for a long time. Then he says, "You're all trying to mix me up." He pauses and changes his answer. "No you're not. It's just me." He puts his hands up to his head and complains about a headache.

I tell him once again that we are all glad he's alive, and ask what he wants to do with his life now.

"I'm going to stay this way," he replies.

"Can you enjoy it?"

"Yes I'm going to enjoy it," he announces with a sense of excitement. "I'm going to do everything I've always wanted to do. I'm gonna sleep. I'm gonna wake up. I'm even going to learn how to eat again. Do you know that? They kept hollering at me to eat but I didn't know how to eat. But I ate. I had corn bread. I wanna laugh but I've got such a headache."

"You also didn't feel like crying before but now you're laughing and crying. Those are both feelings," I explain.

The subject of feelings prompts him to say he feels naked. Then he wraps himself in his bathrobe.

I ask if he can tell me about eating corn bread and he says he hasn't had it for a long time. Then he changes the subject. "I don't know where everything went. They keep telling me but I don't understand."

"What are they telling you?"

"I know Doctor Baird isn't here any more 'cause he ran off. But I can't understand. I want to live so why do they want to kill me again?" He's confused and mixes current time with the time when he was a patient of Doctor Baird. Then he complains about enormous fatigue. "I'm so tired. I feel like I've been through hell." In reality he's emerged from a black hole hell of nothingness into this world like he's been reborn.

"But I'm scared," he says.

"Do you know what you're scared of?"

"No." He pauses, squints at me, and keeps his right hand up to shield his eyes. "I like to look at you. I'm not dreaming. You're not a dream. I did see you, right?"

"Right."

"You're all gold and once you was all white."

This is an interesting description that prompts me to ask about his real birth and suggest that his mother may have worn a white gown.

"Shit. My mother wore maybe a feed sack," he says, clearly disparaging the memory of his mother.

"Mother looks pretty good to a new born baby," I say, hoping he will focus on his own birth, but he prefers to talk about the times he had seen me.

"I saw you before and I didn't like you."

"I wouldn't expect you to like me all the time."

"You caused me to think I'm lying. But I'm not lying."

After he complains again that the lights are too bright, I tell him that it was commendable that he was able to face the pain of being reborn.

He replies that it took a long time for him to finally arrive, and he's not as happy about being here as he hoped. "It's been a long time and I don't think I like it here any longer," he says softly and then lowers his arms. He raises them again to cover his eyes and says, "I had to kill him. I had to. It was in self-defense. He wouldn't even let me listen sometimes."

"That's not entirely true. He wanted you to be here today."

"He did not. He's a liar."

"You are here aren't you?"

"Yes I'm here."

"That's because he wanted you to be here. He brought you over here on Friday."

"He didn't bring me any place. He didn't take me any place!" he insists.

"How would you have gotten over here to my office if he didn't bring you?" I ask.

"I made him come over."

I explain that he and Jay are the same person, but he can't accept that fact so I stop trying to convince him and focus instead on emphasizing he's alive and free. But he can't seem to enjoy that reality because he feels excessive weakness and pain.

I explain that he continues to feel pain because there is a little boy inside of him, which he flatly denies.

"I'm not pregnant and there's no little boy inside me," he insists as he looks down at his hands resting on the arms of the chair.

"There's a memory of a little boy, Jimmy, who was left once and cried a lot," I clarify.

"No! No!" he exclaims, and then insists on avoiding this subject. "I'll take my pain. I'll take my pain. That's okay."

Then James angrily accuses me of being unkind, though he denies being angry, only very tired.

When the session is coming to a close, I announce our next meeting for Thursday and repeat my request that he should make an effort to trust the staff on 4-2-C.

But he objects. "I can't trust them. All they do is lie to me!"

Before we stop he tells me he's afraid he will be killed or sent away and left helpless, or that someone will burn his brains out. Then he puts his hands over his eyes and lowers his head and repeats that he is very tired. As the session ends, James repeatedly announces, "I'm doing the best I can" as Dr. Yoon wheels him out of the studio.

I am pleased that Dr. Yoon came to this session. His presence indicates his interest in understanding a patient on his ward who just survived a suicide attempt. Dr. Yoon also apparently wants to learn more about someone with a diagnosis of multiple personality disorder.

CHAPTER 40

I want to touch you.

December 4, 1975

When we meet again three days later James is like a reborn child waking up after a long sleep, unaware of most of his past. When the session begins he appears excited about discovering a new-found world. "I'm here. I have my own bed. I have my own bar of soap!" he announces. "I don't know what happened all of those years, but I woke up. And I've got a headache. It's lasted for about three days. Ever since I woke up. It pounds and hurts all over."

He looks around to check his immediate environment and says the light hurts his eyes and the sounds of voices are strange. "I can hear myself talk, but it doesn't sound like me. You sound like you're 100,000 miles away. It seems like I'm away, far away but I'm not."

He describes this present existence as very distant from the time he was last in the body four years ago. When I ask about past memories he recalls having his appendix removed at age fifteen while in the eighth grade, but he can't recall any recent memories of his parents visiting him in the hospital.

He prefers to talk about mundane things he needs to do to help fit in. "If I drink orange juice, coffee, and eat a donut and have a cigarette, then I can go someplace, if I don't cause any trouble."

When I ask why he's afraid he might cause trouble he suddenly exclaims, "Why do they scream?"

I reassure him that he is most likely having memories from the past, which prompts him to talk about his last hospitalization when doctors and nurses took care of him. Then he becomes confused, covers his face because the bright ceiling light hurt his eyes, and tells me I appear very small to him.

. Suddenly he gets out of the chair and walks over to the door. He steps out of the room but quickly returns, walks to his chair, sits down, and tells me I look far away.

"You look like you are in the south forties," he says as he scrutinizes me very carefully. Then he becomes excited, "It's not my imagination. I see you. You're in gold."

"What do you mean, I'm in gold?" I ask.

"I knew I saw you in gold. I'm not imagining it."

I am moved by the fact that gold appears to symbolize my importance to him. He continues to be euphoric. "I'm so excited. I want to scream 'I'm here!'" But this excitement quickly ends and is replaced by his unpleasant memory of receiving ECT four years ago. Then he changes the subject once again and says nervously, "I want to touch you." I hold out my arm for him to touch me and see him smile. Touching me may have been his most important new reality experience for this session.

CHAPTER 41

I'm afraid of what I might do. I have a knife under my pillow.

December 11, 1975

James arrives dressed in blue scrubs and a robe, wearing slippers without socks. He sits down, drops his head, rests his clenched hands in his lap, and begins to talk. "That voice is driving me insane. Every time I go to sleep I wake up hollering. Then I'm crying and bawling. I don't know what I'm doing. I get so depressed. I would just like to go back to the darkness where I wouldn't have all this crap. I want to go out (of the hospital) but I know I can't. I'm hungry and thirsty but I'm not thirsty. I want to talk to someone but I don't want to talk to someone. It's driving me out of my wits," he cries.

He tells me he knows his name is James, yet remains confused about the names of staff or patients on the ward. He says his mind is cloudy and his head is in turmoil. "I wake up and it seems like there's a freight train going on inside my head. It's noisy. But I know it's not a train. I'm scared of people but I also want to rip their throats out. If I had a gun I'd blow my goddamn head off. I know I've been there (on the ward) for two weeks and there are people watching me all the time. I'm a damn nuisance."

I listen as he describes himself as a frightened and angry person who hears a voice in his head. He wrings his hands tightly together and continues to complain about being confused and having no purpose. Then he tells me about a memory. "I know I had a seizure. I know what happened. I was threatened if I didn't get out of bed. It scared me so much I fell out of bed and I hurt my arm. I stumbled out and they all grabbed me." He then remembers being told he was getting ECT and struggling to exist before he went into darkness.

He also tells me about a time twenty or more years ago, when he only existed in the form of a thought. "I know I was here as a thought. I had to fight. I couldn't be heard. I couldn't be seen. I had to fight. That's all I know."

"Did you say that was twenty years ago?"

"Even longer ago than when I was born. I try to say (now) that I've been born again but I know this is the same body as when I had my gall bladder and appendicitis." He looks at his body like it's something brand new and says, "It's a skinny, silly, horrible looking body because I've never seen it before."

He also describes other things that are brand new to him, such as the food patients eat every day. When he tries to talk about these things with the staff or other patients they don't understand what he's talking about, which makes him feel worse. "I feel ashamed that I'm even here (alive). That's what I'm trying to say. So what's the sense of being here? I could just as well shoot myself and cease to exist. What's the sense of it all? This is a terrible feeling to have. They look at me and think 'what the hell are you doing here.'"

He tells me he doesn't want to die but doesn't know what to do with himself and begins to shed tears, but says he doesn't want

209

me to see him cry. He also tells me he's angry. "It makes me mad. The only reason I didn't wipe them (the tears) off is because I wanted you to see I'm not crying. It's just damn tears." He takes off his glasses and wipes his face.

When I ask him if he feels like an unwanted newborn he shakes his head. "No I don't feel like a (newborn) baby. More like a one year old," he replies.

"You've been in existence about how long?" I ask.

"I don't know how long," he says but then adds, "Maybe it's been five days. I like five because it's my lucky number." Then he proposes it might be eleven days since he began to exist again.

Today's date is December 11. The number eleven is also symbolic of two people side by side like his parents were. "I'm thinking about my mother and father. They're just two people that had a bunch of goddamn kids," he complains angrily.

"Your mother had (you) James!" I declare.

"I feel I was an unwanted child. But I'm over that. I'm grown up."

"But those feelings aren't likely to be true. They are just your feelings," I assert.

"I don't know. See we're talking about family. And it's Christmas. I want to go home and see Clarence and the family and kids. I remember having Christmas years ago when I was with them and I bought a French poodle for the kids," he says.

"When was that?"

"In 1957. I remember another Christmas and a lot of other Christmases too." But his desire to go home is tempered by his fear

210

of what he might do. "You see I want to go home but how can I go home when I feel like killing myself or someone else. What kind of a person am I if I went home like this?"

I ask James if he seriously is afraid he might kill someone and he assures me he would never do that. I remind him that he is a human being who has a normal desire to be with his family and those who love him.

Then he complains about the voice in his head that torments him. "I'm not going to keep listening to that voice. The next time I hear that voice I'm going to grab out at him. I'll kill him then!" he exclaims.

"You can think about killing him but don't do it. And we're not going to let you do it," I assert, and then ask an important question. "Can you believe that voice is a part of you?" I ask.

"No I can't (believe it)," he insists.

"Maybe the voice in your head is your conscience," I say.

"I guess it's true. I did try to commit suicide then. I did take an overdose."

"It looks like you're caught in a bind."

"It's not easy to pretend everything is all right. I joke with people. I don't even know what I'm doing most of the time. I'm scared to death of who I'm talking to. How long am I going to have to go through this? I was in darkness for four years or more."

He is relieved to know he won't be returned to darkness and then tells me he's grateful to be able to talk with me, and has been looking forward to coming over here so intensely that he's not been able to sleep.

He continues to sit with his head down and then wipes his eyes and tells me he can't continue to feel positive. Then he removes the ring from his left hand and places it on his right little finger. "Yes. It's like when I put this ring on it was me again. But I always wore it on this other (left) finger."

"You used to wear it on your left little finger and now you're wearing it on your right little finger?" I ask, recalling that Jay had worn the ring on his left hand.

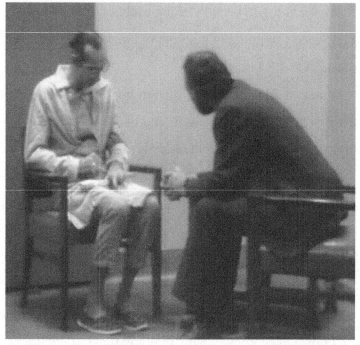

"Well that's what they said," he replies. "Like I always signed my name with my right hand automatically. I didn't think about it. I just did."

I realize that it's quite significant when James wears the ring on his right little finger, because he began wearing it on that finger rather than on his left finger after he survived his attempt to kill

Jay. The significance of the varying locations of that ring will become more apparent as time goes on.

He tells me again that he has a vivid awareness of his bodily functions. He has an enormous appetite and eats everything given to him except for meat. He also says he enjoys going to the bathroom, urinating, and also smoking with a cup of coffee. He tells me he takes the pill prescribed for his epilepsy because it makes him feel freer.

We discuss his need for privacy, and his angry outbursts when people try to get into his room. Intruders make him angry and he wants to be free from constant staff scrutiny, so I suggest he ask the staff to give him some freedom to be by himself. But he's also afraid of being alone because that causes paranoia. "I'm afraid they might take me and put me in building three—the lockup ward."

"Why are you afraid?" I ask.

"I might lash out and hurt someone or might kill myself. I didn't tell you but I have a knife under my pillow." He admits he's kept a table knife because he's afraid someone might attack him, but minimizes the danger because it's only a dull table knife. I give him credit for being honest with me and insist he turn it in, which he agrees to do. Then he tells me about a disturbing patient who came on the ward drunk. "They put him in the quiet room. I can't stand that smell. It makes me vomit."

He says he feels better when he talks to me about what bothers him but can't talk to anyone else because he doesn't trust them. Before the session ends he again brings up the subject that his angry feelings scare him. "I would like to tear their throats out," he exclaims.

I make an interpretation[42] that he has similar angry feelings toward me and he agrees. We come to an end of the session and I remind him we will meet again on Monday. I encourage him to continue feeling positive when he returns to his ward, but he expresses his fear that he will be "doped up" by medicines and "thrown into the quiet room."

I find this session to be very interesting. It is marked by the presence of James, who says he feels reborn although he doesn't act like an infant. He's afraid of his own aggressive instincts, admits to having a table knife under his pillow but doesn't want to hurt anyone. He clearly feels vulnerable, possibly because he no longer has Jay to protect him. There also appears to be a neurological change in the "reborn" James. Rather than having the ring on his left hand as he did before the attempted murder, he now places the ring on his right hand. I believe I am seeing a James I haven't seen before.

CHAPTER 42

His Pathogenic Secret

December 15, 1975

The patient comes into the room wearing a hospital robe and slippers with socks. He is still on suicide precaution and he hates it. He says he feels like running and that he's living in a dream state. I notice he seems confused and reluctant to sign in. When I ask if he plans to write down his name, he says he doesn't know what to sign.

"What name should I call you?"

"I don't know right now. You could probably call me anything."

"How are you going to sign in?"

"Kohlman. I guess that's my name." He tells me that he feels like he's dreaming except that he knows he's been placed on suicide precaution, which makes him uncomfortable and feeling like he wants to run.

"How come you don't want to sign James Kohlman? James is a pretty important person."

"I oughta sign my name James but I have a guilt complex about killing Jay," he replies. "On top of that, I've been told that I tried to commit suicide. I know I tried to rip Darrell's (another patient) throat out. And I'll do it again." He also reports hearing and smelling disturbing things, being confused about who he is,

215

and wishing he was dead. That's why his hospital doctor placed him on a suicidal watch.

I ask him to explain why he's so aggressive, and he responds with tears in his eyes that he doesn't want to go back to the dark place where Jay kept him. "It happened once before in 1971 when I didn't exist," he moans as tears flow faster.

"What comes to your mind about that? When didn't you exist before?"

"I don't want to talk about it," he says but finally answers. "I remember a house on a hill and I walked to work two blocks. I remember being at work and passing out and then being at this hospital."

When I ask for more information he tells me about a job he had in Seattle. "I was the manager for the Mayflower grocery snack bar. A convenience for the customers. I cooked there and managed it and hired my own help and there was a person there who was beautiful. She was cute. Very, very cute," he remembers.

"Did you date her?" I ask.

"I didn't date any of the girls. It was against my policy to date girls that I had responsibility for."

"Did you have fantasies, sexual fantasies?"

"I suppose so. She was very pretty. But I don't want to talk about it. And before when you were talking about me touching my own body. I don't like to touch it. I don't like to even urinate," he exclaims.

I mention the time he became upset when I touched his arm and ask if my touch had triggered disturbing sexual thoughts. The

216

question upsets him and he remains silent. I ask if the question made him feel ashamed.

After a long pause he replies emphatically, "No. No. No. Never!"

"What would you like to talk about?" I ask after another long pause, during which time I see his hands fold and unfold.

"I don't know. I don't know," he repeats.

I ask him to talk about memories that trouble him but he finds it difficult to talk. Then finally he remembers something. "I'm carrying a sack of groceries and it's dark. And it's red. Red." He suddenly stops talking and begins to shed tears.

"It's red what?" I ask.

"I don't know. It's red spots and I begin to hurt all over," he cries.

"What red spots?"

"I don't know. I don't know." He fights to hold back his sobs. "And I wanna run."

"Do you see blood?" I ask.

"No. It's not blood. It's not blood," he shouts, then continues to describe his actions. "I'm standing up." He stops talking and begins to sob.

"What's happening? Are you reliving it right now?" I ask.

"God. God!" he wails. "Goddamn. That's what happened," he sobs.

"What's happening right now?" I repeat, using the present tense to encourage him to relive this painful experience. He brings his hands to his face and wraps his arms around his body, clutching his chest.

"They're grabbing me," he hollers.

"They're grabbing you," I repeat.

He begins sobbing loudly. "Please. Please. Please. They're beating me!"

"What are they doing?"

"Why don't they knock me unconscious? Why do they keep beating me? Oh God. Oh God," he sobs continuously. Between sobs, he begins to painfully relive two men raping him.

"They're both in at the same time. Oh God. And it's a red mackinaw (heavy wool jacket). I can see it. It's a red mackinaw! I never want to be touched again! Never! Never!"

"I can understand why you feel that way James. You're being abused."

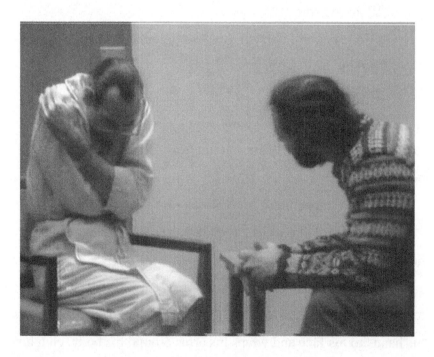

"Never! Never! Never!" He sobs. "I never want them to touch me again. I'm man enough but I cannot take that! I feel filthy! I want to throw up but I can't!"

I offer empathic statements about his horrendous experience while he continues sobbing loudly. Then he sputters, "I'm afraid to tell anyone but I can't keep this secret any longer!" he exclaims. "And then they ran off and left me and you'll do it too," he sobs.

"You were left by those men and no one took care of you? Did you go to the hospital?"

"No. No one ever knew about it. I told two doctors but they didn't listen. I told Gilbert and he ran off. Dr. Baird ran off too," he adds.

He describes himself as worthless and wishes he were dead. "What am I good for?" he asks.

"What do you think?"

"I don't know."

"You've punished yourself all these years by keeping it to yourself and feeling guilty."

He continues to sob while wrapping his arms around his body as if he's holding himself together. "I'm no longer worth anything," he moans.

It's clear he's not only been a victim of the sexual trauma but also of the destructive power of this horrific memory, which therapists in the 1800s referred to as a pathogenic secret.[43] The secret had remained hidden like a cancer that consumed him. His sense of "badness" contaminated his feelings about himself and his feelings about sex. He also had become convinced that his

219

"badness" contaminated others as well.

"And then the only person I loved, died...the only one I cared for."

"Who?"

"Fang. Fanny Hill." James described his dog, his best friend, who died after this tragic event. "It always happens. Every time I have something I love." He goes on to tell me everyone who ever loved him also left him.

"You've thought that people who love you leave you?"

"They do and you're going to do it too. I don't want it any more. I know what's going to happen. Nobody wants me. They'll just use me."

"Like those two men?"

"They were animals. Low class animals. I don't want anyone close to me. I don't want anything anymore. Look what happened. I told her and she knew about it and she died."

"Who?"

"Fang died. Who else did I have in that world! I'm not going back to that world. I don't want that world ever again."

I ask if it's possible for him to forget about those memories and he says he can never forget. I suggest that many people have cared for him but he's convinced they would no longer care if they knew. Then I'm surprised to hear him tell me that Jay has not disappeared. "And there's Jay. I was supposed to kill him. But he's not dead. I've told him to go away but he doesn't. He's still there. He doesn't care about anything except himself."

He continues talking about his sense of worthlessness and

220

shame in spite of my attempts at encouragement. "I can't look at you Dr. Brende," he moans with his head down.

"There's no reason why you have to continue to suffer like this. Can you forgive yourself, James? Just two weeks ago you were beginning to exist and to enjoy it. You have a right to that."

"What am I good for anymore except for animals (like those rapists) to use me. That's what I've always been good for."

"You're a human being and nobody's perfect. Nobody thinks badly of you like you do. You know I don't think badly of you."

"I hope you don't."

"I can understand that this has been tough for you. I can understand why you felt bad and kept people away from you if you've thought that you're not worth much."

"I don't want to get filth all over them," he replies in despair, revealing his sense of toxic shame.[44]

"You mean that you think if you touched me I would be filthy?" I ask.

"Yes. I don't want to make anyone filthy. Please Dr. Brende," he moans.

I confront him with the fact he does not have the power to make me filthy. But logic does not prevail. "I am filthy and it will rub all over you," he insists. "I want to take a shower now, I'm so damn filthy."

In spite of his belief he doesn't deserve to continue seeing me in therapy, I make it very clear that I will keep our therapy sessions going.

"I want to see you. I want to. I told you that ever since I

heard your voice I had a chance. I had a chance to fight. I don't care if I did say that I killed Jay."

To my surprise he tells me the only way to control his unbearable pain is to ask Jay to return and take the pain away. "I want him here right now. He takes away the pain. It's hurting so bad."

"How long do you want him to stay? Is five minutes long enough?"

"I don't care. I want him back! I want him back!" he yells.

"Ok Jay. Why don't you come back for five minutes," I announce, wondering if Jay, the personality James thought he killed November 28, will show up. I wait while James goes into a relaxed state. After about thirty seconds, Jay emerges.

"Hello, Dr. Brende," he announces.

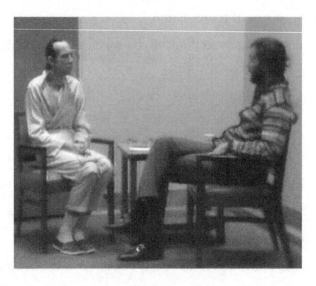

"You're giving James a bad time," I say.

"If he wants it, why not? Why should I care?" he replies cynically.

"I promised James that you would have to go through me rather than pick on him."

"That's okay by me."

"That means if you're angry at him you should tell me. Can you tell me now?" I ask.

Jay superficially agrees.

"Where have you been?" I ask.

"I don't know. I've just been gone."

"When was the last time you remember talking to me?" I ask.

He shrugs his shoulders so I repeat the question but he doesn't answer. Then I admonish Jay for his unaccepting attitude and remind him I only allotted him five minutes to be here. He looks puzzled, shakes his head slowly, and tells me he doesn't want to go back to where he was.

Suddenly James emerges and switches the ring.

"Do you feel better?" I ask.

"Yes, I do but he didn't take away the pain. Is that the reason I don't like that son of a bitch? He feels absolutely nothing, Dr. Brende!"

"Listen, you don't deserve to feel so bad. You deserve to feel better."

"All I want to do is wash, and wash, and wash. The only way is to shower and take baths and get all that filth and smell. That smell!"

"I was wearing a red shirt today. Is that what brought it on?" I ask.

He nods yes.

"Maybe you thought I was that person (the perpetrator). But I'm not."

"You're Dr. Brende," he exclaims.

"For just a moment it seems like I was that person (perpetrator) to you," I repeat.

"Yes, I guess so." He pauses but then tells me again how ashamed he continues to feel.

Our time had come to an end and I insist that we meet in three days. He gets out of his chair with difficulty and staggers out of the room as I say good bye.

I had not expected him to relive this painful trauma. But when his memory of the event was triggered by being touched, James relived the experience of being raped by two men. The assault left him physically and psychologically wounded and overwhelmed with shame. He had never revealed this memory that lay buried in his unconscious like a pathogenic secret. He believed the shame he felt would rub off and hurt others, particularly if he touched them. He thought that his shame killed his pet dog and he thinks it might even kill me.

Ever since the 1800s therapists and healers have known that the pathogenic secret must be expunged like a poison vomited up with a proper emetic. They used confession, hypnosis, and psychotherapeutic methods so that buried traumatic memories could be coaxed into consciousness and spun into words for the purpose of understanding, forgiving, and healing.

CHAPTER 43

They beat me until I was bloody and dirty.
I'd like to find them and rip their throats out.

December 18, 1975

James is escorted into a refurbished recording studio, which now has a curtain backdrop instead of a door in the background. He is dressed in hospital attire with brown pajamas and a robe and appears much improved. He says he's a student now and shows me a paper he's writing about the twelve days of Christmas. He has access to memories he's not had for a long time, and recalls being confirmed in the Catholic Church when he was about twenty-one years old.

He says he has problems linking correct times with events, and can only remember when he's supposed to come to therapy if ham and beans are served for dinner. He also complains that he can't stand the smell of meat. "I just feel sick when meat is around. I cover the meat up and eat all of the other stuff on my tray."

"Meat must remind you of something? Something that's nauseating to you?" I ask.

"It's what those two drunken son-of-a-bitches did. That's all," he exclaims. "They beat me until I was bloody and dirty. I'd like to find them and rip their throats out!" he exclaims.

I commend him for having revealed this painful secret but he warns about the consequences to anyone who has heard his secret, including me. "Do you think that (it will kill) me?" I ask.

"I don't know," he exclaims as he looks around the room in frustration.

"I'm still here aren't I," I emphasize.

He continues to describe the effects of the trauma, stating that he feels broken and contaminated by intrusive thoughts of forcible fellatio. "Sometimes I feel whole and sometimes (I feel like) two halves. I feel like a person that is not stuck together," he says. "I feel like I don't exist during the night any longer. And it feels like it just happened."

I explain there are adverse consequences when a person suppresses a traumatic memory for such a long time, and ask if he can remember the year it happened.

"1969? I don't know." If he is correct, the trauma would have taken place a couple of years after he was discharged from military service.

After I express my empathic support, he says he wants to forget that it happened. He tells me he's enjoying new experiences like learning how to walk, seeing women's bras in magazine ads, and learning for the first time that Americans Neil Armstrong and Buzz Aldrin had gone to the moon in 1969.

Then James repeats his plea that I allow Jay to return and take away his pain. "Just let me put the ring from my right hand to my left hand and let me smoke a cigarette. That will bring him back."

"I will let him come back when he accepts you, but if he does come back he won't be able to take all the pain away," I warn.

This very important session revealed James' new experience of being a person entering a "new world." It also contained symptoms of James' persistent post-traumatic sense of shame and brokenness. Because he doesn't know how to relieve his emotional pain he wants Jay to take it away. It is not clear to me how long James' traumatic memory will continue to torment him. Reviewing literature on this subject, I find that memories linked to painful emotions are the ones that persist. Three areas of the brain are involved in the memory process: prefrontal cortex; the amygdala and fear circuitry; and the hippocampus, or memory circuit. The prefrontal cortex is the unemotional part of the brain that remembers facts but will malfunction or even shut down in the face of a surge of brain chemicals induced by the fear circuitry, the second area of the brain. The third area, the hippocampus or memory circuit, will store emotionally charged portions of the experience as a jumbled, long-term memory.

Jay will soon replace James and his emotionally charged memories. My therapeutic task will be to continue to help James reduce the severity of his traumatic memories. The most prevalent therapeutic approach is memory reconsolidation, which delinks the disturbing memory from painful emotion. I will modify this approach so that Jay and James can share the burden of these memories, but I am not certain how long that will take. [45]

CHAPTER 44

You think love destroys people.

December 22, 1975

James is trembling when he arrives at the studio but becomes more relaxed after he sits down. I remember his struggles with shameful memories last Thursday, so I'm pleased to hear him say he's trying to concentrate on his good memories. For example, he remembers being in the Air Force and going on dates, although he has no memories of having physical contact with women. He also tells me he doesn't know how to define a normal relationship between a man and a woman, so I reassure him he can learn that.

"You'll have to learn what is normal. But I think you look better to me today," I affirm.

"I don't know what it is to feel better," he replies.

When I remind him he told me about good memories from being in the Air Force in Tampa, he counters by reminding me the Air Force kicked him out because of epilepsy.

"It's hard for me to keep going anymore Dr. Brende, you're the only thing that keeps me going," he says.

"I honor all the power you give me," I say. "Do you remember who in your family kept you going? How about your mother?"

"She had too many other kids to pay attention to me," he says.

He has no positive memories of his parents and resented their indifference to his wish for more education. "The only thing they cared about was sex, kids and money," he says cynically.

"You don't talk about having feelings of love in your family," I observe.

"I loved my younger brother. I tried to give my love to him, but he died because he had jaundice when he was nine months old. After he died I know it was my love that destroyed things."

I point out that it was very loving of him to care for his brother, and emphasize that his love could not have killed him. I tell him it's normal to have both loving and angry feelings toward the same person. I also make a transference interpretation that he may have both love and hate feelings toward me.

James nods his head and sobs as he lowers his head in shame.

I insist he was the product of a loving relationship between his parents who brought him into the world, but he only remembers how they fought with each other.

"So do you think you were conceived out of hatred?" I ask.

"I must have been," he exclaims.

To pursue further his obsession that hate is more powerful than love I ask about transference implications. "Do you wonder if I hate you?"

"Yes, I do. You must hate me. I take up your time."

"That must be a terrible feeling. That must be like hell on earth," I state.

"This is hell on earth or anywhere else," he moans, and complains there is no reason for him to keep living. "It's gone now. I have no purpose," he insists sadly as he sits forlornly with his head down.

I rephrase his description of himself and his relationships. "I guess you told me today that you think love destroys people so you keep yourself apart. You don't get close to anyone."

"It (love) does destroy!" he insists.

I encourage him to maintain hope and remind him that I care for him. I also remind him that it's normal to have both good and bad thoughts about someone he cares about.

"If only I could feel the good thoughts and not the bad thoughts. I must have something to keep me alive," he exclaims.

After I make a case that our therapy sessions are a strong force to keep him alive, he looks up at me and shades his eyes. "Sometimes I start going blind because the light gets so damn bright."

After a further discussion, during which I reaffirm how important he is to me and to members of his family, our session comes to a close.

James is convinced that his love is destructive and is unable to comprehend how essential it is for relationships. Both he and Jay can't experience normal relationships or interpersonal attachments as viewed from the diagnostic framework of attachment theory. This problem very likely dates back to childhood. James may not have bonded with his parents, or the relationships were disrupted because of abuse or abandonment.

Their difficulties with attachment now include the inability to trust close relationships for fear they will end painfully. James fears a close or affectionate relationship because he's afraid he'll hurt me. Jay can't establish an emotional attachment because he doesn't "feel" affection and can't depend on anyone for help or support. Thus both James and Jay suffer from problems making or sustaining attachments, although in different ways.[46]

CHAPTER 45

Jay is not dead. He says he wants to give up his protective role.

December 29, 1975

James arrives at the study in hospital garb, wearing blue pajamas and a white robe. He begins the session with objections about patients who can't stop talking about people accused of rape or other patients who said they were raped. "I told them to shut their goddam mouths if they can't say something nice."

Then he complains about hearing Jay's voice. "Jay keeps telling me there's no sense in having feelings? But that's the reason I'm here, because I want feelings."

"Have you told him why feelings are important?"

"He doesn't listen," James complains.

When I ask why feelings are important to him he says, "Because I don't wanna be dead. That's all I am is dead. If I'm going to be dead I want to be really dead."

"If you're dead then wouldn't Jay also be dead?"

"No, he's not dead, I thought he was but he's not."

"If he doesn't have feelings then he's dead by your definition," I say.

"You're right. I have told myself that too."

"But now you say he's not dead."

"No (he's not). Otherwise why does he keep taunting me all the time and aggravating me?"

232

"Well is he still doing it as much as he did before?"

"Yes he's doing it even worse now I think."

"Do you remember I had an agreement with both of you to act as a mediator?"

"I know but I don't ask anymore for anything. I don't even ask him or think about him because of what you've said."

I wait for him to continue.

"He's too sly or cunning because he sneaks up on me."

I point out that Jay may have a good reason to talk but James disagrees.

"He doesn't really talk he just aggravates me. Just taunts me."

"Now if he doesn't talk how do you know he is there?" I ask. "Is it thoughts or ideas or feelings or what?"

"He just tries to make me feel guilty for having feelings. That's all. He keeps telling me I was better off when my purpose in life was only to satisfy other people," he moans sadly.

I assure him that I won't use or abuse him.

But he can't rid his memory of the shame that permeates him. "What happened to me in Seattle is always going through my mind. It makes me feel like a slut and not a male."

"You are a male. You may think you were used as a female but you are a male," I insist.

"I thought I was a male at one time. But I lost it," he tells me sadly.

"I'd like to hear you say 'I'm a man.'"

"I can't do that because it would be a lie."

"Would you like to have a relationship with a woman?" I ask.

"God yes."

"But something is holding you back. You make it sound as if it's impossible to be a man."

"No, I say what's the use (of being a man)?"

His anxiety worsens so I ask James if he would like Jay to come. He nods yes and closes his eyes. After a moment I see a dissociation and a personality I believe is Jay nonchalantly pull out a pack of cigarettes.

"James is a silly fool," he smirks as he gazes into the distance.

"What do you mean?"

"He wants to be happy. He wants to do this and do that. He wants to have feelings and emotions."

"Does he want to have loving feelings?" I ask.

"Oh, I guess he does. But he's so stupid he even wants to have hate feelings," he smirks.

"Can you tell me who James hates?" I ask.

He remains silent and stares into space, but finally tells me about James' problem. "He wants to exist on his own and have his own feelings but they're too painful for him." Then he goes on to complain that he doesn't want to protect James any more as he continues staring into space.

"I wonder why you haven't looked at me since you arrived," I say.

"There is no reason to look at you because I haven't decided about you. I protected him for so many years," he exclaims, apparently wondering if I'm capable of replacing Jay as James' protector.

"Can you let him grow up to be a man so he wouldn't need your protection anymore?" I ask.

"Yes and you can help him. You can teach him. But I wonder if it's too risky for James to be in your care, particularly since I've had years of experience being his protector," Jay says.

I ask Jay two questions: Is he willing to share his knowledge about how I can protect James, and does he feel guilty because he couldn't protect James from being raped?

Jay looks at me, frowns, and says there was no way he could have prevented the rape. Then he thanks me for letting him return.

"I'm glad you could express your feelings about James," I say.

"The only feeling I have is sneakiness," he smirks.

Before the session ends I encourage Jay to take on a new role as one who can help both him and James become united and whole. Jay nods yes as the session ends. I decide not to call for James to return and allow Jay to leave the studio accompanied by the aide.

I will review this session the next day and wonder about the personality switch after James told me that Jay is not dead. When Jay appeared he pulled out a cigarette and made cynical remarks about James, who he called a silly stupid fool for wanting to have feelings. It is very probable that I had interacted with Shea and not

Jay. That could explain why he told me he no longer wanted to be James' protector. I believe that I made a mistake by allowing him to leave the session rather than James.

CHAPTER 46

I thought you were going to let me stay in the body
instead of that stupid son of a bitch!

December 31, 1975

At first I'm surprised when he signs in as Jay rather than James today, but then I remember that it was either he or Shea who left the session instead of James two days ago. At first I wonder if Jay expects to resume his role of protecting James, but then it becomes clear he is not able to do that because of his own unpleasant experiences. He says he's suffering from headaches, disturbing emotions, and voices in his head saying, "Get the hell out of here."

Jay tells me he has no memory of anything since Thanksgiving, which surprises me since I thought he had been present during the last session. In retrospect it *was* Shea rather than Jay. I fill him in on the events that took place on November 28, beginning with his arrival in my office where he collapsed. I explain that James was rushed to intensive care and placed on a ventilator to keep him alive and has been the only personality in the body since that time.

"I better quit saying 'have no fear Jay is here,'" he smirks.

Jay's remark reflects his awareness that he is no longer James' continuous protector. But I praise him for his willingness to return in order to help James during his current struggles.

"I don't particularly like it (helping him out). I'm losing my manners and I'm cussing. I can't cope or tolerate things," he complains.

"Does that mean you're feeling more human?"

"I guess so. I'm not an object to you anymore. I am becoming a person."

"Yes you are."

"I came here today to get out of the agreement I have with you."

"What agreement are you talking about?"

"That I would come back to teach you about helping James grow up."

"I said I wanted to be the mediator between you and James," I explain. "I want to be able to help the two of you solve problems."

"See that makes me mad. If I have a problem I should solve it on my own."

"I will continue to mediate between you two. So I need to talk to James now to find out how he feels. Are you okay if James talks to me?"

"If you want to hear his voice then I'll have to be quiet for a few minutes or close my eyes. That's the only way I can do it," he replies. Jay closes his eyes and sits quietly. James finally emerges, looks around, scowls, and reaches for the pen. Then he carefully covers Jay's signature with the name James.

Rather than appearing jubilant, he looks forlorn. "I have fought so hard. I knew I didn't kill him. I am becoming a nothing. It's becoming darker and darker," he moans.

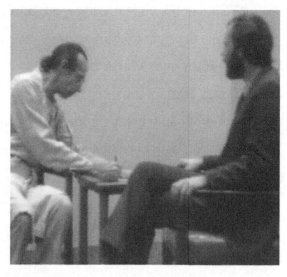

"You seem quite depressed. Are you mad at me because I asked Jay to return to the ward instead of you last time?"

"Jay said you told him to go back to the ward because you were furious with me. I thought you were going to let me stay here (in the body) instead of that stupid son of a bitch," he exclaims angrily.

"I'm not angry with either of you," I explain.

James continues to rant. "He is a liar and a sneak. I had to wait until he went to sleep and when he went to sleep I thought I could take over but I couldn't do anything. He tied me up."

When I ask James if he'd prefer to stay here and feel pain or return to his former dark place he vehemently insists that he wants to remain here.

"Listen James, I have my doubts that you should be in control all of the time. You have to convince Jay and you have to convince me that you should be here all the time."

"I want to be here!" he repeats.

"That's good, you have the right to live. And to feel things."

"I have the right to those feelings. So why can't I have 'em? Jay has no feelings at all. He is nothing! But he doesn't let me exist!" James cries.

I point out that that it's important for him and Jay to learn to get along. "You both need to negotiate with each other so that you can get along better."

"How can I do that?" he asks.

"Would you like me to try to convince him? That's my job to try to help you out. Can I talk to him about it?" I ask.

He agrees to allow Jay to return to the body, but not until I assure him that Jay won't replace him for long. "Absolutely you can come back," I declare. "I'll want to be a mediator between you two," I add.

James frowns but closes his eyes. After a pause he tells me Jay is not around. "I don't feel him here." He continues to wait with eyes closed. After a few more seconds I see the dissociation take place and Jay emerges.

"What do you think just happened?" I ask him.

"I think you heard that voice," he says.

I explain that I had talked with James about my role as mediator and Jay agrees to be open to establishing a good relationship with James. After more discussion about this matter our session comes to a close and he returns to the ward, accompanied by an aide.

CHAPTER 47

He has a vivid nightmare of being raped. Two Jays appear.

January 5, 1976

The patient's hair is in a bun and he appears clean-shaven. He's wearing a robe and PJ's. After signing his name he sits with his left hand over his eyes.

I'm surprised that he has signed in with the name Jim and tell him so. He frowns and says there is something very important I should hear about last night, but he has difficulty putting it into words, so he tries to gesture with his left hand.

"Can you tell me what happened last night?" I ask.

"It felt like I was being held down and taken sexual advantage of by a drunk."

"Do you think it was just a feeling or did it actually happen last night?"

"I don't know. It was so vivid. So alive. It wasn't like most dreams I have."

I ask if he felt like fighting back, and he tells me he must have since the staff placed him on a one-to-one watch. But he also tells me that if he could do the things he wants to do they would put him in a straight jacket.

"Would you kill yourself?" I ask.

He nods. Then I see a subtle dissociation and a different voice speaks. "You see I've always been able to handle every situation. I just say, c'est la vie. What will be will be. But if that was real last night I just can't accept it," he says as he raises both hands in frustration.

Having heard him use the French phrase—c'est la vie—I wonder if I'm talking with Jay or the carefree personality Shea. When I ask who I'm talking to, he says both Jays are present. I'm not clear what he means by that, and go on to explain, as if he hadn't heard it before, that James was emphatic when claimed he'd been raped last night.

Instead of asking questions about the realness of his nightmare, he tells me he's concerned by the fact I called him by the name James. "I know that's my real name but I don't feel that's my name. I feel like a stranger when I write that name down or when I say that's my name." After a long pause he continues. "I'm beginning to feel absolute hatred toward people."

I ask him if he really hates other people but my question seems irrelevant to this personality.

"I really don't feel like killing people. What I want to say is c'est la vie—everything will be okay. I know I used to say that and I still believe it."

242

"But you're changing now. Do you feel things?"

"If you're changing me I don't like it," he complains.

When I remind him he's recently told me he wants to change and see others as human beings he sits quietly for a time, but then finally agrees with me.

I ask his permission to talk with James for a few minutes. He looks at me strangely and asks why I would prefer to say the name James since the voice in his ear has no name. Finally he agrees. "If you wish to hear that voice, then okay." He closes his eyes and remains motionless for about twenty seconds, until his head drops and his hands open up. A different personality appears, who seems to be James, and stares at the floor.

I ask if he can tell me what happened last night.

He continues to sit quietly with head down, looking at his outspread hands. Finally he nods. "I'm not strong like Jay is." Pause. "When I smell alcohol I just don't know what I'm doing," he stammers. He finds it difficult to continue speaking and tries to express himself with hand gestures until he is finally able to talk. "I was right there. I panicked. I was so scared I had to run. I had to go. And I ran. I know I made it to the stairs. These damn shoes I wear are not for running. I fell down the stairs. I don't know for sure. I know that part is true. Everybody was holding me. That drunken fool came right at me!" he cries.

"It sounds to me like (the smell of alcohol) triggered off a memory," I say.

"I know it's a memory. What do you expect me to do?" he exclaims while raising both hands clasped together.

When I clarify that his nightmare was so real that members of the staff restrained him because he was thrashing out of control, he tells me he can't recall what happened.

"Can you believe what I've told you?" I ask.

He grimaces, looks from side to side, raises his clasped hands and struggles to keep from crying. "I want to believe, Dr. Brende," he replies.

"I can understand that you would want to run when you smell alcohol because it's associated with so many past painful memories," I clarify.

He tells me once again that his trauma was so real that he is having trouble living with it. I ask if he has other memories associated with the smell of alcohol, and he tells me he worked in beer joints to earn money to buy clothes for school when he was young. But he was never scared like he is now.

"You really are safe on the ward," I insist.

"I'm not safe anywhere any more," he exclaims. Then he tells me he is always hyper-vigilant, waiting for something bad to happen, which is one of the symptoms of post-traumatic stress disorder (PTSD).[47]

I ask if he feels safe in this room with me but he's uncertain if he can feel safe anywhere now that Jay isn't here to protect him.

"I don't know what to think any more," he says and remains seated with his head down. "I don't understand. Why did I fight like an idiot to be here and talk to you?" he asks, perhaps wondering if I will take Jay's place as his protector.

I point out that when patients and staff see Jay acting pretty normal they assume he's doing well. "You were on a one-to-one watch but when people saw Jay (instead of you) they thought you were doing pretty well. But they didn't realize what's under the surface (was you)."

"I told you he was sneaky and was doing drastic things to keep me from existing."

I ask James if he can still ask Jay to protect him from having bad feelings, but James' only response is to accuse Jay of being a liar who doesn't even know who James is now. But he also says he doesn't want Jay to get into trouble. I'm surprised to hear James say this since it was only thirty-eight days ago when he tried to "kill" Jay. James goes on to say that Jay's problem now is that he can't feel anything.

"I know Jay," he exclaims. "He just doesn't feel. I tried so hard for him to feel. But he just doesn't."

"But James, you haven't wanted him to feel. You wanted him to take away (your feelings) so you wouldn't have to suffer all the time. Would you like to be yourself and feel everything or call on Jay to take it away?" I ask.

"Yes I want to be me. But where would I be? 'Cause I can't handle anything at all. I haven't been able to handle anything all my life," he cries.

"All your life? Since you were born?"

"I guess."

"Well you did fantastically well when you were a nine-year-old boy. You did a lot of things on your own as James."

"That's what I told myself," he says.

"But you haven't wanted to take the credit," I point out as I watch James unclasp his fingers and turn them into fists.

"I'm going to be left here to talk to myself and I can't even understand myself," he moans as he slowly shakes his downcast head.

"As a matter of fact I would like to see you stay as James all day today and tomorrow and until I see you on Thursday," I insist.

He shakes his head. "What am I supposed to do?" he cries.

"Survive!"

"I can't survive. I can't." He wipes his nose with the end of his robe.

I wait for him to continue.

"If you could have it the way you want it between now and Thursday, how much of the time would you like to be the predominant person? I want to hear what you think," I explain.

"I want to be here all the time but I know I can't," he moans.

"Why do you know you can't?" I ask.

"Because I'm so exhausted. I can't think. I don't wanna think."

I repeat my request that James continue his existence in the body until we meet on Thursday, but he answers with a high-pitched tearful response that he's afraid he can't handle the emotional pain. He wipes his tears away. "I don't like what I'm doing here but I just can't control myself."

"You can shed as many tears and be as tense as you want. But you may also want to experiment with having good feelings like you had when I first met you just after Thanksgiving."

"I don't have those good feelings now. I'm even becoming afraid of Jay."

"He has wanted to help you. But you're so angry now because he can't help you like he used to help you."

We continue to talk about his relationship to Jay. Suddenly I'm surprised to see a personality switch and Jay appear. I ask him why he came since I had asked James to remain in the body. He responds by telling me that he had been pretending to be Jay. He goes on to say there are really two Jays, one of which is more flamboyant and expressive of his positive feelings toward me. Since our time has come to a close we don't have time to explore this further, although I assume the flamboyant Jay is actually Shea. Before he leaves the studio I remind him we will meet on Thursday. He stands up, shakes his head, and departs with a psychiatric aide.

As I review this session it's not clear to me why the personality named Jim first signed in. Nor was it clear why the session ended with the announcement there were two Jays. But I will later discover that the one pretending to be Jay, the flamboyant personality, wanted to remain hidden until he believes it will be safe to come out of the closet.

CHAPTER 48

Jim and Shea von Kohlman make entrances

January 12, 1976

We meet in the studio, a very plain room where three chairs are placed near the corner of the room. One of the chairs is empty and is about five feet away from a small table that it faces in the corner of the room. James and I sit in the other two chairs. His chair has its back against a closed door, with the empty chair placed on his right side. I sit at a slight angle about five feet away from James with the empty chair on my left.

The patient is clean-shaven with his hair in a bun. He wears a robe and pajamas, sits down, and signs in as Jay. His left leg is crossed over his right. I mention that it's been a year since I first met him for medication purposes, but his memory is sketchy and I'm not sure if he truly remembers it. He tells me quite glibly that he doesn't want to stay in the hospital any longer. "I want a discharge. I don't like to be put on public display. Some guy was running all over the goddam ward like he does all the time and I couldn't sleep in my room. So I had to sleep in the hallway."

"What would you do if you were to be discharged?" I ask.

"Pack my clothes and leave. Get a cab. I'd care less where I went. I know I used to stay at the Jayhawk (Hotel). I don't know how I got in this damn mess and there's no sense foolin' anyone."

I take notice of the fact that it was Shea who used to stay at the Jayhawk Hotel but I don't pursue that subject. Instead I ask if he remembers what we talked about during last Thursday's session.

"I don't know what's going on and I don't want to think about it. This place is supposed to make you feel better. But I feel worse," he complains and begins to pick at his fingers.

"In what way?"

"I try to figure out what's going on and I just get myself into bigger trouble. I just try not to think about it."

"I was surprised by the end of our meeting last time."

"About what?" he asks.

"About seeing a part of you I hadn't seen before. Do you know what I'm talking about?"

"No."

"Do you remember how the session ended?"

He struggles to remember, then says, "There was a pleasant tone. I don't know."

"It was pleasant at the end. You said you were pretending to be Jay and there was another Jay who was the real Jay."

"I am Jay. And I don't think I'm pretending. This is who I am."

"I wonder why you'd say that? Is it possible there was another part of you existing during that time?"

"I don't remember the weekend until yesterday afternoon."

"I wonder why. Is it possible that there was a part of you, who calls himself the real Jay, who was talking to me just prior to leaving here last Thursday? Do you want to see that tape?"

"I don't know if I want to see it or not," he says, but then after a moment he agrees.

I ask Dick, one of three experienced video camera technicians, to play back the last five minutes of the previous session.

Before we watch the tape I point out that he has recently had several different appearances. "The last time you were here you were clean-shaven. The time before that you were starting to grow a little goatee and today you're not shaven."

"Why should I shave? Mother Nature put it there. Let her take it away." He swings his right arm across his face.

When I acknowledge that he is growing a beard, he replies that he likes beards.

"Do you want to look a little bit like me?" I ask.

He smiles, begins to laugh, and tells me he isn't going to let me catch him off guard. "I don't know what you've been doing to me but I'm not going to let you do it."

Finally Dick has the tape ready for replay. As Jay and I watch it, we see a personality switch on the monitor to an alternate personality who looks like Shea, but Jay doesn't recognize him. "I must be reading a script or something. That doesn't seem like me up there, or I'm drunk. Someone is doing a bad imitation of me." As the tape continues to play a little longer Jay gazes straight ahead with a dazed appearance and I ask Dick to stop the replay. When it ends Jay looks down and pulls at his robe, seemingly disturbed.

"According to him that was Jay. The real Jay," I declare.

"That doesn't seem like me up there. If that's me up there I'm drunker than a skunk and I don't drink. I can't stand that crap," he mumbles. "That's one thing I've learned here for sure that I'm not a drunkard or a dope addict!" he exclaims as he waves his arm across his face.

When I point out it's important for him to find out about the other parts of himself, he asks me if this is why he's having such bad headaches. He continues to frown and tells me he's mad because someone is trying to do a very bad imitation of him.

"You don't like the guy who calls himself the real Jay, huh?"

"No I don't like him. He's not the real Jay."

251

"If you were to name him what would you name him?"

He lifts his hands in despair. "I haven't the slightest idea."

"Well why don't you name him." Then I stand up and pull an empty chair over while explaining, "We'll put that guy in the chair and use our imagination."

"My imagination isn't working so well today," he replies softly as he lowers his head while resting it on his right hand. I ask Jay to talk to the empty chair and tell him what he thinks. But Jay says he can't bring himself to do it.

I prod him to speak and make suggestions as to what he might say.

Jay avoids looking at the chair, looks at the monitor, and complains about feeling sick. Then he insists the film should be destroyed, pulls out his pack of cigarettes, and lights one up. I change tactics after realizing he is not willing to talk to the empty chair and ask him to allow the person who thinks he's the real Jay to talk to me. At first he shakes his head and refuses, but then changes his mind. "Okay, you know him better than I do," he says while raising both hands in frustration. "I'm just a crazy, mixed up, stupid patient. What do I know," he says, and flicks ashes off his cigarette into the ashtray on the table.

Finally Jay becomes agreeable and I ask him to relax. He sits squarely with both feet on the floor, rests his hands in his lap, closes his eyes, and breathes deeply. Suddenly I see his head drop and a smooth dissociation to a different personality take place as he removes the ring from his left hand and switches it to the little finger on his right hand.

After a few moments he lifts his head, opens his eyes, and looks at me.

I ask him about the ring switch and he explains that he always wears the ring on his right hand. Then he reaches for his pen to sign in but quickly stops when he sees Jay's signature.

"It's signed already," he says.

"Did you sign it?"

"No," he replies.

I ask him to go ahead and sign his name anyway and he signs the name James.

I ask if Jay is aware of him and James says, "Yes he's aware of me."

"Are you happy about that?" I ask.

"No. Not really," he says, while anxiously moving his hands back on forth on the arms of the chair.

James tells me he feels confused and depressed. "I wonder why I'm here. I don't wanna be. I thought I had something but I don't have anything." He goes on to tell me he no longer feels excited about living, he can't cope with his bad memories, and he can't feel good about anything.

"You can feel good about being alive," I emphasize.

253

"What is there to be alive for? The past? The future? They have nothing for me," he sighs dejectedly.

"I talked with Jay and he's glad you're alive," I insist.

"Jay? You talked with him?" he exclaims. "I don't trust him. He's planning to skip out of the hospital and leave me here."

"Are you sure about that?"

He does not answer me. Then after a moment I see a subtle dissociation.

"Who are you?" I ask.

"I'm Jimmy. My father called me Jim."

Jim's unexpected appearance prompts me to ask him to tell me more about his father.

"I don't wanna talk about him," he replies morosely.

"Why not?"

"Because he hit me!" Jim exclaims.

I wait for him to continue but he remains silent. Then I ask, "Can you tell me what happened?"

He shakes his head and refuses to talk about the incident, even though I assure him the information will be kept confidential. I will later learn about the disturbing details.

"If he was here now I'd kill him!" he shouts.

In order to help resolve his anger, I explain to Jim he should imagine his father sitting in an empty chair. Then I ask Jim to talk to the person in the chair and tell him how he feels.

"I wish I had a father who cared," Jim moans as he looks down at the floor. Then he looks at the empty chair and exclaims loudly, "I didn't need you! I didn't need Mother either!"

I then ask him to change the scene and have his mother sit in the chair. He looks at the empty chair and complains, "Why didn't you let me grow up with dignity? Why else do you call me Jimmy! Why not call me James? You cheated me for sixteen years out of my birthday. You said my birthday was on the twenty-second (of July) instead of the twenty-third. Where was the help I needed?" he pleads.

After a long pause I ask how he feels about expressing himself so strongly.

With a frown on his face he says, "Okay, I guess."

I assure him things can be different now. "James Kohlman can grow up to be a man."

He doesn't agree. "This is as far as I can grow. I'm no longer a man. You know that," he replies sadly.

"You didn't receive the kind of love and affection you needed when you were a boy to help you grow up," I say with understanding.

He remains silent but I see tension building up in his body, and ask if another part of him can talk about this subject. After a brief time I see him dissociate. His eyes glaze over, his right hand takes the ring off his little finger, toys with it for a few seconds, then places it in his pocket. After a moment he pulls the ring out of his pocket, puts it on his toe, picks up a pen, leans over the table and signs in: Shea Von Kohlman. Then he looks at me. "The other two don't know anything," he sneers.

I'm too astonished to speak.

"I'm the black sheep. I never got married and never had kids," he announces.

To my amazement he shifts his body to the right as he rests both feet on the empty chair and swings his right leg over his left.

Finally I break my silence. I ask about his beginning existence and he tells me he first realized he was gay when he was in his twenties. "I've always done what I've wanted. I played in movies with Kim Novak, who's very pretty, in *Picnic*. I danced on WIBW TV (in Topeka), the Philharmonic Ballet and Tahitian dance."

When I ask him to tell me what's going on between Jay and James he says, "The other two want to leave. The square (James) and the triangular (Jay) want to go."

I remain briefly silent and wait for Shea to continue.

"He doesn't know it but I've been here. I'm going to put on some make-up and take my hair down," he says as he shakes out his hair.

Although he appears to be very comfortable talking openly with me about his sexuality, he also insists this information should remain secret. I listen quietly to his assurance he won't act on his sexual feelings and won't reveal his scandalous dreams.

After this unexpected revelation I ask Shea for his permission to talk to Jay, but he shakes his head. I wait another ten seconds to obtain his approval but Shea smiles, takes off one of his slippers, rubs his foot, and says, "I'm sorry but I'm not going to let the triangular talk to you." I ask if he will agree to place the ring on his left hand but he also refuses to do that. I end the session with Shea present in the body and remind him to attend our next meeting on Thursday. He has a pained expression on his face as he shakes his head, blows his nose, takes the ring from his toe, and puts it in his pocket.

Shea has revealed his homosexuality, and that prompts me to review this subject. As I read about its history, I find differing views about whether or not homosexuality is a pathological condition and whether treatments were found to be helpful. At the turn of the twentieth century, Sigmund Freud did not consider homosexuality to be an abnormal condition. In contrast, psychoanalyst Sandor Rado, a Hungarian émigré to the United States, believed that heterosexuality was the only biological norm. He and other noted psychiatrists considered homosexuality to be a deviation from normal heterosexuality caused by inadequate parenting. A number of psychiatrists reported that they had successfully treated individuals seeking freedom from unwanted homosexual desires. With the rise of gay activism that included mass demonstrations against the American Psychiatric Association (APA) in the early 1970s, the APA removed homosexuality from its list of psychiatric disorders in 1973. The decision to normalize homosexuality has been called a major paradigm shift as it became increasingly viewed as natural and acceptable human behavior. Nonetheless, gay individuals have occasionally sought professional help to escape unwanted sexual desires and behaviors, and some may have succeeded.

I will read about the results of a survey in 2001 of 200 homosexual individuals who were involved in psychotherapy. Before therapy, 99 percent of males and 88 percent of females said they felt lust for or daydreamed about having sex with a member of the same sex. After therapy, there was a reduction in symptoms in both sexes. Thirty-two percent of the males and 5 percent of the females reported fewer same-sex fantasies or daydreams. Twenty-nine percent of males and 63 percent of females reported no or only minimal homosexual feelings, attractions, lustful thoughts, fantasies during masturbation, or homosexual behavior. The author of the survey will conclude that "…contrary to conventional wisdom, some highly motivated individuals using a variety of change efforts can make substantial change in multiple indicators of sexual orientation and achieve good heterosexual function." But he will also caution against misusing the results to justify coercive treatment to change sexual orientation through therapy.

This report will be roundly rejected by homosexual activists and retracted by its author, along with an apology to the gay community eleven years later. The APA and similar mental health organizations will continue to call attempts to change a gay person's sexual orientation ineffective and potentially harmful. They will also urge lawmakers in all states to ban what they label as the harmful and discriminatory practice of conversion therapy.

CHAPTER 49

Shea's Second Appearance: "James was raped.
Nobody can rape me, I'm too willing."

January 15, 1976

The placement of three chairs is the same as last time. One chair is empty and faces a small table in the corner of the room. The other two chairs face each other near the table. I sit at a slight angle about five feet away from James with the empty chair on my left. The patient's appearance is similar to that of his last session. He sits down, signs the name Jay, then crosses his legs tightly with his left leg over the right and looks up at me. "Guess what. I've been made president of the ward," he announces.

"Congratulations," I say with a smile.

"Well, it's the first time in the history of this ward that a person on a one-to-one watch in the 'quiet room' has ever been made a president of the ward!"

We both laugh as I ask him if he actually remembers it. Rather than frankly saying yes or no, he says, "I remember the last two weeks. But I don't really believe all the crap that everyone's been telling me. I don't understand it," referring to the disruptive behavior that caused his doctor to place him on a one-to-one watch.

"But you understand there's 'another you'?" I ask.

He puts his hand up to his head. "That's what you all keep saying. That there's another me. But there's no other me!" he exclaims.

"You know if you sit and relax as you have done in the past, the other you comes out if you allow it to," I reply.

"If you mean the other me may come out if I relax then I will jump up and grab you and try to choke you!" he says sarcastically. "But I'm not going to do that. And I'm not going to stand around and bawl all day. I'm just not going to do those things."

"That's what the quiet room is for. So if the other you comes out bawling or jumping up he can do it in a safe place," I assure him.

He turns up the right side of his mouth with disgust, puts his hands down across his right knee and says, "I don't feel like doing those things myself."

I appeal to his understanding that the other part of him should have an opportunity to speak, but he shakes his head. When I ask if he would be willing to watch a portion of the recording from our last therapy session he makes a joke about not needing to see an instant replay. Finally, however, he agrees to see the videotape[48] and I ask Dick to show the last portion of the previous session. Before we begin to view the session Jay laughs. "Not only are you a doctor of psychiatry, but you're also a TV director."

I smile as I acknowledge his comment while we wait to see the monitor but it quickly becomes apparent that he is not interested in watching it.

"You seem to be so fearful of the other parts of you and can't admit that they exist," I say.

"You know what I've been told. 'You're not a schizophrenic but you have two other personalities. And one of those personalities has two other personalities.'"

"Who told you that?"

"Oh, it's just what everybody said."

"One of the reasons these other personalities stay underground is because you won't allow them to exist," I declare.

In spite of his lack of interest he begins to watch the video display. When he hears the name James he closes his eyes, shakes his head, and mutters he'd rather be "knocked out" than watch it. Finally he reluctantly turns his gaze toward the screen as he crosses his legs and leans his body to the left. "I'm kinda getting sick to my stomach," he complains, but then quickly assures me he'll be okay. He briefly watches the screen but then closes his eyes. He opens them again and tells me there is no way the person on the screen looks like him.

We continue silently watching the screen until Jay gets angry and calls the person he sees a stupid liar. He puts his head down in disgust. "If you say that's me, that's not me. It's someone else!" He lifts both hands to his head, puts them down again, and crosses them firmly as a way of saying he's had enough. "I don't know anything about him. And it's driving me up a wall," he insists. He removes his glasses but quickly puts them on again and insists I shut it off. "I don't have to look at that soap opera up there!" he maintains.

I ask Dick to turn off the videotape monitor and Jay pulls out a cigarette.

"Why are you upset?" I ask.

"I have been way up here," he raises his hand high up over his head and lowers it again, "and now I've fallen. I've got to raise myself up there again to where I'm s'posed to be so I can get out of this damn hospital!" he exclaims.

"I'm very concerned that you would delude yourself into thinking that you're ready to go out of the hospital. You're not ready!" I insist.

I try to enhance his self-regard by reminding him that he was elected ward president. But he is so preoccupied with having "fallen" from his over-idealized opinion of himself that he doesn't listen. He prefers to tell me how important it is for him to get back to normal and regain his patient rights. "I've been more or less hypnotizing myself so that I can get back to where I belong so I can stay out of that quiet room," he tells me. "Do you know where I'm sleeping? In the hallway. I'm between the devil and the deep blue sea."

I am sympathetic to his concern but insist that it's important for me to talk to James to hear his point of view. "I haven't heard from him for two or three days," I assert.

"You say HIM and it was a HIM up there (on the screen.) So it must be HIM. Well, if you can find HIM, you can talk to HIM," he grumbles angrily.

"You're angry with me today, ever since you saw the tape," I say.

"Not just today or for seeing this tape. I was angry when you came in today," he complains. Then Jay quickly changes from being angry to being pseudo-jovial. "I lied today. I told a patient in the group that I was a doctor. A doctor of psychology," he laughs. Then he changes the subject and complains about James, who he refers to as "the little guy" he saw on the TV screen.

"It's rather comical in a way. Let's let the little guy come out," I suggest.

"Who?" he asks.

"James. There's a very lovable side to him."

He shakes his head. "I don't like kids," Jay exclaims abruptly.

"You don't like the kid in you," I say.

"I don't like them period. I like them under two. Between two and nine they have a right to be different. But between nine and twenty-one they should be in a concentration camp."

"That's why James is giving you so much trouble, because you hate him."

"Don't you see why I hate him? He's bawling. Besides that, he steals my ring. And he puts it on the other hand." Jay looks at the ring on his left hand and throws up his hands in despair.

"I need to work with him. He needs my help," I say, appealing to his willingness to care for the child within him.

But Jay continues to reject James, and tells me he wants to put a paper sack over James' damn head.

"Well, let him come right now," I declare.

Jay reluctantly decides to allow James to talk to me. "If you say I can take him away, I want to prove that I can bring him back too. But I'm not listening (to him talk)."

"I'll tell you what he says," I reply.

He shrugs at me. "If you think it's important. I think it's a bunch of garbage myself. The big bawl-baby. Okay, I'll bring him back the same way I got rid of him." Jay sits back, places his hands on the arms of the chair, blinks his eyes, and takes off his glasses. "You can pay the consequences. I'm not even going to be here. I'm going on a short trip, far, far away!" he exclaims and closes his eyes.

I ask him to allow me to use the empty chair technique. "When you bring James back, pretend that he's sitting there in that chair, between us."

"Okay," he replies with a sigh.

He sits rigidly upright in his chair and stares straight ahead. After about twenty seconds, he closes his eyes. I see his mouth quiver and his face assume a different and more somber appearance. Suddenly after ten more seconds, he removes the ring from his left hand, puts it on his right hand, and his facial appearance changes dramatically. His head drops, his eyebrows lift and his eyes seem larger and more childlike. His chin recedes slightly and he shakes his head sadly.

"You're back," I say sympathetically as I see James is present in the body.

He shakes his head and moans. "Don't you see what I'm putting up with? I understand now that he's ready so there's no reason for me to be here."

When I explain to James it's important for me to talk with him he says Jay doesn't approve. "There's no point in it anymore. He says he doesn't want me back here." James shakes his head and begins to cry. "He has an answer for everything and I don't have an answer."

"I don't think you have to answer to him," I declare.

"But I've been around and I've heard him talk. And I've heard you talk to him and no matter what, he has an answer to everything. I'm not that smart."

"Is Jay angry?"

"He keeps hollering at me, Dr. Brende."

"Is he sitting over there watching?" I ask, pointing to the chair that's across from me.

"He's not sitting anywhere," he replies.

I address the chair as a psychodramatist. "Jay, you were going to sit over there and watch and observe. You were not to holler at James," I insist.

James closes his eyes tightly as tears appear from his eyes, run down his cheeks, and hang on the tip of his nose.

"I don't know which way to turn anymore, Dr. Brende."

"You can turn to me," I reply.

He shakes his head sadly and wipes his eyes.

"If Jay won't listen why don't you talk to someone on the staff who will listen?" I ask.

"It's just that I don't know what to say. I don't know anything, that's just the way I am." James goes on to tell me he can't get the trauma memory out of his head, which makes him frightened all the time. "I'm scared of people. I'm even scared of my own shadow. I don't like to cry. You know that. Jay called me a bawl-baby because I cry."

Realizing that fear is often accompanied by anger, I decide to link current emotions to past memories of his father and make a transference interpretation. James agrees that he's angry with his father but disagrees about being angry with me.

When I suggest he may feel affection toward me, James places both hands on his head as if that will prevent it from exploding.

"What's the matter?" I ask.

"Nothing, except that my head hurts."

"Do you know Shea Von Kohlman?" I ask, realizing that Shea's attempts to show affection are distasteful to James.

James takes rapid breaths and drops his hands to his lap. After a brief pause he removes the ring from the little finger on his right hand, places it on his left little finger, and I see a personality who appears to be Jay emerge. He puts on his glasses, looks at me, and says, "James has a terrible headache but I won't feel it. I can't ever feel what James feels. When I dislike someone, I can say, 'you no longer exist,' and that person would cease existing in my mind!"

"You can do that to people?" I ask incredulously.

"Yes."

"Just blank them out?"

"Yes."

"Just like you do with James, huh?"

"Except that it's taken me four days to do it."

"Perhaps James is getting stronger."

"I'm getting weaker," he tells me and then pulls out a cigarette.

"You don't seem weaker," I say.

"I feel as if I'm about to fall off a high plateau to my death."

After a brief discussion about Jay's loss of strength, I ask his permission to speak with another personality. "I'd like to talk to Shea, the flamboyant one. Then after meeting with him for five minutes, I want to talk to you again, before you go back to the ward."

Jay shakes his head, puts his hand to his forehead, and says he doesn't understand. But I persist and ask him to relax. He finally shuts his eyes, relaxes, and begins to count silently. After about twenty-five seconds Shea emerges and reaches over to get a cigarette from the pack that's resting on an adjacent table. He raises his eyebrows, sticks it into his mouth, flicks a match, and lights his cigarette.

"You gave him a snow job didn't you?" He puts the pack of matches back on the table without looking at me. "I like it that you gave him a snow job," he smirks.

"What do you mean, a snow job?"

He reaches down, pulls up the bottom edge of his robe, and wipes off his nose with it.

268

"I've been waiting for ages for him to relax," he says, then readjusts himself in the chair, turns sideways, slouches back against the left arm of the chair, and drapes his right leg over the right armrest. He lifts his cigarette up with his right hand, wipes off his forehead with his left hand, then turns his head away from me.

"You've been waiting for him?" I ask.

"Oh waiting for him and that other square to get into a fight. But they don't get into a fight like they used to," he says.

"That's because they don't want you around."

He shrugs indifferently and leans forward in his chair.

"Why are they so upset by you?" I ask.

"Why?" he asks as he brings his left leg up and places his foot on the seat of the chair. "I don't know. They don't know me for some reason," he says, then reaches down with his left hand, takes off a slipper, and picks at his toes. Then he puts the slipper back on, puts his foot back down on the floor, adjusts his robe, and places his legs together properly.

"That's always the most scary thing," I say, referring to his comment about two personalities fighting.

"What?"

"The unknown."

"But if it wasn't for him, we wouldn't have any excitement." He grins, leans down, and rubs both feet. Then he brings his right leg up and rests the heel on his left knee while slumping back in the chair. "I haven't had any dreams," he sighs.

"You haven't? Tell me about the dreams that you've had before."

"That I've had before?" He tips his head back and looks at the ceiling. "Do you mind if I get up?" he asks as he places his foot back down onto the floor and grins.

"Where do you want to go?"

"I just wanna get up. I've been..." He laughs out loud. "Sittin' or layin'. I just wanna get up." Without waiting for my response he stands up and stretches. "Oh...Oh m' gosh," he says dramatically. "I think I'll sit back down until I get back into shape again." He looks at the cigarette in his right hand. "I know these don't keep their shape." Then he turns to his left side, drapes his left leg over the arm of the chair, and carefully places the cigarette in the ashtray on the table.

"You see I don't want to make a bad recording."

He picks the cigarette up again and scratches his head with a sheepish look on his face. "I don't think I should tell you, but you got kinda naughty," he smirks.

"What did I do?"

"Oh, you kinda..." He closes his eyes and breathes in deeply through his nose as if he were enjoying a sweet aroma. Then he points across the room. "Don't forget that you're way over yonder there and I'm way over yonder here." Then with a shrug of his shoulders and a smirk he says, "So I got naughty? I guess it's naughty." He inhales his cigarette and looks upward with a big grin as he blows smoke out of his nose.

"I haven't done anything to you have I?" he grins, implying sexual behavior.

I shake my head no.

"Okay. So why are you getting so ruffled up about before I've even done anything?"

He looks off to his right and back at me, as if checking for the presence of witnesses. "You're getting all shook up about sumpin'," he grins.

"I want to let you know that there are limitations on sexual behavior. However, I do want you to have the freedom to talk about it," I reply.

"Listen, I'm not a faggot. I might be a queen, but I'm not a faggot," he says with an embarrassed laugh. "I do have some dignity. You know." He raises his eyebrows and scratches the left side of his face with his left hand. "Maybe you don't know," he adds.

"No, you haven't told me."

"About anything?"

"That's right."

"Maybe you don't even know the gay world or anything?" He raises his left hand to rub the back of his head. "Well, there is certain types you know, like there is in any world. And as I said, I might be a queen, but I'm not a faggot." He twists in his chair and leans forward while looking at me. "A faggot is the lowest damn thing in the world. And I'm not that." He looks away from me, leans toward the table on his left, and aggressively rubs the cigarette into the ashtray.

"Considering the fact that James… " I begin to say.

"Is a square," he interrupts me.

"He had been raped in 1968," I continue.

271

"Well, they'd have to rape him." He looks down toward his right, begins to fool with the belt on his robe, then closes it tightly around him.

"And he feels very badly. Is there something he should be ashamed of?" I ask.

"Well, there is! You should never be raped!" He looks at me with a silly grin. "Nobody can rape me, I'm too willing." He bursts out in silly laughter. "If you're willing, you can't be raped. Right?" Then he looks down at himself dressed in a hospital robe and says, "God, I wish I had some clothes on." He reaches up behind his head, unloosens the band that holds his hair in a ponytail, and shakes his hair loose.

Once more I ask Shea to tell me why James is upset.

"I don't know. I think he's kind of silly," he replies.

"But do you like him?" I ask.

"Yes, I do like him in a way."

"He doesn't like you," I emphasize.

"He doesn't know me! Thank God!" Shea asserts loudly.

"Why do you say that?"

"Because of what I've heard of him and seen of him. Maybe it's best that he doesn't know me."

He finally finishes loosening his ponytail with a big sigh of relief, then swings his head backward to whirl his hair back and forth in a sexualized, effeminate manner, and brushes it back with his left hand. Then he brings his head forward.

"Why is it best he doesn't know you?" I ask.

"Because, he's a square."

"You mean he'd be too upset if he knew about you?"

"I don't care about him. I would be too upset if he knew about me! I don't want any squares around me!" he declares with a cynical grin. Then he sighs, takes a comb from his robe pocket, and runs it through his hair.

"Why?" I ask.

"They (squares) don't have any knowledge about anything."

"Would he be very critical?" I ask.

"The only reason he'd be critical is because he doesn't have any knowledge. Listen. Just because I'm a gay queen," he says while pulling the brush from his hair and picking hair from the comb, "that doesn't mean I don't have a lot of knowledge about the studs and the straight kings." He looks up disdainfully. "So am I any different than they are? No! I'm better because I have that knowledge too," he says grandiosely. "The only trouble is that 99 percent of the sons-of-bitches—and that's exactly what they are— that's a good word to use here in America because it's an American word." He doesn't finish the sentence but strokes his hair and swings it around. Then he scratches his scalp. "Oh, God, that feels good," he swoons.

This exhibitionistic description of himself seems more appropriate for the privacy of his own dressing room rather than a studio where we have been engaged in psychotherapy. After a pause he continues. "They could be gay themselves, but they don't have the knowledge or the courage to be that way, unless they're three sheets in the wind. Then they can say, 'Well, I was drunk.'" He continues to comb his hair. "Shiieeet. Three sheets in the wind.

273

You can tell right off the bat. You don't have to go around and try to promote yourself. All you have to do is just walk in."

He waves his hand dramatically and closes his eyes in a flare for attention, and then turns his face partially toward me. "And if they are three sheets in the wind, you know by what their actions are what's going to happen," he says with a sly grin on his face.

I look at the clock, tell Shea our time has come to an end, and ask if I can talk to him again next time. But he ignores me and continues to describe himself.

"I told you already. I told you I was a gay queen," he smirks. "And that explains the whole thing. I think you have enough knowledge to know what that is. That's not quite a homosexual," he says, to instruct me. He springs the teeth of his comb, gestures with his index finger, and continues. "A gay queen is one step below a homosexual. That's about as high as you can go. I haven't made homosexual yet. I've been called a faggot but I'm above that now." He reaches out behind his head with his left hand and strokes his hair. "And I've been called a size queen but I'm no size queen." He puts his leg down and says, "All these words. I keep forgetting. Maybe you don't know."

"I'll tell you what, I've got to talk to Jay now," I say as I look at the clock again.

"Ah sheeeez. Someday I've got to come over here all by my lonesome and talk to you. If you're afraid, you can sit in that room and I'll sit in this room."

"Do I seem afraid?"

"I don't know. I'm not afraid. Alright?" he says with his head down. "So I want to stay for awhile. It's upsetting me. Okay. Okay."

He sits straight up in the chair as he prepares for the unwelcomed end of our time together. "If you want to talk to him, talk to him. I don't care," he complains. Then he lowers his head for about ten seconds and allows the switch to take place. Suddenly I see Jay emerge.

"What are you doing?" I ask as he begins to put the rubber band back on his ponytail.

"I don't know," he replies, unable to explain why his hair is flowing freely. "You told me that if I had to hear the voice that haunts me all the time, I would go away."

"Where did you go?"

"I just went away to relax. I don't know where. Maybe it was in purgatory," he laughs, revealing a blasé attitude about his whereabouts.

Before this session ends, I ask if he knows how many personalities I talked with today.

"Didn't you talk to one voice?" he asks.

"No. Two besides you," I reply.

"Two? Maybe they're right then. One of my schizophrenic personalities is a schizophrenic himself and he has two personalities," he laughs.

"There are two voices I talked to. Do you know their names?" I ask.

"I know one," he says as he lowers his head and puts his left hand up to his forehead.

"Can you say who?"

"Yes, I can say James," he replies reluctantly.

"What about the other one?"

"I don't know anything about the other one."

"Shea. Shea Von Kohlman," I clarify.

"I've seen that name, but I don't know him," he says.

I don't elaborate and bring our session to a close.

I ponder about the possible connection between James' traumatic rape experience and the "birth" of Shea. I review the literature on this subject later and find a frequent connection between childhood sexual abuse and adult homosexuality. There are also reports by a few gay celebrities that they were sexually abused as underage minors. Although it's true there are gay men who were never abused and straight men who never became gay in spite of being abused, statistics gathered by researchers have found a link between childhood sexual abuse, adult psychiatric disorders, and bisexual behavior. I will later see an article reporting that 74 percent of bisexuals had been sexually abused as children.[49] Although I now know that James was the victim of a sexual assault as an adult, I will not learn until later about the details of his childhood trauma.

CHAPTER 50

I want to get rid of HIM. He's a bawl-baby and that irritates other people.

January 22-30, 1976

James has a new hospital doctor who comes to today's session accompanied by a nurse. I welcome their arrival and ask them to find seats in the recording studio to observe what takes place. After Jay signs in, I explain to them that I will interact with Jay for a short time and then talk with his alternate personality. I do not know if Shea will appear today. My remark seems to puzzle the two caregivers, who raise their eyebrows.

I turn my attention to Jay and ask how he is doing. After he gives me a brief but mundane description that he's not doing very well, I request him to allow me to talk to James. He reluctantly agrees, closes his eyes, and relaxes. After a short time I see a personality switch and James emerges. He anxiously looks around, sees the doctor and nurse, and goes into a panic. "No. No. Don't make me go!" he hollers. When I ask why he's upset he says he's afraid of getting shock treatments, but I assure him that won't happen. His hospital doctor also speaks up and promises James there is no plan to give him shock treatments.

I ask James how things are going for him and he complains that nothing is going well. The doctor and his nurse express their concern for James, but also confront him about his aggressive

277

behavior that could get him sent to the quiet room. James objects, expresses his fear of being sent back into darkness, loses control over his rising level of anxiety, and after a brief series of automatisms allows Jay to return to the body. The doctor and his nurse appear shocked to see the personality switch and hear Jay smirk, "I don't want that asshole here. I want to get rid of HIM. And I don't ever want to hear that name again."

I rebuke Jay's disdainful attitude before the session comes to a close. Fortunately he becomes very cooperative and leaves the studio smiling at his new hospital doctor and nurse, who learned a lot more today than they had expected.

Jay's out-of-control behaviors have been of such concern that his hospital doctor and nurse came to a therapy session. They wondered how I might manage his aggressive behaviors and were very surprised to witness the emergence of an alternate personality. They haven't been aware that James has been fighting off takeovers by alternates who cannot tolerate him or even recognize his name. Instead the other personalities have referred to James as HIM. Hopefully these professionals will have gained more insight to help the staff better understand James' behavioral turmoil.

Jay and I meet again eight days later. After signing in, he complains about a number of things that trouble him: he can't remember anything or figure things out like he used to; he is having fainting spells, terrible headaches, nausea, and loss of appetite; he found his toiletries and money in a box but doesn't know how they got there; he believes patients are messing with his stuff when he's sleeping; and he's been told that he gets violent at times and he can only calm himself down by smoking.

I ask if he uses the relaxation technique of counting to ten I've taught him. He says he used to visualize my presence to calm himself but that stopped working. Then he started counting to twenty, which was only briefly effective. When he tried counting to fifty that only worked once. "I've run out of things to do and the only one solution to this whole mess is for me to die," he laments.

"Dying is not the solution," I insist, and recommend that he learn to gain control over the different parts of himself.

He doesn't want to talk about different parts of himself but will talk disparagingly about the "bawl-baby."

"I can't accept any part of me that cries and when he cries that irritates other people. Then they get upset and it becomes a mess. Nothing is solved!" he exclaims.

"The other part of you that cries is a significant part of you and accepting him will help make you a whole person," I explain.

"The reason I can't accept that other part is because I don't like the name," Jay explains.

"It's my job to help you work with that other part you call James because that's the name his parents gave him."

Jay shakes his head and insists once again he can't accept that other part he refuses to name.

Before we finish the session I give Jay credit for having protected James from experiencing painful emotions for many years. I also emphasize how important it will be to help James live with his disagreeable and unpleasant feelings.

CHAPTER 51

Jay has a rebirth experience.

February 2, 1976

Jay has a short goatee and mustache today, and is wearing a robe and pajamas. He seems more reflective, although he continues to feel upset when others talk about his suicide attempt. "I never, never wanted to kill myself!" he insists.

I ask if he remembers what I'd told him about the "suicide attempt," and he vaguely recalls I told him a part of him had tried to kill the other part. But he insists there is no other part.

"Jay, I know there is another part. His name is James and I've talked with him," I declare.

"How come all of a sudden you know him? I don't think anyone else knows him. And you can so easily talk to him? Now don't get me wrong. I know you use hypnosis and you've tried it on me. And maybe you hypnotized me. But I don't know if you have," Jay exclaims.

I assure him I haven't used hypnosis since many months ago. I also praise him for being interested in the other part of him. But he says that other part is creating havoc in his life. He awoke a couple nights ago and found himself standing in the middle of his room. The next day some patients told him they heard a baby crying from his room during the night. He can't understand why these things are happening.

We talk about his memory problems and I remind him he's previously told me he can't remember his early childhood. He tells me he remembers some things, and tells me about an event I haven't heard before. He acted in a play when he was a high school student, and his friends called him Cas because he sounded like a Casanova. But he doesn't remember having a girlfriend and only vaguely recalls discussing marriage with a girl when he was in his twenties.

He pauses as if deep in thought, cracks his knuckles together, then asks about the other part of him. "I know I'm using the pronoun HIM, which is wrong, isn't it? HIM does have a name I guess," he chuckles. "Isn't it funny I really do wanna know but I don't want anyone else to know about it. I guess he got me into trouble." He pauses and looks down at the tips of his fingers touching. Then he puts his left hand up to his chin and flicks his index finger onto his mouth. "The only thing I can remember is that people told me HIM actually committed suicide. But I, as I know myself, did not."

"That other personality you call 'him' is not dead. Would you like to know what he told me?" I ask.

To my surprise Jay says yes, but he also doesn't want me to talk about it. "I don't like to think of me as two different people or objects or whatever you wanna call 'em," he grumbles, gesturing with both of his hands.

"What's the difference between people and objects?" I ask.

"I don't even think I'm a person when they talk about HIM and about me. It makes me seem like I'm not a human any longer.

I know that's not true, but that's just the way I feel," he says, looking perplexed.

I point out that it will help him feel more like a complete human being if he can remember his early life experiences.

He sighs, extends both of his arms toward me and asks if I can teach him how to remember. I explain that he won't want to remember anything that's too painful, but those memories may come back to him when he is ready.

He sighs, looks down and leans on his right elbow. "I've thought of every single way possible to let those things come back. I've thought of mother syndromes, father syndromes, sister and brother syndromes. All of those!" He raises his hands in exasperation.

Rather than continuing to discuss his inability to retrieve memories I ask if he can remember more details about awakening in the middle of his room two nights ago.

"I was just having a nightmare," he explains.

"Is it possible that a part of you was wanting some recognition, and you allowed it to happen during the night so that you would only think it was a nightmare, rather than thinking it was a real part of you?" I ask.

He insists it had to be a nightmare but doesn't know what caused it. But this discussion prompts him to tell me about the time his baby brother died from jaundice, although he can't remember if the baby's death caused any emotional pain.

I point out that he may not remember painful feelings but there is another part of him that does.

He scowls, looks around, then back at me. "Is it HIM?"

"Yes it is. If I were to work with 'him' more wouldn't you feel better?" I ask.

He shifts around in his chair. "Definitely no! You worked with HIM already and now I'm feeling worse. And if you start working with HIM again things will just get even worse," he moans as both hands drop downward in a helpless sinking motion.

Knowing how important it is to get Jay's cooperation, I ask him to advise me about the best way to work with "him." But Jay absolutely refuses and complains that I haven't helped him control his strange behaviors, nightmares, and blocked memories. I jog his memory about our recent session, during which time I helped him rather than help James, Jim, or Jimmy.

Upon hearing those names, he moves restlessly in his seat, closes his eyes, crosses his left leg tightly over the right, and tenses his body until it becomes rigid. Then his left leg begins to flip out and I hear him frantically yell my name, "Dr. Brende!"

"Yes?" I reply.

"I'm sorry, I hear myself hollering and I don't know why."

He remains quiet and I wait for him to continue.

"I enjoyed the meeting on Friday because I wasn't afraid that HIM would pop out and I didn't have to be on guard all the time and protect other people." He points to the door hinge on the wall, prompting me to use the hinge as a metaphor to explain how two things are held together, one of which can swing it back and forth. Then I describe his childhood as being hinged to a stabilizing person, his mother. But the subject of his mother only angers him,

283

and he shakes his head slowly as he describes his mother as too busy to stabilize anyone. "I had my turn and others had their turn. All the others in the family had to go through the same thing I did," he complains, while gesturing to demonstrate the rapid-fire turnover of one younger child pushing an older one out of the way.

"Those are the same feelings you are talking about right now. You're feeling what it's like to be pushed aside."

"I understand that," he responds stoically.

"As an adult, you can understand that. But when you were a little boy you didn't have that understanding," I emphasize.

He seems confused as he ponders the subject. "Well, what do you want me to do? Go around bawling about everything? That doesn't make sense," he declares.

I ask if he recalls bawling as a child and he replies that he gave that up because his mother was too busy to listen. "All I remember about her was that she was pregnant and bare-foot all the time. And if she wasn't pregnant she was holding one (baby) nursing on her breast. That was a way of life," he says, describing how overwhelmed she was with fourteen children. Then he remembers again that he helped his mother care for his baby brother until he died of jaundice. But this memory prompts him to tell me he's convinced the staff wants to get rid of him. "They keep saying why is James Kohlman up here? Sometimes he won't talk to us at all."

Then he closes his eyes, moves his hands back and forth on the arm of the chair, breathes heavily, and plants both feet on the floor. I see a personality shift as James emerges, struggles to speak,

284

and removes the ring from the left hand. "D…D…Dr. Brende," he stammers as he drops his head down.

"Do you want Jay to help you right now?"

"He…he can't," James sobs as he keeps his hands tightly clenched.

He drops his head, tells me that Jay can't help him any longer, and breaks out in spasms of coughing.

"Can you tell me what you're thinking right now?" I ask.

He shakes his head. "I'm trying to forget."

"Can you remember some of the good experiences you had two weeks after Thanksgiving? Let yourself go back and remember."

He shifts in his chair and shakes his head slowly.

"You know that James was your given name. The name that you received when you were born into the world, and I want you to remember that. All these painful things that you are struggling with seem to be problems that Jim or Jimmy had. But you, James, had something special and I want you to remember those special experiences."

He remains silent.

I continue, "Tell me what you remember?"

He doesn't reply.

"Can you remember being born? Can you think back? Tell me what it was like?"

After a long pause he speaks one word, "Cold."

"Cold. What else do you remember?"

"Light. Light. Light. Upside down." Suddenly I see him breathe in gasps.

"You're breathing hard. What's happening now?"

Instead of answering he gets out of his chair and kneels on the rug, oblivious to my presence. I perceive his actions as reliving something from the past since his hands begin to grope on the floor rug for whatever he's lost.

"James, what's happening? How old are you?" I ask.

He continues looking down and begins to point with his finger. Suddenly his hands spread about twelve inches apart as if he were measuring something.

I ask, "What's the matter, James?"

He begins to stammer, "That…that…was…mine," he sobs. "My…my…fire engine…. My…choo…choo…train." His hands move up and down and then apart as if he was measuring the length of the fire engine.

"What's happening to it?"

"He…built…built…" His hands begin to tremble as he opens and closes his fists. Then he waves his arms and breaks down in frustration.

I leave my chair and kneel down on the floor to enter into his reliving experience.[50]

His hands drop onto the floor as he pats the rug and stammers again. "He…built…built…a shed over it."

"He built a shed over it? Why?" I ask.

"He used it to…" He motions with his hands as he tries to describe what he can't put into words. Then he claps his right hand down on his left hand several times.

"He pulled the floor up…the foundation," he sobs. "He used my engine to build the shed."

I'm able to finally understand that his father put his fire engine in the foundation of the shed where it remains buried. I motion with my hands and say instructively, "Let's remove it. Let's take this off and put it over here."

"It's too heavy," he cries.

"I bet I can lift it up."

"It's the whole building. The whole building," he replies.

"I'm stronger than you are. Let me take the building off."

"It's the whole building!" He sobs in despair as his head drops down between his knees and his fists pound the floor.

I assure him again that I can lift up the building and save his choo choo train. He remains on his knees for about a minute while I continue to reassure him. Then I ask him to stand up and sit in his chair again. He manages to do that with some difficulty, but he continues to act as if he's still a small boy.

To counteract his emotional pain I ask if he can retrieve a positive birth memory. "I want you to remember being born, James. Go all the way back to the time when you were born."

His hands drop down from his face and he lifts his head up. I reach over and touch his left shoulder.

"Remember this good feeling," I repeat.

287

He pulls up the hem of his robe and wipes off the moisture dripping from the end of his nose.

"In just a moment you are going to be left with the memory of being born. And then I want Jay to come back and talk to me," I say.

James sits quietly for a moment and after about thirty seconds, takes the ring from the finger on his right hand and transfers it to his left, signaling a personality switch.

"Dr. Brende. See, you did it again!" Jay says as he looks at me. After a pause he continues. "I feel funny," and blows his nose. "Oh, do I have a headache," he complains as he raises his left hand to his forehead.

"Have you been able to learn how to control your headaches by relaxing?" I ask.

"Yes. That's the reason I feel so funny."

"Do you have any good feelings?"

"Yes."

"Can you describe those?"

"I just have a feeling now. I know it's very impulsive." He stops and blows his nose again. I ask him what he wants to do and he suddenly reaches over to touch me. His action surprises me and I flinch. He quickly withdraws in embarrassment.

"I'm sorry," he says.

"You wanted to touch me?[51] I think that's good," I say.

"You jumped," he replies with a painful look on his face. "I don't want to do that. It was stupid. Why do I want to touch you?"

he asks uncomfortably as he appears to have moved from the young James' childlike state to Jay's adult state of mind.

"That's not stupid at all. That's very loving," I say.

"I told you I was impulsive." He raises his hands up to his forehead momentarily and then drops them down to cover his mouth.

"You probably felt like doing that for a long time and suddenly felt like it was all right," I say.

"Maybe it's all right," he replies, then moves his hands restlessly before reaching back up to his forehead. He sighs. "It seems like there's something I wanna…" He stops talking abruptly. Then he stands up. After a moment he sits down again.

"The lights," he says and then covers his eyes. "I'm mixed up! God I am mixed up!" he exclaims.

I explain that James had spent a couple of minutes reliving his birth and said the lights were very bright.

He puts his hands up over his eyes again, then takes them down, frowns and tells me he has a terrible headache and is trying to remember what I said. Then he closes his eyes and asks, "Is our time up?"

"Yes it is," I say.

He nods and stands up with his shirt soaked in perspiration.

I'm very moved when I review the videotape the following day and watch James kneel on the floor and sob because his father buried his fire engine in the building's foundation. I wonder if he relived a true event, or if this was a metaphor in which the buried fire engine symbolized the suppression of his masculine identity, and the foundation symbolized the symbiotic attachment with the maternal object (his mother) from whom he failed to achieve normal separation-individuation.[52] It was important for me to be with him emotionally and physically and help him relive this significant experience. I believed it was essential that his fire engine (his masculine identity) be freed from its burial place in the building's foundation so that he might recover his sense of being a masculine boy.

My intervention had been to role-play a powerful father uncovering the young James' fire engine. Following that I therapeutically facilitated an imagined rebirth experience. When Jay returned to the body he experienced sensory changes that included a desire to touch me, indicating that the boundary between the two personalities is quite permeable now. This significant session was emotionally trying for Jay, who described feeling light-headed and saturated with perspiration.

CHAPTER 52

"Why would I want to touch anyone?" Jay asks.

February 5-9, 1976

Jay comes to the studio wearing a white robe and blue pajamas, and I'm wearing brown slacks and a red and white sweater today. Jay tells me almost immediately that he had a bad night and wonders why his mouth is all chewed up and his lips sore. I wonder if this is related to our emotionally charged last session, and ask Jay if he remembers touching me.

"Why would I want to touch anyone?" he asks, looking befuddled.

I explain that, similar to how James feels, he avoids touch because he is afraid that if he loves someone he will be abandoned.

"Would you please tell me what you mean by this other part. You have called it James so please explain who he is," Jay insists.

"James is the little boy part of you who needs to feel loved."

"That's his problem and I can't help him. In fact I think it's time that you let me out of this hospital!" Jay demands.

We meet again four days later and Jay tells me he abhors the idea that another person might take over his body. He complains of feeling very troubled about the terrible dreams that wake him up, but doesn't believe an alternate personality could be causing such a disturbance in his head. He tells me he has tried to relieve his turmoil by walking down the hall to my office but when he learns I'm not there he feels even worse.

I link his inner turmoil to the subject we talked about during the last session—that he has a conflict with another part of him— the little boy who didn't receive enough love and affection when he was small. Jay's response is to tell me that he has no interest in bemoaning about the past, which he refers to as refusing to cry over spilt milk.

"Not crying over spilt milk is related to a baby not getting attention," I explain. "Maybe the baby (James) cried because his mother wanted to get rid of him," I continue, to stretch the point.

Jay disagrees and refuses to talk about this subject any longer. He insists that I arrange for him to leave the hospital because he doesn't trust any of the patients or staff.

Rather than pursue that topic I ask Jay to let me talk to James. He agrees and after a short time I watch him switch the ring from left to right hand as a signal for James to emerge. After greeting him, I ask his permission to facilitate a rebirth experience again to help him internalize good memories about his own birth, which he agrees to. The intervention appears to be effective as I watch James smile. Before our session comes to a close I ask Jay to return. After he switches his ring from right to left hand I explain what had just happened before Jay leaves the studio.

During today's session, like the previous one, I used an age regression technique to help James experience a sense of being born. I was unaware at the time that rebirthing therapies have been around since the new age movement. A new age spiritual guru named Leonard Orr first developed the technique of rebirthing in the 1960s. Rebirthing sessions were led by trained instructors who focused on helping individuals focus their breathing while envisioning themselves moving through the birth canal. This technique, called conscious energy breathing, was meant for adults and children to reproduce the breathing patterns they first experienced after birth. Some have said rebirthing improved mental focus, stamina, and stress levels. Rebirthing therapy has also been described as an alternative therapy meant to heal persons suffering from reactive attachment disorder, post-traumatic stress disorder, self-destructive behaviors, and drug addictions.[53]

CHAPTER 53

Jay is not ready to recognize that James is a part of him.

February 12-26, 1976

Jay complains that he's depressed and has completely lost his sense of humor. This is not surprising considering the issues we have been dwelling on. I focus again during this session on helping Jay accept there is another part of him. But Jay remains confused and resistant. "I don't want to know about that part and I think it would be a lot better if I could just leave this place," he complains.

"You don't have to let the other part ruin your life. You can both exist at the same time," I insist.

But Jay disagrees and tells me he's not ready for that to happen. Furthermore, he complains that he's been wrongly accused by the staff of trying to kill himself. I explain that he (Jay) did not try to kill himself and that James (the other part of him) was the guilty one.

"If it was the other part that did it, why do I have to take the blame when they tell me I tried to kill myself?" he exclaims.

Before our session ends he informs me that his sister-in-law Betty visited him today before our session, and he appreciated her visit.

We meet two weeks later on Monday, February 23 after I return from a ski vacation. Jay tells me almost immediately that he believes I don't want to see him anymore and he's upset about it.

He tried to relieve his anxiety by walking down to my office on Mondays and Thursdays, which helped him somewhat even though I was not there. He says he woke up last night with tears in his eyes but doesn't know why he was crying. I empathize with his feeling that I had abandoned him. I assure him I am not leaving and definitely want our therapy sessions to continue. I also ask if he remembers any times when he felt abandoned. He tells me he's had memory lapses and found himself at places without knowing how he got there. He also tells me about fragmented memories of finding himself at the Jayhawk Hotel two years ago, and wonders if he had been living there. He has a much clearer memory of moving into a trailer near his parent's house in 1975.

Three days later I meet with Jay and he expresses concern about having emotions. "They make no sense to me," he says. But he's very worried about the emotional turmoil he feels in his head, which I suggest is related to the presence of another personality.

During this session I also clarify his confusion about the significance of the ring switch. There are two different personalities, and each wears the ring on a different hand. I explain that when the ring is on his left hand Jay is present in the body. When the ring is switched to the right hand James is present.

CHAPTER 54

Jay asks if James has come into the body.
He says he wants to understand him.

March 1-11, 1976

During this session Jay tells me he's thinking it may be true that another person takes over his body at times. But the thought of that possibility is so upsetting he wants to run away and get out of the hospital. "No. That's not a good reason to leave the hospital," I emphasize.

To help Jay face the reality of his alternate personality, I ask if he'd like to see James during the last session on the TV screen. But he adamantly refuses. "I don't want anything to do with him. And if you put him up on the TV screen I'd wanna attack him!" Jay exclaims.

I reassure Jay that there will come a time when he'll be able to observe James without wanting to harm him. Then I ask if he will let me talk with James. "Ok. If you wanna talk to him that's your problem. I just don't wanna be here," he says.

I ask him to close his eyes and he agrees. After a short delay I see a personality switch. James opens his eyes and scowls. I ask how he's getting along and he says he's upset because he has been having memories about the time Jay pushed him into darkness after shock treatments. In spite of such a bad memory, James tells me for the first time that he's open to making friends with Jay.

I point out that I want to teach Jay how to share James'
burden of emotional pain, and ask if he will allow Jay to return to
the body. He agrees and Jay emerges.

"I see that you've placed the ring on your left hand," I point
out to Jay.

"Yeah. It feels like a security blanket there," he replies.

For the first time Jay asks if James had just been present in
the body, and also tells me he knows James tried to kill him. In
spite of that, Jay is willing to let James have more time to talk with
me.

We meet again three days later. Jay arrives wearing his usual
hospital attire—blue pajamas and a white robe. I'm wearing a red
shirt today, having forgotten that red can trigger James' anxiety.
After I ask Jay if he will consider accepting James, I hear him tell
me it will be difficult to put up with such a disgusting bawl-baby.
Yet he also tells me for the first time that he would like to
understand James.

Jay appears to look younger today so I ask him about that.
"How old do you feel today Jay?" I ask.

"I feel like I'm in my late twenties. But I've always felt this
way," he replies cheerfully.

"Did your identity begin when you were in the service
during your twenties?" I ask.

"All I can tell you is that I started asking everyone to call me
Jay then."

"Do you have any other memories earlier than that?" I ask.

"Yeah. I can remember back when I was twelve in the sixth grade."

If his earliest memory is age twelve that appears to be when his identity began, even though he didn't start calling himself Jay until he was in his twenties. We spend most of the rest of this session discussing what may happen if he loses his identity as James' protector.

During our next meeting a week later on Thursday, Jay looks tense and tells me he might have had a blackout, and wonders if he hurt anyone, including me. I assure him that I was not aware of anything bad happening. I also inform him I had called his ward and learned that his mood was angry, but also more assertive, which they interpreted to be a sign of improvement.

I'm surprised to hear Jay ask me, for the first time, if he can see the video of the last session. I agree. Jay watches with interest and is only troubled when he hears James talk about being shut into the darkness when he received shock treatments.

CHAPTER 55

Jay recognizes he's a human being and practices writing the name James.

March 15-April 1, 1976

During today's session Jay tells me he sometimes feels emotions, which means he is a human being and not a "thing." However, he's still uncertain if he is really real. "I know you've made me think it's okay to have feelings. But I have one more test to do to prove I'm not a thing," he insists.

"What test to you mean?"

"If I walk out the door of your office I might not exist any longer."

"Do you know the last time a part of you ceased to exist was three or four years ago after you got shock treatments?"

He pauses, then tells me he's still worried that I might subject him to shock treatments. I assure him that I won't do that, and also ask him to assure James there will be no shock treatments.

When we meet a week later on Monday, March 22, Jay tells me he's pleased I did not give James shock treatments. He also tells me he's come to accept that there is indeed another person, and he's been practicing writing that person's name: JAMES. For the first time Jay tells me that his goal is to unite with James and become one person, yet he can't understand how that might be accomplished.

I remind him that if James comes into the body, he will need to feel comfortable giving up his name Jay in order to unite with the other personality and become one person named James. First he assures me the name isn't important, but then changes his mind and says it is important. Then he asks if his therapy sessions will come to an end if James takes over, but I reassure him that won't happen.

I'm pleased that Jay has taken an important step that can lead to his integration with James. I also encourage him to get to know the other Jay (Shea). But Jay shakes his head vigorously. "That's not gonna happen!"

Then I remind Jay that James kept him alive by eating during the ten days when Jay said he didn't eat. "You need to thank James for eating when he comes," I insist.

"I can't hang around when he comes," Jay insists.

"Why do you have to leave?"

Jay says he has three or four different groups of friends that he can get back in touch with, indicating that he has not yet realized he will lose his separate and distinct identity if he and James became one person.

In hopes of facilitating a fusion of the two personalities, I ask Jay if he will sit in a chair on the other side of the room where he can observe if James comes into the body.

He complies.

"James, I want to talk to you," I request. Jay closes his eyes and waits quietly until James opens his eyes and moves the ring from left to right hand.

"How long have you had that ring?" I ask.

"Dr. Baird gave it to me. I liked him at first. Then he gave me a shock treatment and got rid of me," he complains.

"I'm sure that Dr. Baird didn't mean to get rid of you," I explain.

"That's easy to say," he mumbles, and suddenly becomes anxious and tearful.

I ask James what upset him but he loses awareness. His body becomes tremulous, his head drops down, and tears begin to flow from his eyes. I reach over to touch his hand in a gesture of empathy but he doesn't respond. So I ask to talk to Jay, who immediately replaces James and takes the ring from his right and places it onto his left hand. When he notices tears in his own eyes Jay asks if James had injured me. I reassure him James did not hurt me and thank him for his concern. Jay returns to the chair he'd been sitting in, and after several more minutes discussing his worries our session comes to a close.

My expectation that James and Jay might fuse into one identity failed to take place. It didn't happen because all of the criteria for fusion established by Kluft had not occurred. There had not been three stable months of continuous personality existence without a change of behavior. Jay still thought of himself as a separate personality, even though he felt a sense of unity with James. Shea has not given up his wish to continue living.

During our next meeting ten days later the patient arrives wearing his hospital garb—blue pajamas and a white robe—and signs his name Jay. Then he tells me he feels guilty about signing the name Jay, evidence that he realizes James is the name given to him at birth, although he doesn't feel like the real James. I assure him that it's okay to sign his name Jay because it won't change anything.

Jay tells me he's angry about being told he should have emotions. "Emotions have never done anything for anyone," he complains.

"What emotions are you feeling?" I ask.

He has difficulty being specific but acknowledges he feels angry. Then he makes me aware of new symptoms that could be caused by an alternate personality invading his body. "Last night I had a seizure. I woke up laying on the floor and I lost control of my kidneys," he says.

Before the session ends I inform him that I'll be taking a two-week leave of absence.

CHAPTER 56
Discharge and Rehospitalization

April 15, 1976

Jay is not wearing hospital garb today, but has on grey slacks and a blue and white sweater. I learn that his hospital doctor had discharged him during my absence because he seemed normal. But James' appearance of normality ended quickly when he got home. James soon created considerable concern for his family because of memory lapses and aggressive behaviors. Within forty-eight hours they brought him back to the hospital where the doctor readmitted him. The most reasonable explanation for his behavioral collapse was his abrupt loss of hospital structure and predictable meetings with me, which triggered an abandonment depression.[54] But during today's meeting he doesn't acknowledge feelings of loss, but rather feelings of anger because he broke a promise to himself that he would never come back here.

"I didn't want to come back to this hospital because I should be able to work out my own problems."

"And did you?"

"No. And I feel stupid."

"Does it pain you to depend on my help?" I ask.

"Yes, because I don't like to have to depend on anyone. I've never had to rely on anyone except me before."

"This isn't the first time you've had to get help. Weren't you in the hospital four years ago with Dr. Baird when you received shock treatments?"

"I don't remember that."

"I think James remembers it. What do you remember?"

Jay tells me he remembers traveling to the southeast and going to Florida, Georgia, Louisiana, and to the southwest some time before 1975. He remembers returning to Kansas and staying at the Jayhawk Hotel for a year, but remembers very little about that year. It is particularly troubling for him to not remember when he was last hospitalized, which he thinks was in 1972. He tells me how much he hates coming into the hospital again, and that he will bide his time until the doctor discharges him if he just acts normal.

"I wonder if you want to leave again because you don't think you can depend on me since I was away for two weeks," I suggest.

"It doesn't bother me that you were gone. A lot of people have left me. That's why I have to depend on myself," he insists, denying that my absence had anything to do with his return to the hospital.

Jay hates coming into the hospital again and has even talked about terminating therapy. How do we know when therapy should come to an end? Generally speaking, that should occur when a patient's goals have been achieved or when he or she feels that therapy is no longer helpful. If that is the case he or she may choose to find a different therapist. The cost of therapy can be a factor in determining its duration unless the patient is a veteran. Hospital treatment and psychotherapy costs nothing for James because the Veterans Administration pays for it. But if he were to seek medical care in the private sector, it would become more expensive, based on his ability to pay. If he were to have medical insurance, payment would depend on the duration of time necessary for recovery. During the 1970s, insurance paid for long-term psychiatric hospital treatment, which could last up to three years for a patient in the Menninger Hospital. Everything will change in the future. During the early 1990s insurance companies will drastically reduce the length of time they will pay for treatment. During the 2000s, they will pay for five days of acute hospital care for psychiatric patients, and rarely a little longer. Fortunately James will not have to worry about payment because his need for continuing therapy is quite clear. He continues to have memory lapses as well as other factors that require continuing therapy, including the presence of different personalities, each with different goals. At this time James' goal is to understand Jay and become friends with him.

CHAPTER 57

I found wigs and female things in my closet.
I don't know how they got there.

April 26-29, 1976

Jay arrives wearing regular clothes—grey pants and sweater. After he signs in I hear him complain that someone called him a queer after he embraced a patient on the ward. "All I did was give the guy a hug," he insists.

"So someone called you homosexual. Why did that upset you?" I ask.

"It's happened to me before. Dr. Baird called me a homosexual."

"Do you know why?"

"No I don't but if he's gonna call me that I might have to play the part."

"Maybe there is another part of you that was homosexual in the past," I ask.

"Was it James?" he asks me.

"No, not James. It was another part of you," I say, referring to Shea.

"I don't know who that can be and I'm afraid to show affection to anyone because someone might call me a homosexual and I would never commit those kind of acts," he asserts angrily.

"Are you ashamed of those acts?"

"Yes, if I committed 'em. I have friends who are homosexual or prostitutes but they're good people."

"Okay. But let's talk about expressing affection or positive feelings toward someone. Can you talk about that?"

"I don't want those kind of feelings," he says, fearing they're equivalent to sexual behavior.

"But what if there is another part of you that has those feelings?" I ask.

"I have enough trouble with James. Now you tell me there is this other person. How can that be? 'Cause I know James hates homosexuals."

"Would you prefer to be homosexual or heterosexual?"

"Heterosexual! Because I understand that. But then I don't have any interest in sex. You can call me asexual."

"Do you call yourself asexual?"

"That's right. But I should tell you that I've found wigs and female things in my closet. I don't know how they got there. I didn't do anything to bring 'em there."

This is the first time I hear this but I'll eventually learn about it in more detail.

Before the sessions ends he tells me he's afraid he might have had a homosexual experience and doesn't want that to ever happen. I assure him that our task in therapy includes protecting him from doing anything that will be destructive for the well-being of all his personalities.

During our session three days later the homosexual theme comes up again. Jay mentions things that bother him: the color red, the smell of alcohol, and being called a homosexual. "I'm a virgin to the homosexual thing," he says, emphasizing that he knows nothing about homosexuality, doesn't want to be a homosexual, and believes homosexuals don't ever change. However, because of his memory lapses he worries there may have been times when he abused alcohol and carried out homosexual acts.

I bring the focus back once again to his fear of closeness and affection, which he avoids because it's associated with sexuality.

Jay's discovery of female articles in his locker prompts me to read about cross-dressing. I will later find an article published in 1984, wherein the authors study over twenty-five different homosexual cross-dressers. They find cross-dressing per se often begins before puberty in a small minority of boys who fantasize themselves as females. Some cross-dressers grow up to become homosexuals, although the majority don't identify themselves that way until they become adults.

The authors describe homosexual cross-dressers as having personalities on a gradient from being passive at one end to hyper-aggressive and narcissistic at the other end. Both groups tend to be emotionally labile and histrionic. Those on the aggressive end of the gradient may have episodes of crude or violent behaviors. Those on the passive-effeminate side often have a propensity for music, dance, and refined behaviors, which typifies Shea's interests as a twenty-some-year-old. Cross-dressers often have a rich fantasy life that may include being celebrities or stars on the stage and screen. They may visualize themselves as glamour queens with amusing and outrageous impersonations meant to show up straight society as square or pretentious. Those who call themselves drag queens can be preoccupied with costumes and make-up, and often pursue a life style of drag bars and parties.

Cross-dressing homosexuals seek out personal identities that temporarily fulfill their needs for recognition and fulfillment. They hope to consolidate their self-identities with exciting transformation fantasies that will counteract a pervasive sense of deadness, depression and identity-diffusion. These behaviors will momentarily fulfill that purpose but will be repeated frequently and very often become addicting.[55]

CHAPTER 58

It happened in Seattle and I know it was my fault.
I deserve to be punished.

May 3-10, 1976

Jay struggles to write his name when asked to sign in. When I ask him about it he says he doesn't feel like himself. "I'm having a lot of feelings that I never had before."

"What kind of feelings?" I ask.

"I feel scared, angry and very much confused. And I don't know why."

"What do you think is behind it?" I ask.

Jay brings up several things that upset him. First his dreams are very real, which stick in his mind, including dreams about his ring. Second, he doesn't like the red-striped slacks I'm wearing today. Third, he's upset because two people in his group got into a fight that resulted in an injury and drops of blood on the floor.

"Seeing red blood must have triggered a memory from the past, maybe a fight in Seattle or something?" I ask.

Jay looks away from me because of my red-striped slacks and tells me he feels like he's not worth much value.

"I place a great deal of value in you, Jay," I reply sympathetically.

"Don't," he insists.

"Are you afraid something bad will happen if I value you?"

310

"I know every time I value someone then something bad happens," Jay says, and then asks me if I've been drinking.

"No I haven't. Why are you asking?"

He shakes his head. "I don't want to remember that. You wouldn't think much of me," he says.

Since the color red arouses his sensory memory of the rape trauma, I assume it is also associated with the smell of alcohol. I assure him those memories don't influence my opinion of him. "I wouldn't feel any less of you if it happened. I certainly wouldn't punish you, and besides I think you've been punishing yourself for years."

"It happened in Seattle and I know it was my fault. I deserve to be punished," he insists.

"I want you to forgive yourself for things that happened in the past," I assert.

Rather than talk about the rape memory he brings up a different memory. "I can't forgive myself for Fang dying." He hangs his head and  tries to hold back his tears. "I'd be better off if you'd just do away with me," he moans.

"I would never do that."

We spend time talking about his continuing grief about the loss of Fang, his pet dog. Before the session ends we repeat our discussion about his fear of expressing affectionate feelings. I assure him that expressing affection should be good and I make it clear that Shea will not allowed to be sexually active in this hospital because of its destructive effect on James.

When we meet three days later, Jay is wearing old clothes with paint on his trousers, and his hair is in a ponytail shaped like a bun. He talks in a soft voice and tells me he's confused, depressed, and would rather be dead. He gestures with his hands and tells me he can't accept what happened in Seattle. But he also says he wants to feel like his old self and that's why he purchased new dress pants and a shirt. When I ask him where he plans to wear his new clothes he brushes me off and changes the subject.

He closes his eyes and stops talking for a time but then tells me he likes to put on an act. He says he pretends that he is interested in the people who engage him in conversation when, in fact, he isn't. I give him advice about how he can talk to people without putting on an act, and ask if there is a reason he is wearing old clothes spotted with paint rather than the nice dress clothes he purchased. He can't give me a good answer, which makes me wonder if he bought those clothes to put on an act. Perhaps the state of his soiled clothing may reflect his real feelings. "Your depression today is fairly significant. Last time you asked if I could do away with you, and I can see that your feelings associated with that request are still there."

"This is the only time I can sit and think and talk but I don't feel like talking about that."

"It's significant that today you haven't complained about the other personality. Did he buy the clothes?" I ask, referring to Shea.

"There are things I prefer not to discuss," he says. Then he tells me how frightened he is. "I went five days without moving even my eyelids or parts of my body. I made myself do it because it's the only way I knew how to cope with what happened."

"Maybe you kept yourself from moving so you could keep yourself in control. Because every time you let loose of your control a little bit that's scary, since you don't know what's going to happen."

"There is no reason I need to give up control," he insists.

"Over the past month you have taken some risks and you've let me help you. You need to be patient because this is a slow process and you're still struggling with it."

"Why is it so hard?"

"I know it's hard and I can't really answer that question."

He doesn't give me a good answer about why he bought new clothes, which makes me think Shea bought them. After we continue to talk about his depression I look at the clock and let him know we need to talk about this important subject next time.

When we meet a week later on Monday, May 10, he signs in as Jay. I see that he's in a positive mood, particularly since he gives me a fresh flower. But he also complains about his memory lapses. He says he doesn't remember his parents visiting him this past weekend, and only learned about it when the staff told him. He also says he can't recall meeting with me last week.

"I seem to have been bamboozled by whoever came to therapy last time since it was not you," I say. Then he tells me Shea met with me last time and is with me today. He assures me that he's been very discreet and can disguise his presence, but swears he does not want to replace Jay completely. "I let Jay take all the responsibilities because I don't wanna take 'em," he smirks.

CHAPTER 59

*Jay reveals that he and Shea no longer share homosexual desires.
Shea reveals he would like to seduce me.*

May 17, 1976

Jay signs in and tells me early in today's session that he feels scared. He's having dreams so real he can't get them out of his mind. In one dream he tries to take the ring off his finger but he can't. In another dream he is fighting off shock treatments.

I listen to his fears and offer my support. Then I ask to talk with Shea. After a quick dissociation Shea emerges, and I suggest we watch the videotape from our session on May 3, which includes James' reliving the rape trauma in Seattle. Shea watches the session and is superficially sympathetic about James' horrific experience, but also admits he found the event pleasurable.

I ask him to explain why and he says, "If you enjoy it then there's no problem."

"You faced these problems by pretending to enjoy it?" I ask.

"I wasn't pretending," he disagrees.

I ask about his first memories and how he happened to get the name Shea, but he says he can't recall any details, although he says his mother gave him the name.

"I don't understand. Your mother gave you that name?"

"Yeah 'cause she thought I was happy all the time." Shea recalls being a happy-go-lucky teenager, but he wasn't involved in homosexual activity until years later.

I ask if he ever felt bad about becoming sexually active, but he says he learned to put up a front and avoid the truth.

"I wonder how Jay feels about the front you put up. Can you let me talk to him?" I ask.

Shea agrees and after a brief pause I see a dissociation and Jay appears. He quickly tells me Shea's behavior was detestable. It has caused him to feel like he's a homosexual, which he loathes.

I assure him he's not a homosexual and he can be affectionate without having sex.

After this brief discussion Jay tells me he wants to stop talking about this. He shuts his eyes and after a moment I see a dissociation take place. Suddenly I see a man sitting in front of me I have not encountered before.

"What's your name?" I ask.

"I'm Robert Random," he replies.

"It's nice to meet you. Can you tell me who I am?"

"You're Dr. Brende."

"How long have you known me?"

"I don't know," he replies.

He provides no more information about himself so I ask to talk with Jay, who reappears rather quickly. I resume my questions about his relationship with Shea, and learn that they had a close relationship that included sharing surreal recollections of going sex-hunting. Jay tells me the color red used to excite him sexually

316

but not any longer. Now when he sees the color red it scares him and brings back disturbing memories. "I don't wanna remember that night. Not that night. That's why I don't like people who drink or have body odor!" he exclaims.

I ask to talk with Shea once again and Jay willingly allows the switch to take place. When Shea appears he grins at me and says, "I'm horny and I wanna weekend pass."

I make it very clear that neither his hospital doctor nor I will approve a pass to leave the hospital. Furthermore I make it clear that I don't approve of his homosexual behavior because it would likely cause disturbing effects on his other personalities.

He does not object to my disapprovals.

I ask why he feels horny and he laughs. "I don't know if I could seduce you but I'd probably try."

Our time has come to a close, after this session revealed Jay's shared homosexual behavior with Shea during his twenties. It also exposed once again the rape trauma's horrific effect on James, but seems to have caused Jay to turn away from homosexuality, while intensifying Shea's homosexual activity.

Shea's expression of his sexual fantasies prompts me to read about this subject. Sigmund Freud was the first to describe the phenomenon of the erotic transference and theorized that it draws on and transfers earlier life experiences onto the therapist. His observations were based on a female patient's love fantasies toward a male therapist, and I wonder if his theory would also apply to homosexuals. As I search the literature about erotic transference in a homosexual patient there is very little mention of

317

it. I find references involving a homosexual male patient expressing sexual fantasies to a homosexual therapist. But I find none directed toward a straight therapist. The therapist must always value the therapeutic relationship as essential and recognize the possibility there may be legitimate love. But the therapist must also be aware of other motives for the patient's erotic transference. Freud recognized that women might use the erotic transference in an attempt to compromise the physician's authority, avoid feeling inferior, and equalize the therapeutic relationship. While there have been reports of true love occurring between patient and therapist they've primarily occurred when the relationship was heterosexual.[56]

CHAPTER 60

*There were times I woke up in bed with a man
and ran home like a scared chicken.*

May 20-24, 1976

The patient arrives wearing black slacks and a white shirt.
He signs in as Jay and begins the session on a positive note, telling
me he feels relaxed, hasn't had any nightmares, and was granted a
pass to go fishing with a group of patients and staff at a nearby
lake. When I ask if he recalls the last session, he remembers we
talked about homosexuality and also that Dr. Baird once diagnosed
him as being homosexual. He remembers being upset when he
learned about that diagnosis and insisted he's not one. Any
reminders of being raped, including seeing the color red, cause him
to feel like running and screaming, but he's able to calm himself
down by counting to ten. Of interest is the fact that he tells me he's
recently been aware of homosexual thoughts, but the idea of
having sex with a man is abhorrent to him, and he avoids talking
about sex with anyone except me.

I point out to him that his sexuality may be unclear since
he's reported dreams and perceptions that show both heterosexual
and homosexual desires.

"That's true," he says. "But I don't like to think about being
homosexual. And I'm glad I passed out when that rape happened
in Seattle because I don't wanna remember it."

We spend considerable time talking about his recurring traumatic memories, his poor self-esteem, and his desire to become whole. As our session comes to a close I encourage him to continue pursuing his goal. "It's possible to maintain your self-esteem and become entirely whole like you want to be and, in the future, remember only that which you want to remember. That should be our goal."

When we meet four days later Jay appears depressed. He says that he can't clear his mind and wonders if he can get shock treatments again to block the thoughts and memories like four years ago. "Dr. Brende, there's a fight going on inside my head. There are two thoughts fighting each other and I can't stop 'em."

"Can you tell me more about the thoughts?"

"There's one about wanting to have sex and another that's fighting against it 'cause it makes me sick. And I keep remembering the red jacket."

"What do you remember?"

Jay tells me he remembers the rape in some detail, which indicates the presence of a porous boundary between him and James, the victim personality who experienced it. "There were two drunken Indians and the biggest wore a red jacket. And I can't stop smelling the alcohol on his breath."

"I haven't heard you say before that they were two drunken Indians. When did you remember that?" I ask.

"I don't know. I never saw them before or after."

"You continue to have bad memories and also concerns about your own sexual orientation," I say.

"I know. I've started looking at males and wonder what it would feel like to have sex with them. It makes me feel like a queer but I know I'm not. And I know I can't solve this on my own."

"I agree you can't solve this on your own."

"How can you help me?" he asks.

At this point I ask a question pertaining to the transference since it's important to clarify all potential conflicts. "I'm wondering if you may have sexual feelings toward me?" I ask.

Jay frowns. "No I don't!" he insists. "I don't like those thoughts and when I have 'em I feel like I'm losing." Jay gazes downward and appears to be deep in thought. He turns his head away and says, "I didn't tell you this before but there have been times when I woke up and found myself in bed with a man."

"What did you do?"

"I ran home like a scared chicken and then I showered for hours and hours," he says shamefully.

I provide empathic support for him and then, realizing our time is close to ending, reluctantly let him know I'll be absent for ten days. Jay is clearly disturbed about that information and spontaneously dissociates. I see his head drop as he switches to James. I'm saddened to see him begin to cry and reach my hand over to provide emotional support. He holds on to my hand and remains in the body for a brief time before switching back to Jay, who wipes his eyes and looks at me.

"You know that James finds it difficult to deal with my absence. But you provide a great deal of support for him," I say.

"Yeah he has trouble when you're gone."

Before the session comes to an end I make an observation about each personality's responses to my absence: Jay has never wanted to depend on anyone, including me. By doing that he can avoid feeling abandoned. James needs to depend on me, consequently he's very vulnerable to feelings of abandonment.

CHAPTER 61

Shea says, "I feel I could be replaced by a vacancy. Permanently!"

June 3-7, 1976

When Jay arrives for our first session after my ten-day absence, he tells me that he thought we were supposed to meet last Monday. He asked an escort to accompany him to the studio but when he didn't find me there he went to my office. After discovering I wasn't in my office he felt confused. One part of him could not believe I was gone and wanted to remain there, but the other part felt abandoned and wanted to run away. "I felt like I was living in two different worlds!" he exclaims.

This incident exposed the two personalities' reactions to real or potential abandonment. James experienced intense emotional pain while Jay, who has always denied feeling anything, can now for the first time sense James' experience of loss.

When we meet again four days later I'm surprised to see him sign the name Shea. After meeting Shea during my early sessions with Jay, I was unaware of his presence until he reappeared six months ago during a session on January 12, and signed in as Shea von Kohlman. I've seen him twice after that but this is the first time he has signed in at the beginning of a session. I acknowledge his presence and, at my request, he tells me more about his early life. Although I have heard James' childhood memories, Shea's memories are slightly different. He remembers having a good relationship with his parents and growing up on a farm where they raised a number of pets and farm animals.

When I ask if he remembers our last meeting he says, "It feels like one hundred years ago but I think it was last week."

I ask about his relationship to James, and he tells me that he has some awareness of James' feelings but has no awareness of his own, although he has recently begun to feel scared.

"When are you scared?" I ask.

"When it's real dark. Sometimes I like the dark but mostly I don't like it."

"Why did you sign your name Shea today?"

"I don't know. I just signed it that way."

"In other words you don't want me to know who you are?" I ask.

"That's why I have mixed feelings about you because you know me better than anyone else."

I mention that he's not been here very often and has apparently been replaced many times.

"I feel I could be replaced by a vacancy. Permanently!" he asserts.

"What does that mean?"

"If I wasn't here someone else would be here. I like to be here but I won't get in a fist fight about it."

"There are times you're not here. Maybe that's the vacancy."

"Yeah. And that makes me mad."

I ask him if he knows anything about his other personalities, and he answers that he only knows who he is. "I know what I am and the reason I am. I am an un-understandable homosexual."

"How did you become homosexual?" I ask.

"I tried being heterosexual and it was a bunch of garbage. Then after what happened in Seattle there was nothing I could do about it."

"What happened in Seattle was very traumatic. What do you remember?"

"It wasn't traumatic for me but I remember being held down with bodies laying on me. The closeness was almost pleasant." He pauses, then continues with a smirk, "Maybe I was willing."

"I wonder, were you and Jay starved for physical closeness growing up?"

"Maybe so. But in our family I didn't really want closeness."

"Do you have mixed feelings physical closeness?"

"I have mixed feelings about my parents," he replies. After a long pause he changes the subject and asks why he's having constant thoughts about two different philosophies, when he used to have only one philosophy. I ask him if he would like my assistance to help him better understand but he rejects my offer. "I don't think I'm worth it. I lie all the time anyway. I've messed up my life. How can you help me with that?" he asks in frustration.

Shea is asking for help for the first time to understand his messed up his life and his two different philosophies, which are really his different "selves." Is this a step closer to an integration I wonder?

CHAPTER 62

*He draws himself as two parts. One part is crying
and another part is sarcastic.*

June 17, 1976

The patient arrives wearing casual clothes. After sitting down, he looks at me and says he wants to sign the name Robert Random.

"Why?" I ask.

"I like the name Robert."

"You can sign that name but you also need to sign your legal name," I reply.

He signs two names: James and Robert Random. Then he puts the pen down, looks at me and complains. "I don't like the name James."

I'm surprised to see a new personality and ask him why he's here.

"I don't know," he replies.

"There must be some reason," I say.

"Sure. I'm a wild man, very high-strung, obnoxious, and I can sit around for hours and not say a word. Or I can cry," he replies sarcastically.

"If I haven't talked to you before what do you want me to call you?"

"Call me Kohlman."

"Okay Kohlman. Why don't you tell me about yourself?"

His answer is brief. "I was in the military and I got medically retired due to epilepsy."

"I know you're receiving a medication for epilepsy. But since that's not a problem any more, how would you describe your problem now?"

"I don't know. I feel pretty scattered. I sure know my dreams are scattered."

"Scattered? Into how many parts?"

He tells me he feels scattered into two parts. One part is crying and another part is sarcastic.

I bring out a chalkboard and ask him to draw the parts. He gets out his chair and walks over to the chalkboard. He draws two small oblong circles, one slightly larger than the other. They are disconnected and one is higher and larger than the other. I assume they represent two different personalities.

I suggest that they represent two parts of himself and ask him if I can talk to the bigger and more intact part.

He nods, closes his eyes, and waits. I see a smooth dissociation develop and a familiar personality opens his eyes. "I'm Jay. I think you want to talk to me," he announces.

"Why did you come today?" I ask.

"Because you can help me find a reason for being here, and tell me why I have scary dreams that are so real they actually happen," he replies.

We spend the rest of the session reviewing his history, which is somewhat similar to what Shea told me last time. I wonder if Shea is phasing himself out. Before our session ends I remind him that our treatment goal has been to help him feel whole.

I had asked him to draw what I believed were two parts of himself on a chalkboard for a therapeutic purpose, illustrating how art therapy can be an effective adjunct to psychotherapy. It's described as one of the expressive therapies that include dance, movement, music, poetry, and psychodrama. An art therapist can use one of the mediums—pencil, paint, crayon, collage, or sculpture—to delve more deeply into a patient's thoughts and emotions to uncover important issues or conflicts that haven't been put into words.[57]

CHAPTER 63

*Since Saturday everyone has asked me, "Who are you
and where did you come from? I don't understand."*

June 19, 1976.

Shea arrives today looking well dressed in blue pants, a
white shirt and a wig. After signing in he tells me he spent $300 on
new clothes so he can dress and leave quickly before someone
leaves him. It is now five months from his appearance on January
12 and I suspect, from recent things he has said, that he expects to
be leaving the body soon. He insists that he doesn't want to
maintain ties with anyone who might leave him. "Anything or
anyone I ever got attached to either left or died. But that's never
going to happen again because I will always leave first," he insists.

I face the challenge of convincing him that I have no plans to
leave but he doesn't believe me.

Why are you wearing a wig?" I ask to change the subject.

"I've got two wigs. I need a wig because it makes me feel
twenty-eight or twenty-nine. Without a wig I feel like I'm ninety
years old."

"You're not even close to that age. Do you remember what
year you were born?"

"I can only remember back to 1968 or 1969. But I'm not
interested in talking about my age."

"Do you know how old you really are?"

"You make me feel like I need a wheelchair asking these questions about age. And don't push me. I don't like to be pushed. That absolutely irritates me."

"Asking your age is pushing you?"

"Since last Saturday everyone has asked me who I am and where I came from. I don't understand it."

"Apparently the other patients haven't seen you in a wig. Why are you wearing a wig now?"

"It goes with these clothes. And I wanna look decent for this meeting. I can't remember when I've seen you last."

I'm surprised he can't remember coming to a therapy session, since his most recent appearance was our last meeting on June 7. But it's easy to see why the patients don't recognize him since his flamboyant appearance and effeminate gesturing make him appear dramatically different today.

"I try not to remember things. All memories end up bad," he insists.

"If you can't remember them how do you know they end up bad?"

"What about my memories of being in this hospital? I don't have any good memories about it."

"Do you remember Dr. Baird? And Gilbert?"

"I try not to. They left as I recall."

"And you think I'm going to leave?"

"It doesn't matter what I think because I'll leave you first."

"I know you've had losses and other painful things happen that you don't want to remember. Do you think you're running from painful feelings in the past?"

"Maybe."

"How were you able to run away from the painful rape experience in Seattle in 1968?"

"That was easy. I became a homosexual."

It's surprising to hear Shea say that he became a homosexual after being raped in Seattle and that his memories only go back to 1968 or 1969. Is it possible that Shea's existence began after the rape, even though I remember hearing him say during an earlier session that he first became a homosexual during his twenties while he was in the Air Force? Or did the rape primarily exaggerate the differences between James, the victim, and Shea, the homosexual? Shea describes the rape as a pleasurable experience and James describes it as a horrendous trauma that caused shame and post-traumatic symptoms ever since.

"Maybe that was your way of dealing with it. But how has James dealt with it?" I ask.

"He can't deal with it. He believes love is destructive," Shea says.

"If you're equating sex and love I don't believe love destroyed James in 1968. It was the rape. And that had nothing to do with sex!" I exclaim.

"Well since you're talking about love and sex I believe there's love for love, love for sex, and sex for no love."

"Meaningful sexual relationships only happen when there are meaningful loving relationships. And for you to have sex with another male would be destructive for you and for James now," I emphasize.

"I'll think about that."

I ask him to think about James' painful experiences of abandonment and other traumas, but he is not interested in talking about that. Neither does he want me to mention James' name.

"I know James is my real name. But hearing that name is upsetting," he insists.

"Why?"

"He's part of a family that I don't wanna be part of."

"So are you are outsider to that family?"

"Yes! I definitely am."

"Talking about your relationship to James is a crucial part of your therapy. But before we stop today let me tell you again that I will not be leaving, which should be reassuring for you and for James."

CHAPTER 64

Jay tries to forget Seattle because it makes him feel dirty.

June 21-24, 1976

After signing in Jay tells me he has no memory that he even met with me last Thursday and feels confused.

"Do you remember when you last saw me?" I ask.

"Last Monday," he replies, clearly indicating he was absent when Shea met with me last time.

"Since you weren't at the session last Thursday would you like to see the tape?" I ask.

Jay frowns slightly but then nods his head and tells me he would like to see it. Dick immediately agrees to play the tape. Jay begins to view it and seems to recognize Shea, but quickly becomes annoyed when he sees Robert Random.

"That person is crazier than I am and it makes me angry to see it!" he exclaims.

"Do you think you have feelings now you didn't have before?" I ask.

He squints and tells me he doesn't know about feelings and can't understand what's happening to him. Then I tell Jay that Shea met with me last time and said he was a homosexual.

"I don't like it! That's for sure. It makes me feel dirty when I remember Seattle. I'd like to kill those sonofabitching rapists!" he exclaims.

I listen to Jay tell me he feels dirty when remembering what happened in Seattle, although he claims that he has no feelings about it. I explain that Shea has wrongly equated sex with love. "Shea's homosexuality has been destructive to him. He says sex and love are equivalent but I disagree. It's important to be able to love someone without needing sex. What do you think is the normal relationship between love and sex?" I ask.

Jay reveals his own confusion about this subject and states he can't think of love without also thinking about sex. But he also says he's always tried to love people for what they are.

Before the session ends I ask Jay if he will allow me to talk with James. He says he has no objection and he'd like a break. So Jay closes his eyes and after a moment I see a dissociation. A personality emerges who appears to be James. After my brief visit with him I ask Jay to return so that he can leave this session feeling positive.

We meet again three days later. Jay tells me that he is depressed and feels like he has no purpose other than to be the one who fills in when James is gone.

I ask him to be more specific and he tells me that he feels like running away, but realizes he can't do that. I ask if he has requested anti-depressant medication from his hospital doctor.

He shakes his head. "I don't want medication 'cause I'm scared to take it."

"What are some other ways you can cope with your depressed feelings?" I ask.

"The problem is that I'm alive. If I was dead I wouldn't have any problems," he says morbidly. "I feel like a phony. All I do is play a role to be whatever people want," he complains.

"Would you rather be a whole person?"

"Maybe being a whole person isn't worth having bad feelings. I'd rather play roles."

"Are you playing roles with me?" I ask.

"Do you think I'm playing roles with you? I feel like I've lost control. I can't even switch roles when I want to."

"Why do you want to switch roles?"

"Because it's easy. Sometimes it's easy to be Jay and sometimes it's easy to be Shea. Sometimes I wish I was just Shea."

"If you were Shea that might be easy because Shea doesn't have any feelings."

Jay tells me he is not a homosexual and can't pretend to be Shea. Furthermore, he doesn't want to play roles or games with me. I give him credit for his honesty and let him know I'm aware of the difficulty he may have keeping track of the different personalities. I also let him know I'm aware he's scared to depend on someone else, and that he's also afraid to love or be loved.

Before the session closes I assure him again that I am not going to leave or discontinue therapy.

During this session Shea's depiction of his exaggerated homosexual behavior, which began after James was raped could be described by the idiom: "If you can't lick them, join 'em." In psychological terms his behavior fit the description of the mental defense called "identification with the aggressor."

335

This same mental defense has also been described as the Stockholm syndrome, based on an actual event in 1973 when two men held four people hostage for six days after a bank robbery in Stockholm, Sweden. After the hostages were released, they refused to testify against their captors and even began raising money for their defense. This exemplified how victims identified with their persecutors. This same phenomenon was experienced by Patty Hearst, who was kidnapped in 1974 by a terrorist organization called the Symbionese Army. She later participated with them during a bank robbery and was brought to trial. Although she was convicted and sentenced to seven years in prison, many people believed she was a victim of the Stockholm syndrome.

CHAPTER 65
Shea has a premonition he'll be pushed off into darkness.

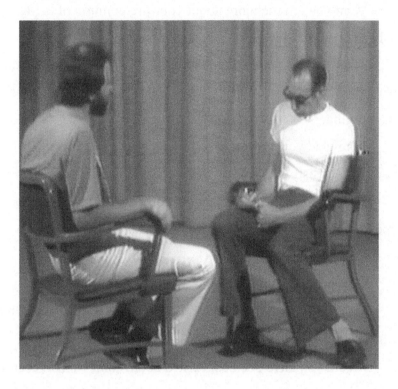

June 25, 1976

He has a flashy appearance today, wearing classy blue jeans and a white shirt and sunglasses.

He signs in as Shea and almost immediately tells me he's had a premonition he'll be pushed off a cliff into darkness. He also says he was told this morning that he had a very disturbing nightmare last night that scared everyone. He became so disruptive that the doctor on call ordered medication to calm him down. He refused to take it just like he refused his prescribed medications earlier in the evening.

"Are you feeling suicidal?" I ask.

"No I'm not."

"Can you tell me more about your premonition of being pushed off a cliff?"

"That's easy. I won't be here," he replies. Then he tells me his nightmare was so disturbing he asked to talk to a social worker this morning.

"I'm glad you asked for help. Why don't you also talk to me about it?" I insist.

"I didn't even know the social worker and I don't wanna depend on you or anybody else for help. But can you answer a question?" he asks.

"Sure. What's your question?"

"Why do you think I refused to take medications last night?" he asks.

"Well, you have been concerned about some things recently. One concern was that you might take an overdose. It happened once before you know," I explain.

"They keep telling me that. When did that happen?"

"It happened the day after Thanksgiving."

Talking about this subject, about which he claims to have no memory, triggers considerable anxiety. "They say I only have that much to go before I go into darkness," he moans while displaying two fingers close together.

I ask him to tell me more specifically about what he's afraid will happen, and he replies that he just won't be here.

"Where will you be?" I ask.

"I'm not sure. I just know I'll be off a cliff into the darkness."

I ask if something happened to upset him yesterday, and he replies there were a lot of things but the worst was getting a haircut. "I thought it was amusing while it was being done," he explains.

"How do you mean?"

"Have you ever had your hair cut by a nervous barber? That was amusing to me," he smirks and then continues. "I've seen situation comedies where a guy acts very nervous and he doesn't know where to start or where to stop and his scissors are snapping like an alligator's jaw. It's amusing at first but after awhile it becomes sordid."

"So were you watching the haircut from a distance?" I ask.

"Yeah. But then I'm right there. Which is hard to understand. That's why I think these are nightmares."

"Was that a nightmare when you watched your hair get cut?" I ask.

"Yes it was. I felt like I was being pushed. Not dragged. Not coached. Not beckoned. Just pushed."

"By whom?" I ask.

"I don't know. I'm just being pushed by a bunch of people. They push and then they go off and have a coffee break and they come back and start pushing again."

"Where to? Pushing you away somewhere?"

"Well, yeah!" he exclaims.

"Over a cliff?" I ask, still finding it hard to understand.

"That's the feeling I have."

"What's the feeling? Fear?"

"It's not a good sensation."

"You could be killed?" I ask.

"I don't think I'm going to be killed. Have you ever jumped out of an airplane? It's something you won't forget. And then you'll have another sensation when you are jerked by your parachute before you hit the ground. And it's like being pushed off a cliff. And there's nothing else there. It's a beautiful place. I'd like to go there."

"Where is this place?"

"It's just black. It's a BLACK black. Right around the black it's kinda white. And it has silver dust sprinkled all through it."

"Hum."

"I'd love to paint it. But I think you'd have to be a genius to get it just like I see it."

"You can see it?"

"Yes. I can see it almost all the time lately since this feeling came up." He pauses and then asks, "Do you know why I wanted to meet with you today?"

"No, but I know you said yesterday you were upset and scared. Does it have anything to do with your relationship with me?" I ask.

"I'm not sure."

"It may be related to having positive feelings toward me and feeling afraid that you will lose our relationship."

"I'd be left in no man's land. Sure I like to see you. Even with my dark glasses on."

Before our session comes to a close he mentions that he had come to the studio to see me yesterday but was surprised when I wasn't there. Perhaps he wanted to say goodbye.

CHAPTER 66

Jay tells me Shea has disappeared.
Jim relives a trauma of being struck.

June 28, 1976

The patient comes to today's session wearing a tan jumpsuit and signs in as Jay. He tells me he's been struggling with fear during the day and nightmares at night. He had one about Seattle that was so real he woke up drenched in sweat. "I feel so scared and I have to go hide from everyone because I get so upset. I don't know what I'm doing and it's upsetting."

"Is there anything else that might be scaring you?" I ask.

"He said he loved me."

"Who said he loved you?"

"He did. And I don't need it."

"Who's he?"

"Like it's a voice but it's not a voice. He looks like me but he's much younger than I am. I just don't understand."

"Can you be more specific about him?"

"I try to understand him but I can't understand him any longer. I can't tolerate him."

"You can't tolerate that he loves you?" I ask.

"I don't need problems," he replies.

"Love is a problem?" I ask.

"Yes. Love is a problem."

I wonder if the voice he hears is a younger Shea or the memory of his father or other family member. Then he tells me how painful it is to lose someone or something he loves. "I remember feeling pain when the Air Force told me they didn't need me any more. I felt abandoned. It was a terrible pain."

"It's terrible to be abandoned," I agree.

"But you learn to live with it," he says in resignation.

"But it's even worse if you have to keep those feelings to yourself and not tell anyone," I reply.

"But I'm feeling guilty about saying these things to you," he says, and then adds that if he feels guilty that brings on self-pity, which he abhors. Furthermore he doesn't want me to pity him.

I ask him if his family members expressed love to each other and he replies that his mother was loving but he didn't trust her.

"Love never will be honest," he bemoans as he lifts his arms but keeps his eyes downcast.

"Do you think I have loving feelings toward you?" I ask.

"I don't know. I'm confused," he replies and lowers his head.

"I see that you have tears in your eyes."

"That's what they are. They're tears. I'm not bawling. They're just tears that's all. I'm not a bawl-baby. I'm just not a bawl-baby," he insists.

"I never said you were. But I think you've heard people call you a bawl-baby."

"I am not. I'm not," he insists while struggling to hold back his tears. His eyes remain closed and his right arm moves up and down with his right hand hanging limp.

I ask him to remember a time when he was called a bawl-baby but he remains silent. Yet his tears flow.

"You're crying now. The tears are coming down," I say and ask him to describe his feelings. "Can you tell me what's happening?"

Rather than speak he continues to cry and raises his right hand to caress the side of his face.

"What's happening?" I ask.

Finally he speaks. "It won't hurt. It won't hurt."

"What's happening?" I repeat as I reach out with my left arm and touch his right shoulder.

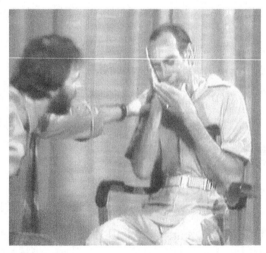

I see him begin to dissociate. To my surprise he begins to relive a painful childhood event.

"It won't hurt," he blubbers.

"What won't hurt?" I ask.

"I just wanted his hand. I just wanted the hand," he mumbles.

I repeat his words as a mirroring technique.

"I just wanted his hand. Why did it turn into such a heavy door?" he moans. He brings his hands up to each side of his face in an attempt to comfort himself, but his eyes remain closed.

"What do you mean by heavy door? Did you hit your head on it?" I ask, uncertain about what he's reliving.

"No it's not a door."

In order to clarify, I ask him to tell me what's happening and where it's taking place.

"I'm in the yard," he states.

"How old are you?"

"Seven," he mumbles softly.

"Seven? Something happened that hurt you. And you didn't get the kind of sympathy you wanted?"

His eyes open and tears stop flowing. He remains silent but his face is pained.

"Did someone hit you?" I ask, knowing that a door was not the offending object.

"Daddy hit me," he replies softly.

"I'm sorry. You didn't want to be hit. You loved your Daddy and you wanted his love."

"Yes," he whispers.

"He loved you too but he had difficulty expressing it," I say, giving his father the benefit of a positive perspective.

"I just wanted his hand," he repeats softly.

"And he hurt you. Physically and emotionally," I say empathically, but then make corrective statements to provide a healing experience. "Can you imagine that he is caring for you and saying, 'Jim, I'm sorry I hit you.' Let yourself imagine that is happening right now. He's really sorry and he wants to be loving toward you, because you deserve more than being hit. You deserve affection. I want you to believe that."

 His face and body appear frozen in place—almost catatonic—as his hands remain close to his face and his eyes stare blankly downward. It appears to be James' physiological response to the experience of being struck by his father—a cessation of movement, which seems like catatonia.

"You've always been afraid of affection but you don't have to be afraid any more," I continue.

He remains physically motionless.

"Are you listening to me?" I ask softly.

He nods slightly.

"Okay. Don't let yourself be afraid of affection."

"I'm not afraid of affection," he replies, but I see him smile slightly as his hands come together in a prayerful motion, his face becomes mournful, and his hands pull apart. I also hear a change in his attitude, which makes me believe I'm talking to a different personality.

"I can understand why Jim would be afraid," I explain.

He nods his head and closes his eyes.

I see a subtle dissociation and I ask, "Who are you?"

He breaks the silence and says, "I can't hang on any longer." I see him struggle to speak as the ring moves to the little finger on his left hand, indicating the presence of Shea. He laughs in a weird way and closes his eyes. I hear no more sound. He is gone!

After a brief time Jay, having replaced Shea, returns to the body but does not speak. Before the session comes to a close he picks up the picture he had given me. Then he leaves the studio with an escort.

Later in the day I reviewed the tape of this unusual session and picked out the key elements: Jay came to the session and reported a scary nightmare about his rape trauma in Seattle. He expressed his fear of giving or receiving love because it has been associated with memories of sexual exploitation, physical injury, and rejection. He relived an experience of being struck in the head by his father, whom he thought loved him. Then his body stiffened and I saw a cessation of movement that seemed like catatonia, a condition I have encountered in occasional psychiatric patients during my career. What was unique about James' catatonia is that it was a likely response to his traumatic memory of being struck by his father. Individuals exposed to extreme stress typically respond with heightened sympathetic nervous system activity, causing a rapid heart rate. James experienced something less common—a freeze response that spread throughout his body via the parasympathetic nervous system, and caused a slowing of all physiological functions, like a catatonia.

CHAPTER 67

There has been a major personality shift.
"Shea's dead," Jay announces.

June 30-July 1, 1976

This significant session on June 30 is marked by Jay's appearance at my office door for an unscheduled meeting. "Shea is dead!" he announces and goes on to tell me Shea disappeared two days ago and is no longer in the body.

I'm not surprised to hear this since Shea had told me during his last meeting with me five days ago he expected to drop off a cliff into nothingness. I'm struck by the fact that Shea's "death" occurred just six months after Jay was "killed."

Jay tells me today that he feels different. "I'm trying to be a human being but I'd like to know if someone has taken away my feelings," he says.

I'm very pleased to hear Jay say he wants to learn how to be a human being, but not surprised to hear him say he can't feel anything, because his role as James' protector required him to block out all emotions.

Although Jay complains he can't feel emotions I explain that I would expect him to grieve the loss of Shea—a part of him. I also assure him that he will eventually feel reborn and experience loving feelings.

After this short and unscheduled session I escort him through Building Two and down the corridor to Building Four, where I find his hospital doctor and request that Jay come to the studio tomorrow.

On the following morning, Thursday, July 1, I receive a call from the patient's hospital doctor telling me that James tried to harm himself by hitting his head against the wall, and made demands to leave the hospital against the doctor's advice this morning. As a result James was placed on a one-to-one suicide watch. But his doctor also wants me to see James in therapy today.

I watch my patient being escorted by an aide into the studio. He's wearing hospital garb—pajamas and robe—evidence of the change in his status. After sitting down and hesitatingly signing Jay, he begins to speak in an earnest, low-pitched voice. "I guess there is something I must do!"

"What's that?" I ask.

"To have feelings like a human being I guess."

He appears confused and anxious, saying he's uncertain about what it means to be a human being. I explain that being human means to have feelings that aren't just unpleasant, like anger, but also positive feelings of love and joy. However, Jay can't absorb this information because it seems too foreign for him.

"I woke up this morning and it seemed like I had to harm myself," he explains. Then he pauses, shakes his head, closes his eyes, clasps his hands together and appears to have difficulty collecting his thoughts. He speaks in a halting voice. "I keep thinking I had to stab him so I did something else. I harmed myself instead."

I attempt to clarify. "What I hear you saying is that your feelings of love and anger are coming out in the form of thoughts of killing somebody or yourself. That's the anger side. I know you're afraid of that. What about the love side?"

He struggles to understand the idea of experiencing love. "I don't know. It seems like somebody was there this morning," he stutters. "Please don't go locking me up now."

I assure him that the staff placed him on a one-to-one suicide watch because they want to keep him safe. "It's done in love. Do you know why? Your doctor told me you were hurting yourself and wanted to leave the hospital against his advice."

His tears begin to flow. "But I have to get away because it seems like I'm going back to where I was and I don't wanna go back there." He frowns, rubs his forehead and struggles to keep his eyes open. "I feel very tired. I have a headache, and I don't feel like eating," he complains.

"I think your body is expressing feelings of pain but also of lost love because of things that have happened to you," I explain.

He frowns, stares at his feet, and closes his eyes. Then he looks at me. "Love is love. What do I know about that? I keep thinking someone else had those feelings."

"Can you tell me who the person was who had those loving feelings?" I ask, assuming he's referring to Shea.

"I don't wanna say," he replies.

"I don't understand. You've told me the name of the person before."

"Yes. And I did bring you the thing he left," Jay says, referring to the picture Shea had made to give me. "I'm not confused. I know he's dead. There's no body. There's nothing. There's just nothing." He places his hands up to his head and wipes his eyes.

"Let me tell you what's dead. It's the part of you that you didn't want," I explain.

"I think I know. That memory (of Shea's presence) is coming back."

"Can you tell me what or who you think you didn't want?"

He tells me he tried to explain to people on the ward that he is not Shea and not a homosexual. "I am not what they said I was and I couldn't convince them otherwise. And when I tried to, they kept telling me I was talking off the wall," he says.

"When was that? What did they say?"

"That I was a queer or a fairy or a homosexual." He shakes his head sadly and places his hand to his forehead again.

"Do you know why Shea was homosexual?" I ask.

"No. I don't think I really know. I only wanna guess."

"What do you guess?"

"He told me that it was not his free choice and that others wanted him to be that way. He also told me it's important for me to be a normal human being. So I'm trying to show everybody that I really am a human being. Not just act like one, but I am one!" he exclaims.

"I think that Shea would appreciate your doing that very much because he had trouble acting like a normal human being."

"I keep feeling that they liked him so much that they didn't want me around," he says sadly, realizing Shea had been more entertaining to the other patients than he was.

"That's why you needed Shea, because he felt confident and people liked him. You felt inferior and so you used Shea to cover up your low self-esteem. Now that Shea's gone and not here to help you, you're wondering if you have the strength—if you can do it alone," I explain.

"Why must I fight to prove that I am a human being?" he asks. "I'm sorry but saying that will get me in trouble."

"Why do you think you will get into trouble?" I ask.

"Every time I told anyone I was a human being I got into trouble," he replies.

"Maybe you're wondering what my response to you would be if you are a human being?" I ask to clarify the transference.

He doesn't reply and waits for me to continue.

"If you're a human being, I would expect that you'd have loving feelings toward people," I say.

"But I was told that I only had loving feelings toward you," he says with his eyes closed and his hands rubbing his temples. He continues, "Shea told me that he loved you and loved me."

"You're afraid of having those same feelings?" I ask.

"Because love is different for me compared to what Shea had," he stammers.

"Can you elaborate how it was different?"

"You can love without having…" He hesitates.

"Without having sex?" I ask.

"Yes."

"Shea knew that too," I explain.

"No, he didn't."

"With me he did. He loved me and he didn't have sex with me," I clarify.

"I'm glad that he didn't have that with you," Jay exclaims.

"The same thing is possible for you."

"Then to love becomes wrong. And if I love it's wrong and they will take other things from me."

"Do you think I might expect something else from you?" I ask, wondering if he's afraid I might sexually abuse him.

"I don't know what to expect, Dr. Brende."

"Do you expect to be abused by a person you have loving feelings for?"

He nods yes.

"Let me assure you that I won't abuse you and I'll accept your love."

"As a human being?" he asks.

"Yes. As a human being, and I won't abuse you or misuse you."

He pauses, then apologizes for feeling confused and not being able to express love like a human being. He lifts his right hand over his eyes and tells me it's too hard to be human and to keep from hurting someone.

I assure him that he can trust me and I won't let him hurt anyone. My assurance seems to empower him to continue his efforts to stay alive.

"I'm going to eat. I'm going to keep taking my medication. I'm going to sleep. And I want my clothes again," he says slowly but emphatically.

I assure him I'm pleased he is committed to being alive. I also clarify the reality of his situation—that he will only get his clothes back after his hospital doctor believes he's no longer at risk to hurt himself.

He tells me he can't remember trying to hurt himself, and doesn't remember much of yesterday, including the fact I walked him back to his ward after our meeting.

To help clarify his lost memories I explain I had talked with the members of the hospital staff about his need to remain in the hospital. Jay replies he doesn't trust his hospital doctor to not give him shock treatments, but I assure him that won't happen and encourage him to test his doctor and staff to see for himself that they are trustworthy. We conclude this session by talking about his desire to feel love and affection and I hear him say that he wants to cry.

Jay had walked down to my office yesterday to tell me that Shea died. He also said he sensed something different inside him and wondered if someone took away his feelings. I suspect that Jay feels emotionally numb, which is the first phase of the grieving process. Today his hospital doctor called to say he placed Jay on suicide watch because he stabbed himself. Jay is grieving the loss

355

of a person he's been very close to, even though that person is a part of himself. Jay and Shea were so close it was nearly impossible for most patients to tell them apart. Those who saw Jay every day continued to call him a homosexual, which infuriated him. Although he described himself as being gay during his twenties, he came to be ashamed of Shea's homosexuality because it reflected on him. I pointed out to Jay that his grief is also about losing the part of him that expressed affection, which is important if he wants to feel like a human being. The session ended on this significant theme—love and affection—which will be the most important issue I will pursue as therapy progresses.

CHAPTER 68

He is struggling for an identity and
wants to know if loving feelings are normal.

July 6-8, 1976

He arrives wearing hospital garb—blue pajamas and a white robe—and begins the session by telling me he's afraid to go to sleep. "I keep dreaming about Seattle and there is always the color red. And I get hit by an iron door that knocks me over. Then I feel pain on my right side. After that I can't feel anything and then I feel like an animal that's been beaten."

Although he signed in as Jay, I point out that he appears different today, and he tells me he feels confused about his identity. "I don't know who I am and I don't know what to do. I can't go back to what I was before but I can't go forward either," he laments.

"The problem is that you aren't free from the past. And you need help to go back there in your mind and resolve the issues that have kept you from being a whole person." I go on to explain that being a whole person includes having loving relationships, something he needs help to understand.

"Am I a grown-up human being?" he asks.

I nod yes.

"I don't know what a grown-up person is supposed to feel," he moans.

"You'll learn. I think that you often feel like a mixed up young boy," I reply.

I see his eyes wander upward and I ask if he's looking at something. He tells me that he sees things in the atmosphere—coolness and hotness. Then his gaze turns downward and he asks if a human being can love.

"Yes, human beings have the capacity to love," I reply.

"I know that Shea loved Jay," he says. "I also think he loved you."

"I am very glad that you're aware of Shea's love."

He looks down at the floor and his body appears to tighten up. "I feel all tied up inside. I don't know how to feel free," he says. Then he adds, "I feel like a moron when I'm like this."

I tell him I'm aware that his tension is most likely a physiological grief response to losing Shea, and he tells me he agrees.

Before we close the session I explain that his emotions are confusing for him now, but as time goes on he'll understand.

When we meet two days later he arrives wearing blue pajamas and a hospital robe and signs in with the name James. He is confused because the patients talk to him as if he is Shea, and don't believe him when he insists he is not Shea and disavows homosexuality. Although he is ashamed of Shea's homosexuality, I encourage him to accept Shea's feelings of love and affection. "Love and affection are not bad emotions and it's normal to have those feelings, even toward me," I say. I also encourage him to develop relationships with real persons, and hang on to real people like me.

When I bring up the past—that James' father had difficulty expressing love—he becomes anxious and his body tightens up. I respond by empathically touching the side of his head, which helps James to relax. This is clearly an improvement from times past when such a touch would have caused him to recoil.

I received my psychiatric training in a setting where touching or the expression of love from therapist to patient had a negative connotation. But I know that James, as he expresses the emotional distress of a child, needs to know that his therapist has loving feelings for him and touch is acceptable. As I review the literature I find articles supporting touch as important for normal human development, communication, and healing. In the words of Ashley Montagu, touch is one of the most essential elements of emotional growth from the time of birth. Touch has also had an important place in therapy and physical healing as far back as the 1930s. Marion Rosen, a physical therapist who worked with individuals undergoing psychoanalysis in Germany during that time, found touch therapy helped some individuals access unconscious memories and forgotten past events. Her approach was based on the principle that chronic muscular tension was the body's way of blocking undesirable emotions. It was accepted by other therapists, and the Rosen Method became an established therapeutic approach.

Bioenergetic Analysis, developed in the 1950s by Alexander Lowen, was also grounded in the idea that chronic muscle tensions in the body served as a way to block emotional expression. Body-based psychotherapy was also taught by the Hartford Family Institute, which utilized the "here and now" approach of Gestalt Therapy. Individuals who received hands-on therapy reported physical and mental restoration. Dr. Lubin-Alpert, one of the founders of the Hartford Family Institute, felt that it was much more important to provide an appropriate therapeutic touch than to withhold it. "Not to touch any clients at any time can be experienced as abusive as the original neglect to the young infant inside the adult client."[58]

CHAPTER 69

He reaches out to touch me. "You are my friend and therapist.
I love you Dr. Brende."

July 16, 1976

Jay signs in but appears distressed and immediately tells me
his head hurts. I ask his permission to gently touch the area that
hurts and he pulls away slightly. Then he nods his head yes and I
reach over, touch his head, and suggest the pain is leaving. I'm
pleased to hear him say, "It doesn't hurt now."

Then I observe him change his ring to his other hand,
indicating that a dissociation is taking place. After a moment a
personality appears who seems very childlike. He tells me he is
Jim and is seven years old. I am very surprised when he begins to
relive a traumatic memory of asking his daddy to hold his hand but
then being slapped by his father, who calls him a bastard. This is
very different from previous sessions, when Jim seemed to have a
close relationship with his father.

This very traumatic reliving experience propels him out of
the chair. I help him sit back down and encourage him to
remember something positive about being with his father. "Your
father wants to hold your hand," I say while touching his hand
gently.

"Bastards don't have fathers," he replies sadly.

I place my hand over his hand and position it on the side of his head. Then I suggest, "Let this touch help the pain go away."

"No it can't. Please, you make the pain go away," he whimpers.

I reach over and touch the side of his head while telling him this is meant to be a loving touch that will take the pain away.

He reaches out to touch my hand and says, "You're my friend. I love you Dr. Brende."

The patient tells me that the ring is not his and asks me to keep it, which surprises me. I'm very moved to hear him tell me he loves me.

I recognize that James' core sense of self must be grounded in love. He first received unconditional love from his mother as the foundation for his identity. I also believe he received significant love from his father. But his cohesive sense of self, fashioned by those loving relationships, was fragmented by trauma and abandonment and he became a "multiple." Jay, a protective personality, defended him from further trauma but he was emotionally detached and lacked the capacity to experience or give love. Shea's exaggerated homosexual behavior, which began after James was raped, was also devoid of genuine love.

James is like a child who will respond to a loving touch and interpersonal expressions of love. Love has been defined in different ways: unconditional love, familial love, sexual love, and friendship love. He needs all of these, but primarily unconditional love such as he received at birth and first year of his life. His mother provided an emotional bond and loving touch during that

362

time to reduce fear and physical discomfort. A loving touch enhances a person's body image and self-awareness. A loving touch can also reduce the emotional and physical impact of trauma and abuse. The instinctive need for human touch and loving affection persists at every stage of life.

How will the expression of love affect my therapeutic relationship with James? There are a number of articles asserting that the conveyance of romantic or sexual love violates the client's trust in the therapist, which I wholeheartedly agree with. There is less literature written about the unique quality of love a therapist may express for his or her client. I am able to find authors who emphasize the importance of maintaining deep respect and caring for their clients throughout the course of therapy. Carl Rogers, the well-known therapist from the 1950s, referred to the therapist's love as unconditional positive regard. He said therapists and counselors must value their client's emotions, thoughts, perceptions, and deepest secrets. Yet this unconditional positive regard must also challenge the client's beliefs and misperceptions when they prohibit him from living a fulfilled and actualized life. Such unconditional love provided by the therapist can enable the client to begin to love and accept himself.[59]

CHAPTER 70

He says he's a bastard without a father
and thinks he came from a mystical entity.

July 19, 1976

I watch him come into the studio with the assistance of an aide. I can see that his appearance is child-like. He sits down and stares at the sign-in sheet, looking confused. After a long period of hesitation he signs "KOHLN." Then he tells me his body hurts all over and he's bleeding from the rectum, which I'm unable to confirm. He seems fearful and tells me he does everything the staff wants him to do so that he won't be sent to the quiet room. He makes his bed, washes his face, eats his food, brushes his teeth, and shaves.

He says he feels a lot of pain in his body and tries to make it go away by caressing the right side of his head. Then he tells me David is able to make the pain go away. I am unclear who he is referring to, so I ask for more information. He says they became friends when he was in the hospital four years ago. "Dr. Baird found out and said that we couldn't talk to each other any more. But I trusted David. He never hurt me. After awhile he could make the hurt go away. He told me to play along with their silly games. Then I got lost and I forgot about him. Now I remember everything."

His voice is heavy with sadness as he places his hand up to the right side of his head. I ask if he can remember feeling this way as a child.

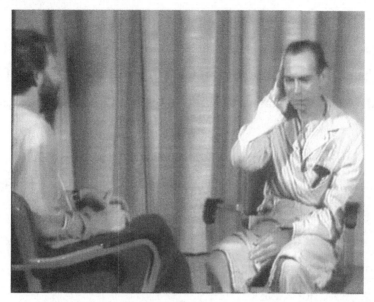

He tells me he can remember that his life was taken away by someone he thought was his father. "I thought he was my daddy but he wasn't," he tells me.

"Who was he if he wasn't your daddy?" I ask.

"I don't know. He always made my mother pregnant," he stutters. "So I went to my mother and…" He begins to cry softly. "She wouldn't listen." His voice trails off as his facial expression takes on a look of terror while he continues to soothe himself by caressing the right side of his head

"What did you ask your mother?"

"I asked her what bastard meant." Suddenly he becomes agitated and stands up. "She said that bastards don't have fathers." He appears confused and moves his head from side to side. "I

365

don't understand why my brother had that man for a father. I thought I should listen to what everyone's saying: 'Do your best. Try. And he'll be your daddy too and you won't be a bastard.'"

The tears stream down his face. He turns to his left then looks back to his right. His begins to caress his right arm with his left hand. Then he lifts his right hand to caress the right side of his head. After a few minutes he moves his hand to his face, wipes off moisture, and returns to his chair.

I hear a change in his voice as he says, "It's okay Dr. Brende. I don't have to cry." Then he calmly sits down, but stands up again after a moment and begins to cry. I see him soothe himself and sit down calmly. "Don't let anyone know. Don't let anyone know that you care," he says.

"Why not?" I ask.

"Because they'll make them go away?"

"Who?"

"All of them," he says almost inaudibly. His right hand slowly comes down from the right side of his face and drops to his lap as he comes out of his trance-like state.

I ask more questions about his loss of close personal relationships. "When somebody cared, was it taken away from you? Is that why you've found it difficult to be close to somebody on the ward?"

He replies that people don't help him feel safe, and laugh at him because he's afraid of the dark. "Horrible things happen in the dark," he says as he reaches up to caress his head.

"What kinds of horrible things?" I ask.

He doesn't answer.

"Do mothers and fathers make love and fathers make their wives pregnant in the dark?" I ask.

"I don't know."

"You just told me that your father was always getting your mother pregnant. Although you said it differently. You said that the man in the house always got your mother pregnant."

He remains silent with his head bowed. "Yeah," he replies softly.

"Can you tell me more about it?"

"It was nothing. I'm tired of lying to people."

"You were tired of buying your father's love?" I ask.

"I had no father," he replies abruptly.

"Then how did you arrive? Did you only come just from your mother?"

He lowers his hand to his head and tells me he keeps his mother at a distance and doesn't want to buy her love any more. When he tried to please his parents he had nothing to give them or to anyone else. "I gave myself but not willingly. But I had nothing more to give but my body. But now my body is worn out and I have nothing else to give. I have nothing else to give but my life." He begins to cry.

"Can you tell me what you mean when you said that you gave your body?"

He doesn't reply and appears overwhelmed by his tears. Then he tells me his friend David was the only person who didn't want his body. Suddenly he breaks down and sobs.

"When did you have to give your body?" I ask, speculating that he was a helpless recipient of Shea's homosexual behavior.

"So many times that I don't know. Sometimes they took it and I fought. Sometimes they took it and there was no one around for me to say anything to. What else could I do if they wanted it but to let them have it. Now it's worthless." He continues to sob and holds his hands out, palms up as if surrendering. "All I have is my life. Are they trying to take away my life too?"

"Who?"

"Everyone."

"Are you wondering if I want to take it away from you too?"

"I don't know," he sobs.

The subject of not having a father but only a mother remains to be explored. "You said that you didn't have a father but only a mother. Was your mother a virgin?"

"No."

"Were you the product of a virgin birth?"

"No."

"Who impregnated your mother? Was it that man?"

"No. If he did, I wouldn't be a bastard and he would be my father," he cries.

"If he didn't do you think someone else did?"

"You'd just laugh and say I'm crazy. I don't understand it all," he replies while holding his head in his hands.

"I'm your therapist and it's my job to help you understand."

He pauses and looks at me. "You're not a Lot are you?"

"What's a Lot?"

"Those without bodies."

"Could you explain that to me?"

He puts his hands down and blows his nose. Then he tells me he doesn't understand what Lots are. He thinks they are different thoughts that show up when it is dark. Sometimes they are like human thoughts and sometimes they aren't. They will change colors and vanish.

I ask for more details, and he says he's only seen them on three occasions, but they appear to be white with a blue halo. He's too confused to say much more, so I change the subject and ask about his mother's love for him. But he shakes his head and claims she didn't love him.

"Your mother told me that you were her favorite son and your father told me the same thing," I say in disagreement.

"I have no father," he exclaims once again as he shakes his head.

I challenge his belief and tell him that I had met with his parents more than once, and heard his father and mother say how proud they were of their son.

He continues to look down in silence, indicating that I have not changed his mind, so I pursue his delusion that he is not a real person because he's the product of an illicit relationship between his mother and a man. "Do you want to deny your existence in order to protect your mother?" I ask. "If that's true, then you must have a great deal of love for your mother. You go to great lengths, even to sacrifice yourself to protect her," I insist.

He continues to slowly caress the right side of his head, but his face remains expressionless.

"What are you thinking?" I ask.

He drops his gaze and slowly shakes his head. He furrows his brow, swallows, and finally responds. "If I must sacrifice myself for something does that mean I'm being tortured?" He frowns intently.

"Can you tell me what you mean?" I ask.

His definition of torture is to endure terrible nightmares, which he says are planted in his brain day and night. "They frighten me until I'm numb. Then I become so afraid and so confused. They threaten me and laugh. I don't know how to play their games anymore."

He disagrees with my interpretation that he feels compelled to sacrifice himself as a way of protecting his mother from the shame of illicit love. He also struggles to understand my assertion that his shame about having loving feelings toward his mother is like his shame about having loving feelings toward me. He continues to sit quietly while I reemphasize that love is not shameful. Finally he seems to recognize the significance of his loving relationship with me. He turns his face upward, continues to sit motionless, and looks intently at me.

"What are you thinking?" I ask.

"You are real?" he asks profoundly.

"I am real!" I assert.

He looks down and then up at me and asks another profound question. "May I touch you?"

"Yes."

He reaches out slowly but then draws back. I extend my hand out to him. He begins to sob but starts to reach toward me again. "I don't want to hurt you," he pleads. I watch as his hand remains still an inch from mine. Then he withdraws it.

"You can't hurt me." I assure him.

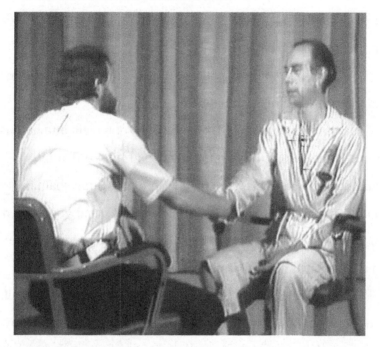

He reaches out again, touches my hand briefly, then withdraws it and begins to sob. He brings his handkerchief to his face and wipes his eyes. Suddenly he stops crying, looks at the ceiling, then gazes down at my hand again.

"It's okay to touch me and find out that I'm real," I say while keeping my hand extended.

"You're real?" he asks again and reaches out to grasp my hand. "I'm not hurting you?"

"No, you're not," I insist.

He withdraws his hand and says, "I'm sorry that I'm carrying on." Still finding it hard to believe he asks, "Do you exist? Really?"

"I exist," I state clearly.

"I know you do but I'm afraid that if I say so they'll say 'No you're not real.'" He reaches out again and repeats, "You're real! I won't tell them. They won't know anything."

"When you're ready, you can tell them," I say, assuming that he is referring to other personalities.

He withdraws his hand, then reaches out again and begins to sob in a combination of pain and joy. Then I insist that his experience of being born is real and there is nothing shameful about his birth. "If you can allow me to be real, and you to be real, then you can allow the memory of your birth from your mother to be a real and meaningful memory."

To my surprise he suddenly gets out of his chair and walks out of the room. I call out and then follow him. He responds by returning to his chair. After standing there momentarily he sits back down.

"Why did you leave?" I ask.

He remains silent.

"I guess you're not ready for that. It upset you."

He replies inaudibly about something, and I realize that I need to modify my previous statement. "I guess I should change what I said. I am more real than your mother is and I guess your mother isn't quite real to you yet."

372

Rather than respond to my statement he asks, "You're not a Lot?"

"No I'm not a Lot."

He looks puzzled, looks down and then looks back up at me and says he won't tell anyone that I'm real.

I assure him that no one will take me away because I'm a real person, but he insists that no one will believe that. So I ask the aide who accompanied him to the studio to verify that I'm real. When she enters the room he looks up at her and asks. "Who do you see besides me?"

"I see Dr. Brende. He's sitting in the chair," she asserts.

With widened eyes he reaches over, touches my hand, and looks at her. "He's real. Don't tell anyone!" he exclaims.

"If you are afraid that if she tells someone they'll take me away, I can assure you that won't happen," I insist.

"But it always does," he declares and closes his eyes tightly. Then he reaches out again to touch my hand for the fifth time and grasps it tightly, holding on until it is time for him to leave.

CHAPTER 71

James wonders if he and I are real.

July 22, 197

James enters the studio before me. After looking around, he sits down calmly and surveys the room. Then he bows his head, clasps his hands and rests them in his lap. When I enter he immediately stands up. His first words are, "You're real, right?"

"Yes, I'm real. So are you," I reply.

He reaches over to the table near his chair, picks up the permission slip, and seems confused as to what to do. Then he looks at me and struggles with his words.

"I…uh…don't know…I get kind of a little mixed up." He looks at me again and asks if I'm real once more. When I reaffirm that I am indeed real he seems relieved enough to change the subject and tell me about a visit he had with his brother. Then he looks at the red striped shirt I'm wearing and asks if he is in danger of being hurt. After I reassure him that the color red won't hurt him he seems to feel that it's safe to be a real person.

He tells me about his routine as a patient, as if he is learning it for the first time. "I know what to do. I get up and go to the bathroom and wash my face and hands. I eat and then we have this meeting. I shave and then we clean the kitchen. We have a meeting and then we eat. When my hand itches I know I come to see you."

I ask about the itch on his hand.

"I have the feeling that when my hands itch I'm going to see someone real. Someone that I know," he says.

"Who else besides me do you know that's real?"

"Well, Pappy (brother), and Betty I know is really real. I get confused about you," he says, and then adds that he can close his eyes and still see me in his mind.

His perceptual capabilities are confused since he finds it difficult to tell the difference between persons and furniture. He also struggles to understand the meanings of words. "When someone says 'read out loud those words' I can't. Some words I can."

"I wonder why that is?"

"I get so confused. They all laugh or say that I don't know what I'm talking about so I don't say anything. Then they get mad. But I don't want to make people mad."

"Who are you talking about? Who are they?"

"They?" He pauses and answers with a perplexed look on his face. "They're not the real 'un-reals,' but they're the 'un-reals,'" he says.

Although I don't clearly understand what he means I think he's finding it difficult to distinguish between the "more real" individuals he sees on the ward compared to the "un-reals" he sees in his mind. "They sometimes look like…" he starts to say but then squirms in his chair. "I get all anxious and I don't know. Maybe they want my mind. If they do, why don't they say so?"

"Your mind? I wonder why they might want your mind?"

"I don't have anything else."

375

"You're describing it as if you had something they would take from you."

He nods.

"No one took you away. And you are real! You had a white tie on. And I touched you and I didn't go through you."

"That's right. So if I'm real and they couldn't take me away from you, they won't take your mind!" I declare.

He is trying to make sense of things and tells me he doesn't know what "they" want, possibly referring to the hallucinated voices of past personalities. He says he's frustrated because he can't talk to them or ask what they want. "They keep saying, 'What's this? Who? What?' Then they start to scream and holler and I tell them I don't know what they want," he says.

"Now when you start to feel confused, it should help you when you can remember the things that are really real," I propose to him.

"But it doesn't help so much anymore."

"Can you explain?"

He goes on to tell me he feels better when he remembers Pappy and Betty because they take the hurt away, but not the pain.

I'm confused by his use of two similar words— pain and hurt—which must have different meanings for him, but I assure him he doesn't appear to be in pain today.

"I didn't want to let anyone know it because if they see that I'm in pain, they make me go into darkness," he explains, and then repeats himself several times. "If they know I'm in pain, they make me go into darkness!"

"Are you in pain?" I ask.

"I am!" he insists.

"Right now?"

"Yes!" he exclaims.

It's still unclear to me: How can I make his hurt go away yet also cause pain? I wonder if his pain is caused by my absences and relieved when I'm not absent. When I ask if I can make his hurt go away now, he nods his head yes but with a perplexed look on his face. "Are you going to make me go into darkness?" he asks. His question leads me to believe he's afraid I will replace him and make him go into darkness as Jay did.

"If you were to tell me that you had pain, would you be afraid that I would put you into darkness?" I ask.

He looks at me silently for a while and then says, "You have a beard and you're thin and you're not going to hurt me, are you?"

I assure him I won't hurt him, but also ask again why he is afraid I would put him into darkness.

I see the frightened look on his face and his eyes dart back and forth, so I assure him he won't go into darkness.

Then he tells me there are two different kinds of darkness. "One darkness is that there is darkness; (the other is) I am in darkness. Does that sound right? I'm in darkness and then sometimes it's dark."

I ask him again to clarify the relationship between pain, hurt, and going into darkness.

He hesitates, catches his breath and opens his mouth. Nothing comes out.

"Are you afraid that if you told me you hurt, I would put you into darkness?" I ask.

He nods yes.

"And if you said you didn't hurt, what would you be afraid of then?" I ask.

"Then you would go away and I would be alone," he replies. After a brief pause, his chin quivers and he yells, "Brende?" as if he's afraid I am leaving.

"You don't want that to happen," I clarify.

"No, I don't."

"Brende?" He looks at me. "See you're here. See you're here. And you have a beard."

"I'm real. I'm not in darkness," I state clearly.

"No," he agrees but looks perplexed.

I clarify that one of the reasons he came today was to learn if they had taken me away.

He agrees.

"I guess that proves to you how strong I am," I assert.

"That's right!" he exclaims then closes his eyes. "I'm screaming," he announces loudly, although I don't hear any screams. Then he opens his eyes wide and announces that he sees me like he sees David, which is confusing since I'm the only person here.

"It's not only that you see me but I'm also real," I say, clarifying my presence is not a hallucination. Then I ask if he can tell me where David lives.

He struggles to recollect until he finally remembers that David lives near Arkansas City. Then he focuses again on my reality. "But you're real. Can I touch you?" he asks. After I nod yes he reaches over to grasp my extended hand. "I can touch you! And you're real!" he repeats firmly.

"Yes."

"And I'm not hurting you?"

"No."

"And you're not mad?"

"No."

"Okay. Everything is okay then right?" he asks.

He's elated to hear my assurance that I'm all right. I ask him how he expects to feel during the next three days. He pauses and can only answer, "You're real and I'm here," indicating that he can only focus on the immediate present and not the future.

"You'll probably see me during the next three days," I say, referring to his ability to visualize my face.

"Yes, and I hear you too," he says.

I point out that he'll be able to remember my voice and my appearance in order to remember that I'm a real person.

"That's not bad, is it?"

"That's not bad and it's important to you."

"Just like (the color) red won't hurt me?"

"No, and you're finding out that loving feelings are important and they won't drive people away. Those loving feelings in relationship to me are okay to have."

He frowns, looks down, and begins to talk but seems unable to get the words out. After a brief silence he says, "I won't tell anyone." Then he looks to his left out of the corner of his eye, apparently afraid someone has heard me mention our loving relationship.

He tells me again that expressing loving feelings will cause something bad to happen, but I reassure him nothing bad will happen to either of us.

"Yes," he says and nods his head several times. "You're here and you're strong and I can touch you and I'm not so afraid. I just don't listen to what they all say," he says.

"That's right. You don't have to listen to them if it's upsetting for you."

"Yes, because I get all confused and things go all wrong."

When I point out that it's time to stop he responds, "I don't know time. It's so important to everyone but I don't know time. I wish I knew time." Then he adds, "You're real. May I touch you one more time?" He reaches over to grasp my outstretched hand again and then stands up. As he walks out of the studio he continues to look back at me as if needing to reaffirm my presence.

During this session it's clear that he has a tentative hold on reality. Like a newly born child, he visualizes my presence as if I'm a maternal figure who can provide the necessary strength to prevent him from returning to darkness. According to object-relations theorists, an individual begins life in a symbiotic relationship with the mother before recognizing he is a separate being with a unique self-identity. His identity continues to develop through the process of separation-individuation when he learns new things about himself and the world he seeks to explore. James appears to be starting the separation-individuation process.[60]

CHAPTER 72

James' early beginning. I give him a pen and he writes down the letters LAOT.

July 23, 1976

Today is James' birthday. He was born forty years ago on this date, although he doesn't seem to be aware of it. He left yesterday's session with considerable anxiety, so I had requested an extra session for today. He appears to be confused about the time and place because he immediately tells me he doesn't want any shock treatments to put him out of existence again. "I don't want to go back into darkness," he sobs. "I'm glad I'm here. It's painful, but I'm glad I'm here."

I ask him to sign the permission slip and after a struggle he finally signs James. He seems upset and I ask if he will tell me what's troubling him.

"I thought you were mad at me because you thought I was dumb. So I ran away," he stammers between sobs.

I point out that he is not dumb, but may have been running away from loving feelings because he wrongly believes those feelings are wrong. I also clarify that I am really real. I offer him a tissue to wipe his tears, and also assure him I won't abandon or punish him. Furthermore, I won't give him shock treatments like he received four years ago.

382

"Sometimes it seems like a war just started," he moans as he shakes his head helplessly, "and sometimes I say things and they get mad because I don't know what they mean."

"You're frightened," I observe.

"Yes, and I don't understand what I'm frightened about."

"You're frightened that I might leave you. And you needed to come over here today to see if I was still here," I say.

"When I close my eyes, you're here," he says, referring to his ability to visualize my presence. He continues to cry so I reach over to touch his right shoulder, which causes him to move away slightly. He tells me that I take away his hurt but also make pain, so I assure him I won't hurt him.

He opens his eyes and asks, "Are you real in the light?"

I assure him again that I'm real, and also predict he will repeat this question many times. "You may have to keep coming back to find out I'm real. And that's all right. And you may keep coming back to find out that I'm not mad."

"I'm not mad at you," he sobs.

"It wouldn't make any difference if you were. I would still be here."

He places his hands softly on both sides of his head as if to cradle it.

"I don't know what I've done to be punished," he cries as he lowers his left hand and keeps his right hand on the side of his head as a way of comforting himself, or caressing the place where he was struck as a child.

"When they start to punish you, you tell them that I said there's no reason for you to be punished," I assert.

He points to my red shirt and says, "Red doesn't hurt. But it reminds me of my pain."

"You don't have to remember that anymore."

"When they want to punish me, I can tell them that my friend Brende said, you don't need to be punished, and you are a friend. A friend. Not like Doctor Baird."

"Yes, I'm a friend."

He appears to relax as his hands and body become less tense.

I notice that he's perspiring and ask him, "Are you sweating?"

"That's not the word. It's perspiration. But I'm not being snotty by saying that word. You're not mad at me, are you?"

He tells me he's afraid of using certain words, but I assure him he can use any words he wants to use and I won't be mad. He also tells me he's glad I'm here where he can see my face and hear my voice.

He looks and talks like a young James who is experiencing a rebirth. I consider this a remarkable event that I've never witnessed in a patient before. But his "entrance" into becoming a person remains precarious. He continues to express his fear that "the others" will be mad at him if he gets stronger, while at the same time they will be angry because he's too weak and unable to do many things for himself.

He says he can't remember when to brush his teeth, but he can remember when it is time to see me when his right hand begins

384

to itch. He says his nurse continues to remind him to keep his appointments with me on Monday, Wednesday and Friday. But he says he doesn't know what those words mean.

I emphasize that it's important for him to learn how to survive in this world and that he can trust in others to provide guidance. "The staff won't let you down," I assure him. As I point out that this is a fragile time for him, he sits quietly with a puzzled look on his face, gazes to his left, changes subjects, and says he wants to write something for me. I give him a pen and he writes down the letters LAOT.

"What does Laot mean?" I ask.

"That means Laot (pronounced Lot) and I told you the other day that's what I thought you are."

"Are Laots good or bad?" I ask.

"I don't know." Then he pauses a minute as he struggles to find a word. "Fantabulous! That's what you are and what David is. It's hard to explain," he says, implying that David and I are both Laots.

"The next time we meet, I want you to tell me more about it," I say, as our time is about to run out.

Before we end the session he asks, "Can I do one more thing?"

"Sure."

He extends his right hand saying he would like to touch me as he did last time. I reach over and firmly grasp his hand.

"Can we do another thing? Can we go out of the light?" he asks.

Continuing to hold my hand, he leads me to the other part of the studio where the light is not shining, which is significant since he made the statement earlier that I was only real while I am in the light. Now he discovers that I'm as real in the dark as I am in the light.

CHAPTER 73

He asks me if I'm a Lot; today he spells it LATOT.

July 26-29, 1976

The patient enters the studio accompanied by an aide. He says he is so confused that he wants to scream, and seems to be having difficulty distinguishing this time from when he was hospitalized four years ago. I remind him that this time is different from the past, and he won't be left in the dark like he was before.

"I'm fighting in the dark. I want to stay in the light where I have a beginning," he says sadly.

I reach out to touch him and ask if his hurt has gone away, but he replies that the pain is still there. "I feel pain, but that's good because it means I'm alive," he says.

"I believe that you're having feelings like a young child might have. One who feels loved. I know that hasn't been your experience before."

"You are good to chase away the darkness and bring the light. Now I feel like I'm here and there."

"Where is there?"

"There is where the Lots are," he says. When I ask him to spell Lot he writes LATOT, a change from last time when he spelled Laot. As I look at the word I realize that LATOT is TOTAL backwards.

I ask for further clarification as to the location of there and he replies, "There is there but it's not here."

"Does that mean all of you is not here?" I ask.

"I don't know. I'm here but I'm there too. I want to be human. I want a body. I want a mind and a body."

"Newborns don't have the mind they need. It becomes developed as they grow older," I explain.

He continues to say things that must be important to him, but he lacks the vocabulary to tell me clearly what he means. Finally, when he says he wants the waste removed from his mind and body, I understand he wants to be clean.

When our time comes to an end I assure him that he will learn more words as time goes on.

During our meeting three days later on Thursday, July 29, I notice that he is tearful and still can't speak without difficulty. He struggles to tell me that he feels scared all the time and doesn't know who to trust. I am sympathetic to his feelings and ask him if we should meet more frequently, even if it's for shorter times, to help him with his fear.

He tells me it helps him to remember David, but he is fearful that "they" will take David away from him. I don't discourage him, but since David is not involved in his life now, I encourage him to imagine my presence to help his anxiety. But talking about this stirs apprehension, which is evident in his body language, so I reach out for him to grasp my hand.

He hangs on to me while asking if I'm a Lot. I ask him to spell the word as I did during a previous session. I hand him a pen

388

and paper and he spells L A T O T. When I ask where he comes from, his answer fits with what he has described a few days before. "From space."

This diagram depicts changes that have taken place in James' basic sense of self. His "rebirth" grew out of the loving relationship between patient and therapist. Shea has apparently left the body for good. Jay is still present for periodic appearances. Jim and Jimmy remain hidden as sub personalities. Latot is a new entity who will become more important as time goes on.

CHAPTER 74

He wants to grow a beard like me.

Friday July 30, 1976

The young James is wearing hospital garb of blue pajamas and a white robe. He's struggling to find himself, and because of his sense of helplessness he continues looking to me for guidance. He says he wants to be unconfused like me, so he tries to hear my voice in his mind for guidance whenever he is confused. He doesn't always know the words to describe his activities, although there are things he does automatically. "I was doing something and didn't know the reason why. I know I was shaving with an electric shaver and I wanna be like you but I don't want to be you. And that's the reason why." He points to his unshaven face and to the beard on my face.

"Do you want a beard?"

"Yes," he replies.

"Do you sometimes feel like you might be me?" I ask.

"Yes," he replies.

I'm pleased that he would like to grow a beard like me. That indicates he is moving forward in the process of individuation, like a young boy seeking to identify with his father. He also wants to learn new things and find the meanings of words. But as he moves forward he also needs the freedom to move backward and obtain my support. In psychological terms, this has been described as "regression in the service of the ego."

"I know the times I want to come here. If I want to cry I'll cry because I want to. I can say things I don't know what I'm saying but I say it because of a feeling I should say it. I want to jump up and down and clap my hands and I can do that without being punished," he says. After a pause he continues. "I cried this morning because I want to. It was a funny feeling. A feeling in my stomach."

Then he talks about the fact he knows what people are, but not things. "You are people and I am people," he says.

"And what are things?"

"But I'm not sure what things are," he says.

"They're objects. Some are different from others."

I ask him to give me an example and he knows to point out the Kleenex box on the table.

I encourage him to continue to learn new words, and suggest that when he learns a new word he should try to remember it. He becomes anxious and says he's afraid of losing what he has gained, and gets out of his chair and turns his back to me. I can see him become tremulous and I reach over to touch the back of his right arm, which reduces his anxiety and enables him to sit down again. He tells me that the only way he could keep from losing himself in the past was to run away, because he didn't know what else to do. I assume that meant he left the body via dissociation.

I ask if holding on to people helps his anxiety but he shakes his head no. I remind him that he held onto my hand yesterday,

391

which seemed to help him. He agrees, and tells me he can often visualize my presence but it's better to meet with me. I point out it's good he has a memory of me.

He nods his head, but then frowns and asks, "Is that wrong?"

"No. It's not wrong," I assert.

When our session has ended I say "I'll see you Monday," but my words confuse him. So I repeat, "We will meet together on Monday. That's only three days away."

In order to help him cope with his anxiety about leaving our session, I ask him to repeat these instructions to himself: "I can close my eyes and remember that I am real and you are real."

I praise him for his desire to continue learning and his response brings tears to my eyes. "There is a word I'm thinking of," he says haltingly, then adds, "thank you."

"You're welcome," I respond.

"It pleases me…for what…has been done," he says with broken English.

"Those are the right words to express your feelings," I reply with a smile.

After telling him our time is over I reach out and shake his hand.

CHAPTER 75

What have we been through and where do we go from here?

We have reached a significant phase in the therapeutic process: He now feels reborn. The young James has emerged from his "contamination" by unwanted alternate personalities to discover he is a human being. But he is uncertain who his parents are. Is he an offspring of LATOT, a spiritual entity who lives in space somewhere? Or is his "rebirth" the result of the power of love between patient and therapist? How did the changes within this individual take place during the 16 months from the time therapy began on March 23, 1975?

My original goal was to discover why James had amnesia for a period of two weeks. After using hypnosis during my first two meetings, I discovered that James had four alternate personalities—Jay, Jim, Jimmy, and Shea. The predominant personality was Jay, and I proceeded to meet with him regularly in psychotherapy two or more times a week. I found evidence of physiologic changes related to the two personalities Jay and James. James appeared to be associated with brain activity in the right cerebral hemisphere and Jay in the left cerebral hemisphere. These two personalities struggled for control over several months, during which time I saw automatic movements called psychological automatisms triggered by brainwave abnormalities. James finally emerged from his prison of darkness where he believed Jay had placed him four years earlier when he received shock treatments (ECT). But James was convinced that his only way to remain free was to kill Jay, so he gave him an overdose of pills he had stockpiled. It was discovered later that he had been stockpiling his medications to the point that the overdose would have killed him without intervention. Jay actually had a premonition of his own death and was temporarily displaced at the time of the overdose, only to emerge again at a later time, convinced he had murdered James.

When James awoke after he "killed" Jay he appeared like a reborn child. But his growth was stymied because of unexpected events. The most disturbing was a traumatic homosexual rape that occurred after he was discharged from military service and which he relived during a therapy session nine months after therapy had begun. Although this was the most significant of James' traumatic experiences the first one took place at age seven when his father struck him and caused a split in James' identity. Jay took over as a protective personality at that time and became predominant in his role as the' protector. Jay did not feel emotional or physical pain until he eventually began to fuse with James at a later time during therapy.

Shea von Kohlman was a flamboyant homosexual who claimed to have begun his existence at the time of the traumatic rape that victimized James. Shea appeared several times during therapy and even tried to seduce me before he eventually left the body. Prior to the rape, Jay had apparently co-existed with Shea at some level, and carried on ordinary life activities as a member of the Air Force for ten years until he received a medical discharge because of an intractable seizure disorder.

My psychotherapeutic work with this remarkable individual thus far has relied on my understanding of dynamic psychotherapy and early growth and development, as well as my experience as a trained medical hypnotist. However, I did not expect that I would find myself entering into an area that psychiatric training had not prepared me for—the development of a loving bond which paralleled that found between a mother and young child. But it had to take place before James could experience his "rebirth." As this young man grows up, the process of therapy will bring new surprises.

ENDNOTES

[1] L.D. Butler, R.E.F. Duran, P. Jasiukaitis, C. Koopman, and D. Spiegel, "Hypnotizability and Traumatic Experience: A Diathesis-stress Model of Dissociative Symptomatology," *American Journal of Psychiatry* 153, No. 7 (July, 1996).

[2] The official diagnosis of multiple personality disorder would appear in the diagnostic manual (DSM-III) in 1980. That diagnosis would change later to dissociative identity disorder. *DSM IV: Diagnostic and Statistical Manual* (Washington DC: American Psychiatric Press, 1994).

[3] The use of hypnosis to reveal the hidden presence of multiple personalities has been reported by several authors including Dr. Ralph Allison. R.B. Allison and T. Schwartz, *Minds In Many Pieces: Revealing the Spiritual Side of Multiple Personality Disorder* (New York: Wade Publications, 1980). R.P. Kluft, "Varieties of Hypnotic Intervention in the Treatment of Multiple Personalities," *American Journal of Clinical Hypnosis* 24, No. 4 (1982): 230-240.

[4] M.H. Cogdon, J. Hain, and I.J. Stevenson, "A Case of Multiple Personality Illustrating the Transition from Role Playing," *Journal of Nervous and Mental Disease* 132, No. 6 (1961): 497-504.

[5] Psychiatrist David Spiegel calls hypnosis a useful tool in uncovering and recalling traumatic events in a patient with multiple personalities. Noted expert in the treatment of patients with dissociative disorders, psychiatrist Richard Kluft has frequently used hypnosis to treat his patients. David Spiegel, "Dissociation, Double Binds, and Post-traumatic Stress," in *Treatment of Multiple Personality Disorder*, ed. Bennett G. Braun (Washington DC, APA Press, 1986). R.P. Kluft, "The use of Hypnosis with Dissociative Disorders," *Psychiatric Medicine* 10, no. 4 (1992): 31-46.

[6] In normal individuals either of the right- and left-brain hemispheres can function in a lateralization process temporarily for specific purposes. In this patient one side of his body persistently functioned differently indicating the presence of fixed lateralization. This suggested an absence of inter-hemisphere communication caused by blockage at the level of the corpus callosum connecting the two hemispheres.

[7] Different personalities have been reported to respond differently to the same medications. "Numerous clinicians have made anecdotal reports of differential responses to medication across different personalities. These medications include anxiolytics, sedative-hypnotics, antidepressants, antipsychotics, and narcotic pain medication. This same phenomenon has been seen with

alcohol and other substances of abuse." Philip M. Coons, "Psychophysiologic Aspects of Multiple Personality Disorder: A Review," *Dissociation* 1, No. 1 (March 1988): 47-53.

[8] F.W. Putnam, J.J. Guroff, E.K. Silberman, L. Barban, and R.M. Post, "The Clinical Phenomenology of Multiple Personality Disorder: Review of 100 Recent Cases of Multiple Personality Disorder," *Journal of Clinical Psychiatry* 47, No. 2 (1986): 85-93.

[9] Shea's histrionic gestures and emotional flamboyance reflect behavior that has been referred to as "Labelle Indifference" by Pierre Janet (1859-1947), a pioneering French psychologist, philosopher and psychotherapist in the field of dissociation and traumatic memory. H.F. Ellenberger, *The Discovery of the Unconscious: The History and Evolution of Dynamic Psychiatry* (New York: Basic Books, 1970).

[10] Brain researchers have demonstrated that timekeeping functions in the brain are found in the basal ganglia and right parietal cortex.

[11] Joel Paris, "The Rise and Fall of Dissociative Identity Disorder," *The Journal of Nervous and Mental Disease* 200, No. 12 (2012).

[12] His former physician prescribed this patient Dilantin, an anticonvulsant, and Librium, a mild tranquilizer. His hospital

399

doctor continued to prescribe these, and I continued to provide follow-up prescriptions for him as an outpatient. According to doctors who have treated individuals with multiple personality disorder, medications are only helpful when targeting specific symptoms like depression, insomnia, pain, etc. They have been described as "shock absorbers" rather than curative. Carolyn Spring, "What Role Does Medication Play in Treating Dissociative Identity Disorder?" *Journal of Trauma and Dissociation* 12, No.2 (July 1, 2012): 115-187.

[13] Research studies using neuroimaging (PET) have found that the perception of pain is linked to the amygdala within the limbic system, predominantly in the right cerebral hemisphere where emotions are also located. Thus the presence of distressful emotions linked to pain signals can be marooned in the limbic system, which may explain why Jay does not feel pain.

[14] Thorazine (Chlorpromazine) is an antipsychotic medication that was first developed in 1952 to treat schizophrenia more effectively than any other drug available at the time. It was eventually replaced by other antipsychotic drugs with fewer side effects. Dilantin (Phenytoin) was first approved for use in 1953 to control tonic-clonic epileptic seizures. It has continued to be used successfully over many years.

[15] Automatisms are spontaneous verbal or motor behaviors, which in this patient are automatic movements of his limbs. These are also referred to as motor automatisms, and my last for several seconds or longer.

[16] Pierre Marie Félix Janet first described psychological automatisms during the 19th century in patients suffering from hysteria and dissociations caused by emotional trauma. He is ranked alongside William James and Wilhelm Wundt as one of the founding fathers of psychology. Ellenberger, *Discovery of the Unconscious*.

[17] J.A. Chu et al., "Guidelines for Treating Dissociative Identity Disorder in Adults, Third Revision," *Journal of Trauma and Dissociation* 12, No. 2 (2011): 115-187.

[18] Glen O. Gabbard, *Long-term Psychodynamic Psychotherapy: A Basic Text* (Washington DC: American Psychiatric Publications, 2011).

[19] The lateralization of brain function refers to the way some neurological functions or cognitive processes tend to be more dominant in one side of the brain or cerebral hemisphere than the other. Each of the two hemispheres is linked with motor functions on the opposite side of the body. The left hemisphere is also linked to speech, cognitive organization, and right-handedness, while the

right hemisphere is more frequently associated with emotional expression.

[20] In the book *I'm OK—You're OK*, the principles of transactional analysis and parent, adult, and child ego states were described by the author for the purpose of understanding interpersonal relationships between children and their parents, called transactions. A child growing up in a very disturbed family may have introjected or incorporated a critical or victimizing parent ego state and a pathological child ego state linked to the emotions of fear, grief, and shame associated with abandonment or victimization. Thomas Harris, *I'm OK—You're OK: The Principles of Transactional Analysis* (New York: Harper, 1967).

[21] Splitting is a term mental health practitioners use to describe the behavior often found in patients diagnosed with borderline personality disorder, who attempt to pit the "bad" staff against the "good" doctor on an inpatient psychiatric ward, or other healthcare facilities.

[22] When James observes the videotape four years later he can't remember this session. But he comments that he is not God and never believed in God. He also brings up the name "Lot," a spiritual-like entity he will later spell LATOT (Total spelled backwards) who possesses some god-like qualities, and eventually functions as the predominant personality at a later time.

[23] Early childhood memories may be significant to help understand the roots of emotional and psychological conflicts. When those recollections involve personal events, they are referred to as autobiographical memories. Freud argued that such events may not be available for recollection if they are traumatic in nature. They persist instead in the unconscious mind as repressed memories, and can be the source of psychiatric symptoms. Favorable therapeutic outcomes in adulthood hinge on successfully retrieving these memories. Neuroimaging PET studies have shown that the storage of such memories primarily involves the pre-frontal cortex in the right cerebral hemisphere. However, the hippocampus is a key region in the medial temporal lobe. It processes information through the hippocampus for short-term memory to be encoded into a long-term memory. The long-term memory does not remain stored permanently in the hippocampus. M.I. Howe and M.L. Courage, "On Resolving the Enigma of Infantile Amnesia," *Psychological Bulletin* 113, No. 2 (1993): 305-326. Asaf Gilboa, "Autobiographical and Episodic Memory—One And The Same? Evidence from Prefrontal Activation in Neuroimaging Studies," *Neuropsychologia* 42 (2004): 1336-1349, https://doi.org/10.1016/j.neuropsychologia.2004.02.2014.

[24] ECT has had limited use in the treatment of dissociative identity disorder. There is a report of the successful use of ECT on a patient with multiple personalities who also suffered from major

depression. There was also a report of ECT used to facilitate integration of alternates in a patient with dissociative identity disorder, after having been treated unsuccessfully for a number of years with psychotherapy and medication. When ECT was applied over a prolonged period of two years, there appeared to be an integration of several alternate personalities. C. DeBattista, H.B. Solvason, and D. Spiegel, "ECT in Dissociative Identity Disorder and Comorbid Depression," *Journal of ECT* 14, No. 4 (1998): 275-9. Kyle D. Webster, Susan Michalowski, and Thomas E. Hranilovich, "Multimodal Treatment with ECT for Identity Integration in a Patient With Dissociative Identity Disorder, Complex Post-traumatic Stress Disorder, and Major Depressive Disorder: A Rare Case Report," *Frontiers In Psychiatry* 9, No. 275 (June 2018).

[25] In spite of ECT's primary effectiveness as a treatment for major depression and certain other disorders, there have been reports about its adverse effects on the brain. For example, ECT has been found to cause neurological changes: A study in *Proceedings of the National Academy of Science* in March 2012 reported a considerable "decrease in functional connectivity" between the prefrontal lobes of the brain (verbal, intellectual, organizational) and other parts of the brain following ECT. Professor Peter Sterling from the University of Pennsylvania department of Neuroscience testified at a mental health hearing in New York that "ECT unquestionably damages the brain." And ECT advocate

Harold Sackeim reported in the *Journal of ECT* that "virtually all patients experience some degree of persistent and, likely, permanent retrograde amnesia." Ernest Hemingway told his wife he couldn't live with the memory loss caused by ECT and committed suicide at age 61 on July 2, 1961, the day after his 36th shock treatment for persistent deep depression. Harold Sackeim, Testimony at a Hearing on ECT before the New York Assembly Standing Committee on Mental Health, Mental Retardation, and Developmental Disabilities, (2001). "Shocking Treatment, How ECT Works," *The Economist*, September 15, 2005.

[26] T.H. Steven Moffic, "We Are Still Flying Over the Cuckoo's Nest," *Psychiatric Times* 7, no. 31 (July 1, 2014).

[27] In French, *c'est la vie* means "that's life," borrowed into English as an idiom to express acceptance or resignation, much like *oh well*.

[28] Many therapists, particularly those using hypnotic techniques, have reported instances of hypnotic regression and revivification (reliving a past experience) in patients who suffer from past traumatic events or other psychological problems. The emotional intensity of reliving the experience as it takes place in the "here and now" is made more realistic when the therapist uses the present tense. This experience may be reflected by the patient's altered breathing pattern, change in facial expression, and evidence

of altered muscular tension. Jerome M Schneck, "Special Aspects of Hypnotic Regression and Revivification," *International Journal of Clinical and Experimental Hypnosis* 8, No. 1 (1960).

[29] I first learned about the ISH when participating with Dr. Ralph Allison in a training seminar about multiple personality disorder for the American Psychiatric Association in May 1976. Dr. Allison had treated several patients with multiple personalities, each of whom had a personality he called an ISH. Before learning about the ISH, I had already discovered that Jay served a protective purpose because he had no awareness of physical or emotional pain, and no memory of past traumatic events. Six months after the beginning of therapy, he began to sense the presence of a personality who had been abandoned. He also allowed James to eventually reveal himself as suffering from painful emotions and memories related to being a victim of physical rejection and sexual abuse. R.F. Kluft, "An Introduction to Multiple Personality Disorder," *Psychiatric Annals* 14, No. 1 (January 1984).

[30] According to medical experts, tears not only have an emotional healing capacity, they also have a physiological effect as they keep the eyes moist, remove irritants, and secrete antibodies to fight bacterial infections. Researchers have found that ordinary tears are comprised of nearly pure water, while tears related to grief and emotional pain contain stress hormones that had accumulated during times of distress. Other studies have found that crying

stimulates the production of endorphins, which have positive mood altering effects. Judith Orloff, *The Empath's Survival Guide: Life Strategies for Sensitive People* (Louisville: Sounds True, 2017).

[31] John Bowlby, *The Making and Breaking of Affectional Bonds* (London: Tavistock Publications, 1977). Gregory J. Jurkovic, "Characterizing the Magnitudes of the Relation between Parentification and Psychopathology: A meta-analysis," *Journal of Clinical Psychology* 67, No.1 (2011). Gregory J. Jurkovic, *Lost childhoods: The Plight of the Parentified Child* (New York: Brunner/Mazel, 1997).

[32] Deirdre Barrett, "Dreams in Dissociative Disorders," *Dreaming: Journal of the Association for the Study of Dreams* 4, No. 3 (1994). C.C. Sizemore, *A Mind of My Own* (New York: William Morrow, NY, 1989). H.F. Ellenberger, *The Discovery of the Unconscious: The History and Evolution of Dynamic Psychiatry* (New York: Basic Books, 1970).

[33] Christine "Chris" Sizemore was an American woman diagnosed with multiple personality disorder, now known as dissociative identity disorder. Her case was depicted in the book *The Three Faces of Eve*, written by her psychiatrists, Corbett H. Thigpen and Hervey M. Cleckley, upon which a film was based. She continued to have symptoms and went to several different psychiatrists. Finally, after four years of treatment with Dr. Tony

Tsitos, her eighth therapist, the personalities came together—integrated—like pieces of a puzzle, in July 1974. She went public with her true identity as Chris Sizemore after that time. She co-wrote (with James Poling) *Strangers in My Body: The Final Face of Eve*, using the pseudonym of Evelyn Lancaster in 1958, and also wrote *I'm Eve,* with Elen Sain Pittillo, and *A Mind of My Own.* I had the opportunity to hear her speak about her experiences at a meeting of the American Psychiatric Association special forum on multiple personalities. C.H. Thigpen and H.M. Cleckley, *The Three Faces of Eve* (New York: McGraw-Hill, 1957). Evelyn Lancaster, *The Final Face of Eve* (London: Secker & Warburg, 1958). Chris Costner Sizemore, *I'm Eve* (New York: Jove Books, 1977). Chris Costner Sizemore, *A Mind of My Own* (New York: William Morrow, NY, 1989).

[34] Jay relies on his cognitive functioning to suppress emotional expression personified by James. His perception of time is interesting. He says it has no meaning to him and that it extends indefinitely. But he says now that he has a sense time will end very shortly for him.

[35] Patients who have been traumatized in the past are at risk for self-injurious behaviors during adult life. Reenactments and recollections of previous traumas often induce emotional and physiological numbing experiences. Extreme fear accompanied by physical pain may trigger the release of endogenous opioids, which

cause physical and emotional numbing. The presence of these neurotransmitters tends to block the perception of pain, and enable individuals to carry-on survival behavior. High levels of opioids, however, may impair the encoding of experience and declarative memory, since they also inhibit the level of arousal necessary to promote memory. In addition, this can also cause changes in the hippocampus, where long-term memories are stored, and thus impair learning and cognitive functioning. K. Menning, "A Psychoanalytic Study of the Significance of Self-mutilation," *Psychoanalytic Quarterly* 4, No. 3 (1935): 408-466. Kristalyn Salters-Pedneault, "Self Mutilation and Borderline Personality Disorder," Verywell Mind, updated March 23, 2020, https://www.verywellmind.com/self-mutilation-425484. T.P. Beauchaine and S.P. Hinshaw, eds., "The Development of Borderline Personality Disorder and Self-injurious Behavior," *Child and Adolescent Psychopathology* (New York: John Wiley & Sons, 2008): 510-539.

[36] William Drake, "The Empty Chair Technique And Why Therapists Use It," Betterhelp, updated June 3, 2020, https://www.betterhelp.com/advice/therapy/what-is-the-empty-chair-technique-and-why-do-therapists-use-it/.

[37] Putnam et al., "Review of 100 Recent Cases," 285-93.

[38] The defense presented evidence of a written conversation between the two personalities when Mr. A planned to see his doctor because of fear of losing his job. These two personalities wrote the following to each other:

Mr. A: "I talked to Dr. (B) this morning. I don't think that it has helped much. I feel like I am being cut off at the (agency where I work) and I don't know why. I have been only a week and a half with only twelve hours sleep."

Billy Ray: "You stupid mother.....r (if you tell that to the doctor) that's when I take over completely and finally you don't stand a chance. I'll show that stupid doctor a thing or two."

Mr. A: "I must get through to Dr. D. He must know how serious this is. I have an idea what he (Billy Ray) is going to do and it's deadly to my family."

Billy Ray: "I won't let you squeal on me Stupid. I control you. You may fight it sometime but you're not strong enough nor will I let you get so."

Mr. A wrote back in large print: "Please Help Me!!"

Dr. Irwin N. Perr was the defense's consulting psychiatrist and the author of the article describing this case. Irwin N. Perr, "Crime and Multiple Personality Disorder: A Case History and Discussion," *The Bulletin of the American Academy of Psychiatry and the Law* 19, No. 2 (1991).

[39] Richard F Kluft, "Treatment of Multiple Personality Disorder: a Study of Thirty-three Cases," *Psychiatric Clinics of North America* 7, No.1 (1984): 9-29.

[40] In contrast to the notion that the goal is fusion into one personality, sometimes the goal may be to achieve fusions of a very few who will work together in a cooperative relationship. Heather B., "D.I.D. I Do That? Thoughts on Dissociative Identity Disorder," Psychcentral, July 8, 2018, (post is no longer available on this site).

[41] Ward Hill Lamon, *Recollections of Abraham Lincoln, 1847-1865*, published 1911, reported by Dale M. Kushner, Psychology Today, posted Feb 28, 2000, https://www.psychologytoday.com/us/blog/ transcending-the-past/202002/can-dreams-be-prophetic.

[42] Pertaining to transference, I've been trained to always look for both positive and negative elements of the patient-therapist relationship that are linked to important persons in the patient's past. According to an esteemed psychoanalyst and author, Dr. Glen Gabbard, "A transference interpretation is a very important intervention in psychotherapy." He maintains that it's important to understand that the patient's world of childhood relationships can be repeated in the here-and-now interaction with the therapist, and transferred into that relationship without the patient being aware of

it. In such cases the therapist can interpret the transference situation in order to make something conscious that has been unconscious. Glen O. Gabbard, *Long-term Psychodynamic Psychotherapy: A Basic Text* (Washington DC: American Psychiatric Publications, Inc., 2014).

[43] The description of pathogenic secrets causing specific symptoms including post-traumatic stress and dissociative disorders can be traced back to Pierre Janet, Freud, and other therapists who followed them. These practitioners used confession, hypnosis, psychoanalysis and other psychotherapeutic methods to incite individuals to remember and talk about their painful memories. They learned that when painful emotional toxins buried in the unconscious are coaxed into consciousness and spun into words, those who have been wounded by their traumas are better able to integrate their memories into consciousness, experience healing, and overcome shame. Margaret Lock and Vinh-Kim Nguyen, "The Pathogenic Secret as a Mode of Subjection," *An Anthropology of Biomedicine* (New York: Wiley Publishers, 2010.)

[44] Toxic shame is different from a temporary feeling of guilt caused by a specific wrong action. Rather, toxic shame is a paralyzing and irrational feeling of worthlessness, humiliation, and self-loathing, caused by traumatizing experiences such as sexual abuse or violence associated with rejection and abandonment. The bearer of toxic shame tends to believe it can be transmitted to

others, like a contagious disease. Claudia Black, "Toxic Shame," Psychology Today, posted June 4, 2010, https://www.psychologytoday.com/us/blog/ the-many-faces-addiction/201006/understanding-the-pain-abandonment.

[45] James Hopper and David Lisak, "Why Rape and Trauma Survivors Have Fragmented and Incomplete Memories," Time, Dec 9, 2014, https://time.com/3625414/rape-trauma-brain-memory/. Lee Breislouer, "Time heals wounds, but how long does it take?" Headspace, July 17, 2017, https://www.headspace.com/blog/2017/07/17/time-heals-wounds/.

[46] Attachment theory involves the way you form intimate and emotional bonds with others. Psychologist John Bowlby developed the theory while studying babies who became very upset when separated from a parent. Babies need a parent or other caregiver to take care of their basic needs. Bowlby found they used what he called attachment behaviors, such as crying, searching, and holding on to their parent, to prevent separation or to find a lost parent. Bowlby's study of attachment in children laid the foundation for later research on attachment in adults. *The Diagnostic and Statistical Manual of Mental Disorders* recognizes two main attachment disorders diagnosed in children between the ages of nine months and five years. The first, reactive attachment disorder (RAD), is characterized by emotional withdrawal from caregivers. The second is disinhibited social engagement disorder

(DSED). Children with DSED might wander off, approach strangers with no hesitation, and hug or touch unknown adults easily. As a person ages, he or she develops a unique attachment style, based largely on the attachment behaviors learned as a child. This attachment style can have a big impact on how someone forms relationships as an adult. There is no formal diagnosis for attachment disorder in adults. But there are different attachment styles in adulthood: secure-insecure, anxious-preoccupied, dismissive-avoidant, and fearful-avoidant attachment styles. "How Attachment Issues Impact Your Relationships," Healthline, February19, 2019, https://www.healthline.com/health/attachment-disorder-in-adults.

[47] Post-traumatic symptoms may include disturbing thoughts, nightmares, reliving experiences (flashbacks); intense psychological and physiological distress upon exposure to events which are reminders of, or memories of, the trauma; attempts to avoid reminders of the trauma; and increased fight-or-flight responses in the form of panic attacks and aggressive outbursts. According to psychiatrist David Spiegel, multiple personality disorder can be conceptualized as a post-traumatic stress disorder that arises in response to repeated episodes of trauma. Treatments can include specific approaches to reduce post-traumatic symptoms as well as classical therapeutic principles. David Spiegel, "Multiple Personality as a Post-traumatic Stress

Disorder," *Psychiatric Clinics of North America* 7, No. 1 (March 1984).

[48] I found videotaping therapy sessions to be valuable for several reasons. Most importantly, I could review and transcribe the contents to paper. Second, my patient could observe his behavior to determine its consistency with self-perception. Third, I could learn if my interventions were accurate and helpful. Fourth, I could show taped sessions to my consultant for his feedback at certain times. After reviewing the literature I also found additional reasons. Videotaping is useful to establish patient diagnoses. It's an objective way to help young therapists improve their techniques. It demonstrates psychotherapy sessions for individual, group, family, and couples. It may help patients see themselves and their therapists more realistically, and observe how behavior is linked to underlying feelings. Surprisingly, patients are usually more amenable to videotaping sessions than therapists, who may be sensitive to observing their own shortcomings. Michael C. Albert, "Videotaping Psychotherapy," *The Journal of Psychotherapy Practice and Research* 5, No. 2 (1996): 93-105.

[49] Research presented by Cheryl Dobinson, MA, and Stewart Landers, JD, MCP, from their two separate studies, reported that bisexuals suffered from depression and anxiety in higher rates than heterosexuals or lesbians and gay men. In terms of attempting or thinking of attempting suicide, bisexual men were 7 times higher,

while gay men were 4 times higher, than straight men; bisexual women were 6 times higher, while lesbian women were 4 times higher than straight women. An Australian study revealed that middle-aged bisexual women were 24 times more likely to engage in self-harm, such as cutting, than straight women, as a coping mechanism. Dobinson's research revealed that only 26 percent of bisexuals did not experience child sexual abuse, while 74 percent of them reported being victims. Cheryl Dobinson and Stewart Landers, Bi Health Summit Chicago Conference, website report of the conference, presented on August 14, 2009, post is no longer active.

[50] Helping a patient to relive a significant experience from the past has its origins in hypnosis whereby a therapist, via the presence of an altered state of consciousness, can facilitate the retrieval of a memory. The first time I facilitated a patient's age regression occurred when I was a medical practitioner hoping to treat a young woman with a chronic gastrointestinal disorder. When I hypnotized her, I unexpectedly saw her spontaneously regress and re-experience a traumatic event at age five. I was so surprised at seeing this happen that I wanted to learn more about the mind and body connection. Thus I decided to seek special training in psychiatry a year later at the Karl Menninger School of Psychiatry. I have since learned that some therapists encourage age regression during the course of treatment, with or without hypnosis, for the

purpose of enabling their patients to relive early distressing experiences that had been the cause of their problems.

[51] I received my psychiatric training in a setting where patient-therapist physical contact had a negative connotation. However, there is considerable data in the literature supporting the importance of touch for normal human development, communication, and healing. For that reason I know that this patient, as he feels child-like, needs to experience touch with his therapist. Ashley Montagu, *Touching. The Human Significance of the Skin* (New York: Harper and Rowe, 1978).

[52] Understanding the normal phases of early growth and development is important for a therapist. In a normal mother child relationship, the child begins the process of separation-individuation at about four to five months of life. At about fifteen months of age the child becomes aware of increasing separation from his mother, and about age two has established a personal identity and can hold a stable mental representation of the mother or other caregiver. The completion of the separation-individuation phase also depends on a positive relationship with the father, who establishes a healthy male identification with his son as well as an enhanced sense of autonomy.

[53] This therapeutic approach became very controversial after it resulted in the death of a ten-year-old girl. Candace Newmaker

died during a seventy-minute session, in which she was wrapped from head to toe and surrounded by pillows. Despite the girl's cries that she was suffocating, the therapists continued to push her in an attempt to simulate uterine contractions. The episode had been videotaped and was used in court against the therapists, who were convicted of reckless child abuse resulting in death, and sentenced to sixteen to forty-eight years' imprisonment. A law, known as Candace's law, prohibiting the use of "rebirthing" techniques by mental health professionals, was signed by Colorado governor Bill Owens in 2001. Candace had been diagnosed with reactive detachment disorder, a psychiatric illness thought to be caused by the failure of normal bonding with a parent or caregiver during infancy. Deborah Josefson, "Rebirthing Therapy Banned After Girl Died in Seventy Minute Struggle," *BMJ : British Medical Journal* 322, No.7293, 2001: 1014, https://www.ncbi.nlm.nih.gov/pmc/articles/PMC1174742/.

[54] Upon learning of James' experiences of abandonment I become sensitized to a predominant theme a therapist often faces during therapy for a patient with unresolved grief and depression. That patient is likely to have suffered from early life experiences of repetitive trauma and loss, often linked later in life to a range of disturbances in functioning and psychopathology, including dissociative identity disorder. The emotional wounds have been referred to by some authors as toxic shame. Abandonment depression is a description previously used by my consultant and

friend, Dr. Donald Rinsley, who described this as a sense of emptiness and meaninglessness resulting from the child's failure to achieve normal separation-individuation from the symbiotic bond established with his mother at a young age. As a result the child is unable to reach the normal depressive position, with a resultant incapacity to mourn. This failure results in repeated but disappointing attempts throughout life to re-establish and separate from that bond, thus suffering recurring episodes of abandonment depression following interpersonal separations or loss. Donald B. Rinsley, *Developmental Pathogenesis and Treatment of Borderline and Narcissistic Personalities* (New York: Aronson, 1989).

[55] Ethel Spector Person and Lionel Ovesey, "Homosexual Cross-dressers," *Journal of the American Academy of Psychoanalysis* 12, No. 2 (1984): 167-186.

[56] Ethel Spector Person, "How To Work Through Erotic Transference," *Psychiatric Times* 20, No. 7 (July 1, 2003).

[57] Katharina Star, "Treating Anxiety With Art Therapy," Verywell Mind, updated February 18, 2020, https://www.verywellmind.com/art-therapy-for-anxiety-2584282. Susan Hogan, *Healing Arts: The History of Art Therapy* (London and Philadelphia: Jessica Kingsley Publishers, 2001).

[58] Montagu, *Touching*. Dwight Norwood, "Touch in Therapy: Helpful or Harmful? One Therapist's Perspective," Good Therapy, June 29, 2017, https://www.goodtherapy.org/blog/touch-in-therapy-helpful-or-harmful-one-therapists-perspective-0629175.

[59] Christopher Berglund, "Loving Touch Is Key to Healthy Brain Development," Psychology Today, posted Oct 9, 2013, https://www.psychologytoday.com/us/blog/the-athletes-way/201310/loving-touch-is-key-healthy-brain-development. Carl R. Rogers, *Client-Centered Therapy* (Boston: Houghton-Mifflin, 1956). Bob Edelstein, "Love and Psychotherapy, A Unique Kind of Love," Psychology Today, posted May 14, 2016, https://www.psychologytoday.com/us/blog/authentic-engagement/201605/love-and-psychotherapy.

[60] JF Masterson and AR Lieberman, eds., *A Therapist's Guide to the Personality Disorders* (Phoenix: Zeig Tucker & Theisen Inc., 2004).

ACKNOWLEDGEMENTS

There are many people who helped me with this project, beginning in 1975 when the team at the audio-visual studio at the Colmery O'Neil VA Medical Center in Topeka agreed to videotape my therapy sessions with James. I want to thank Jim Wright, Dick Shackelford, and Karla Westmoreland for their camera and production work, which enabled them to make almost 300 recordings on one-inch videotape cassettes. Following a year of recording, I began to purchase those cassettes for $25 apiece in order to resist the VA administration's wish to shut down our operation as a cost saving measure. After I left Topeka in 1983 I kept in touch with Jim and Dick at the Topeka VA, who told me that administrators wanted to have those videocassettes reused to free up room for other recordings. That didn't happen and four years later when I was a psychiatrist at Bay Pines, FL VA Medical Center, I obtained a $15,000 VA research grant to secure those cassettes and keep them from being stored away and forgotten.

I want to thank a number of professionals who helped me during my time as a VA psychiatrist. My friend and colleague, Dr. Donald Rinsley, was my primary consultant and co-author of two papers about this case. Dr. Sam Bradshaw was the Chief of

Psychiatry at Colmery O'Neil VA Medical in Topeka who allowed me to devote considerable time to this project. Dr. Bernie Berkowitz, Chief of Psychiatry at Bay Pines VA Medical Center, alerted me to the availability of grant money that I could use to have the James Tapes transferred to my care at Bay Pines VA in 1987. I'm thankful that Dr. Harold Voth, a former consultant of mine, and Chief of Staff at the Topeka VA at that time, was able to facilitate the transfer.

Although many of these one-inch cassettes were lost because of deterioration over the years, the majority of them remained intact and could be viewed on VCR equipment. My attention was focused on other professional work so I asked my stepson, Derek Kershner, who was living and working in Columbus, Georgia in 2001, to convert the cassettes to DVDs. I purchased the necessary equipment and Derek spent hundreds of hours watching with fascination as he made the conversions over a two-year period of time. Several years later he down loaded all of these 255 DVDs to a computer where I've been able to view them while writing this book. The one-inch videocassettes were all eventually lost.

My wife Jackie was helpful in so many different ways with encouragement, making suggestions for changes, and reminding me multiple times to get organized. She suggested that the book would benefit if I included something personal. So I consulted with my oldest daughter Kareen who looked in her diary and found a family trip we took in July 1975, which I described at the end of chapter 15.

I wish to thank computer whiz and graphic artist Patricia Chong, who improved my design of the fragmented figure for the book's cover and provided telephone assistance for my computer work numerous times when I needed it.

Finally I am thankful to have found my very talented editor, Linda Ingerly, after Francis "Ziggy" Zigmund, a fellow jazz trombonist, raved to me about her editorial work for his books. She has guided me with her thoroughness, her creative ideas, her integration of the cover content and photos, and her final uploading for publication.

Keep reading for a sneak peak of

THE JAMES TAPES
Book Two

The James Tapes
Book Two

The patient arrives today dressed in hospital garb—a robe and pajamas. He has the appearance of a young boy marked by a look of innocent confusion. His skin is pale and his eyes seem almost blank. He sits down and signs the permission slip "J   Kohlman."

I ask him why there is a space after the letter J instead of the name James. "You have a given name, don't you?"

"I think I do but I just don't know."

"Can't you use the name you were given by your mother?"

"I don't think I have one. I think there was a woman there but she couldn't have been," he stutters.

"Couldn't have been what?"

"A mother to me," he adds. His face takes on a puzzled look and he shakes his head repeatedly.

"You may feel she wasn't a mother like you would have liked. But you have a name. You were given a name when you were born."

"That brings up another thing. When was I born?" he asks, his face revealing a mixture of confusion, fear, and curiosity.

"When do you think?" I ask.

Rather than answer the question he yells, "I wanna run! But I don't wanna run. I wanna stay right here and I wanna scream!"

"I wonder why you want to scream? Can you remember anything in your past that caused you to feel this way?"

He shakes his head as the tears begin to flow down his face. After a long pause he finally relaxes and tells me about the time when he stood barefoot in a room in the family barn with a brood of baby chickens. Then he remembers the time he ran to his father's side but was slapped in the face and called a bad name. He fights to keep from crying and stammers words I can't make out. Then he shouts words that his father apparently used. "You stay right here you . . . you . . . !" After a pause he frowns, looks at the floor and stutters. "I . . . I . . . I should have k. . . k . . . killed him right then and there. That's what I should have done. Then I wouldn't have had to fight. I wouldn't have had so much pain." He places his right hand onto the right side of his face as the tears come. "Maybe then I . . . I . . . would know who to trust and who not to trust and I . . . I . . . wouldn't be so afraid to s . . . s . . . say what I feel," he stammers between irregular breaths.

I ask him if he is feeling pain right now and he replies yes. Then I ask if his pain reminds him of any other situations. He begins to gently massage the spot where his father hit him with his right hand. Then he answers haltingly that he wants to be able to feel love as well as hate.

"I know you want to have the feelings that a real person has. And you are a real person because you have a body." But that seems to confuse him so I point out he also has a mind.

He shakes his head, apparently not understanding that a person's mind and body are connected. "That can't be. I'm not here then. I can see myself as I see myself now, but I am not here," he insists. He begins to stand up but then sits back down and tells me he doesn't want to be on the other side of the room looking at himself, a description of an "out of body experience (OBE)" which he's had in the past. "I want to be here! I want to be here! I don't want to be over there anymore! I want to be here!" he sobs. His face is contorted as the tears pour down his cheeks, impeding his ability to continue talking. He clenches his fists and tells me again that he wants to be right here and he wants to have feelings. But he's afraid he will be threatened or called names if anyone knows he has feelings.

I hand him another tissue to wipe his tears and ask how I can help him feel better.

He wipes his eyes and repeats that he wants to be a person who has feelings.

I point out that it can help him to experience touch. "The last time you were here I touched you and you felt much more relaxed."

"Yes. And I want to know that I can be touched and you aren't going to hit me or beat me."

I reach over and touch his right arm.

His body stiffens but he looks carefully at me. "I'd like to be able to touch you," he says.

I extend an open hand.

He reaches over to grasp it. "It's not wrong. It might be silly but it's not wrong," he says.

About the Author

Dr. Joel Osler Brende worked as a psychiatrist for over thirty-five years, specializing in the treatment of individuals with post-traumatic and dissociative disorders. He worked at the Karl Menninger School of Psychiatry as a psychotherapist and instructor in clinical hypnosis, for the VA as a staff psychiatrist in an outpatient clinic in Topeka KS, and director of the recovery unit in Florida. He was a tenured professor and department chairman of psychiatry at the Mercer University School of Medicine.

Dr. Brende is the co-author of the book, *Vietnam Veterans, the Road to Recovery*, and authored chapters for multiple books in the area of trauma recovery, including *Dissociative Disorders in Vietnam Combat Veterans*. He has also written over twenty journal articles and served on the peer review editorial staff for psychiatric journals including the *Journal for Traumatic Stress*. He was a presenter for numerous workshops and conferences, including an episode for the news show 20/20 on multiple personality disorder.

Dr. Brende currently lives in Kansas City with his wife and dog Brooklyn.

$$9\overline{)368} \quad \frac{41}{9} \quad \frac{^{41}}{30}$$

$$\begin{array}{r} 41 \\ 9\overline{)368} \\ 36 \end{array} \qquad \begin{array}{r} 41 \\ 30 \\ \hline 1230 \end{array} \qquad \begin{array}{r} 3^{28} \\ 9 \\ \hline 29.52 \end{array} \qquad \begin{array}{r} 3^{00}_{9} \\ 27^{00} \end{array}$$